THE RATH OF THE SYNODS

The Rath of the Synods,
Tara, Co. Meath: excavations by Seán P. Ó Ríordáin

Eoin Grogan

With contributions by Caroline Velzian Donaghy and Seamus Caulfield

Drawings by Ursula Mattenberger and Eoin Grogan

UCD School of Archaeology

Word*well*

in association with the UCD School of Archaeology

In loving memory of Mary ('Minnie') Grogan

First published in 2008
Wordwell Ltd (in association with the UCD School of Archaeology)
Media House, South County Business Park, Leopardstown, Dublin 18
Copyright © Wordwell

Academic editor: Muiris O'Sullivan

ISBN 978-1-905569-24-3

British Library Cataloguing-in-Publication Data.
A catalogue record for this book is available from the British Library.

This book has been produced with the aid of a grant from the Heritage Council.

Typeset in Ireland by Wordwell Ltd

Cover design: Nick Maxwell and Nicole McKenna

Copy-editing: Emer Condit

Printed by Graficas Castuera, Spain

CONTENTS

SUMMARY

This is a report on the archaeological excavations at the Rath of the Synods (*Ráith na Senad*) on the Hill of Tara, Co. Meath, Ireland. The excavations were directed by Seán P. Ó Ríordáin, then Professor of Celtic Archaeology at University College Dublin, who spent two summers at the site (1952 and 1953). His discoveries are supported here by post-excavation research and a series of radiocarbon determinations from samples collected by his team.

The earliest recorded human activity at the Rath of the Synods took place during the late Neolithic and can be associated with the primary use of the megalithic tomb at the nearby Mound of the Hostages, with which it is contemporary. A significant phase in the life of the complex occurred during the Iron Age, in the final centuries BC, continuing into the mid-first millennium AD. In the earlier Iron Age (in the centuries after 400 BC) a number of palisade enclosures were constructed, leaving a general figure-of-eight trace. A small number of Iron Age artefacts were recovered from this complex. Later in the Iron Age, during the second to fourth centuries AD, a considerable amount of activity took place at the centre of the site: post-built structures were erected and Roman glass and pottery were deposited. The Roman assemblage is not typical of what would be expected on a contemporary provincial Roman site in Britain. The Tara material is more specialised, consisting of drinking vessels. A feature of the evidence from the Rath of the Synods is the occurrence of burials, some associated with a barrow of unknown prehistoric date but assumed to be Iron Age, and some occurring in a flat cemetery close to the centre of the multivallate enclosure. These might conceivably have been broadly contemporary but it is more likely that they reflect a sequence of burial activity, or at least more than one phase. Radiocarbon analysis suggests that one of the extended burials dates from as late as the thirteenth century AD.

Chapter 1 introduces the site, sets out the context of the excavations and outlines the difficulties of publishing from an old excavation archive. Chapter 2, based heavily on the traditional approaches of stratigraphy and typology, attempts to unravel the earlier Iron Age sequence of activity at the site. Chapter 3 deals with the burials from the site, Chapter 4 provides detailed information on the complex dubbed 'the residential enclosure', and Chapter 5 discusses various aspects of the enclosure. There follows, in Chapter 6, a general discussion of the Rath of the Synods. The reader's attention is drawn in particular to Appendix J, dealing with radiocarbon dating, which provides significant chronological data that emerged after Dr Eoin Grogan had completed the text.

ACKNOWLEDGEMENTS

As specified in Eoin Grogan's opening chapter, where many of his collaborators are acknowledged by name, the current volume is a product of generations of research, beginning with Ó Ríordáin and his excavation team in 1952 and 1953. The Rath of the Synods post-excavation project has been facilitated in various ways by Ó Ríordáin's successors as Head of Archaeology in UCD, most recently by George Eogan (1979–95), Barry Raftery (1997–2001) and Gabriel Cooney (2001–4). For a time Seamus Caulfield was centrally involved. Eoin Grogan, an experienced field archaeologist with a long and distinguished publication record, has worked on the excavation archive since the 1980s.

I have come late to the undertaking, my role being to guide it to completion and publication, and I would like to place on record the patience, approachability and general cooperation of Eoin Grogan in this process. The final stages of the scheme, including the radiocarbon-dating programme, could not have been completed without the understanding and financial support of the Heritage Council and the efficiency of its Archaeology Officer, Ian Doyle. In the UCD School of Archaeology, indispensable behind-the-scenes work on the final document was contributed by Conor McDermott, Kim Rice, Jessica Smyth and Deborah O'Sullivan, usually late into the evenings and frequently under intense pressure to meet deadlines. In November 2007, Roman pottery specialist Dr Jeremy Evans travelled from Birmingham to examine the ceramic fragments from the site. His discussions with Dr Grogan and Dr Linda Mulvin (UCD School of Art History and Cultural Policy) have provided additional validation for elements of the final text, his pottery report (Appendix G) complementing Ed Bourke's glass report (Appendix C) and providing some interesting parallel findings. A report on some charcoal samples has been provided by Lorna O'Donnell, and bone samples used for radiocarbon dating were examined by Jonny Geber prior to being sent to QUB. The UCD School of Archaeology is grateful to the Queen's University Radiocarbon Laboratory for its cooperation in processing these samples.

A draft of the final report was submitted to an anonymous external reader, to whom a special word of gratitude is due for detailed comments throughout the text and invaluable general suggestions. As in the production of the Mound of the Hostages volume, the professionalism of Nick Maxwell and Emer Condit at Wordwell Books has made life easier for all concerned.

This project has been proceeding intermittently for close to 60 years, and it is inevitable that some of those who helped along the way will have been overlooked. Their contribution, although anonymous, is appreciated. Finally, gratitude is extended to the funding agencies that have contributed to the Rath of the Synods project down the years, not least the Office of Public Works, the Heritage Council, Meath County Council and University College Dublin.

Muiris O'Sullivan
UCD School of Archaeology

PREFACE

Following the publication of its sister volume on the Mound of the Hostages (O'Sullivan 2005), this report is yet another milestone in the archaeological investigation of the Hill of Tara. Excavations at the Rath of the Synods were directed by Seán P. Ó Ríordáin during the summers of 1952 and 1953. His intentions were partly to rescue as much information as possible from the debris of the eccentric British-Israelite search for the Ark of the Covenant half a century earlier and partly to launch a more extensive programme of investigation on the Hill of Tara. In 1955 he turned his attention to the Mound of the Hostages, where he continued in 1956. Ó Ríordáin's early death in the spring of 1957 interrupted the programme, although his excavations at the Mound of the Hostages were completed by Ruaidhrí de Valera in 1959.

When the excavation archive from the Rath of the Synods was addressed with renewed purpose in the 1980s, inevitable difficulties were encountered. It was a challenge to trace some of the material from the excavations, and the permatrace supporting annotated drawings from the 1950s was found to have degraded to such an extent that important information had probably been lost. That so much has been rescued is a tribute to the painstaking work of Noel Dunne and Eoin Grogan in particular. In the 1990s Tara was selected as one of the key Discovery Programme research projects, leading to

the publication of an archaeological survey (Newman 1997) and a number of specialised studies (Bhreathnach 1995a; 1995b; Fenwick and Newman 2002). Excavations directed by Helen Roche in the 1990s re-examined cuttings made across the ditch of Ráith na Ríg by Ó Ríordáin during the course of his excavations at the adjacent Rath of the Synods. Roche's investigations clarified aspects of the older excavation and confirmed that the large enclosure known as Ráith na Ríg dates from the Iron Age. The appearance of the Mound of the Hostages monograph in 2005 prompted a final drive to bring the Rath of the Synods project to publication.

The completion of a third volume, reviewing and contextualising the outcome of the excavations, will conclude this publication project. Field survey, geophysical survey and the recently completed LIDAR survey provide important Discovery Programme insights that would have been barely imaginable in Ó Ríordáin's time. From a research perspective, our understanding of Tara in its local setting is also being expanded significantly by the archaeological excavations along the M3 corridor to the east of the Hill. The scene is undoubtedly being set for strategic reflection on the future nature and direction of investigations at the Hill of Tara.

Muiris O'Sullivan

LIST OF ILLUSTRATIONS

Frontispiece—Taoiseach Eamon de Valera, accompanied by Professor Seán P. Ó Ríordáin, turning the first sod at the Rath of the Synods, 21 June 1952.

CHAPTER 1

County Meath

DUNDALK

Raffin

Nanny

Blackwater

Knowth

Boyne

Tara

Delvin

Boyne

Carbury Hill

N

30km

Rath Grainne

Rath Caelchon

Teach Miodhchuarta
or Old Hall

H   i   l   l   o   f   T   a   r   a

Rath na Seanaidh
or King's Chair

St. Patrick's
Church

Teach Mairisen

Dumha na ngiall

Rath Riogh
Forradh

Seamhrach
(Well)

Teach Cormaic

Rath Riogh
or Cathair Crofinn

D E E N

C A S T L E B O Y

(E. D. Tara)

Rath Laoghaire

Rath of the Synods

INTRODUCTION

Abstract

This report presents the results of Seán P. Ó Ríordáin's unpublished excavations carried out in the 1950s at the Rath of the Synods. The site had a complex sequence of ritual, funerary and domestic activity which is divided into four main phases. The earliest is undated but is represented by a ditched enclosure that may be of the Bronze Age or Iron Age, while the second dates from the late Iron Age and consists of a series of ritual or ceremonial enclosures with strong parallels at Emain Macha and Dún Ailinne. In the third phase there are two cemeteries, one contained in a barrow and the other unprotected, of the early centuries AD. The domestic enclosure of the Rath of the Synods itself was built and occupied in the fourth phase. There is a substantial and significant material assemblage from the site. While in the third phase this reflects a very strong element of contact with Roman Britain in the third to fourth century AD, disentangling the native from the Romano-British contribution is especially complex as no other Irish site has produced a comparable set of evidence. The material suggests, however, either interaction between the occupants and allied or related communities in Britain or possibly the domestic site of a family from the fringes of the Roman world.

While there was considerable difficulty in dealing with the archival record of an earlier excavation, we have attempted to present Ó Ríordáin's own interpretation. Nevertheless, while respecting his scholarship, more recent research has advanced our understanding of the periods in question and we have reassessed the evidence in this light. Every effort has been made to assess all the available material, including the uncontexted finds.

Introduction

The archaeological complex at Tara (Fig. 1.1) occupies the summit and upper slopes of the Hill of Tara, with expansive panoramic views despite its relatively low elevation (*c.* 152m). The Rath of the Synods (*Ráith na Senad*) is in the townland of Castletown Tara (OS 31:16:6) (85.5, 07.7) (NGR 292017 259795), on the northern edge of the hill summit on level ground and immediately north of the hillfort, Rath na Ríogh (*Ráith na Ríg*), in the townland of Castleboy (RMP 31:33:5) (NGR 291968 259598) (Figs 1.1, 1.2, 1.3 and 1.7).

The pre-excavation (and present) appearance of the Rath of the Synods is of a generally circular trivallate enclosure that incorporates an earlier barrow on the western side between its ramparts (Figs 1.2 and 1.4). On the eastern side the graveyard of St Patrick's Church of Ireland parish church, which was rebuilt in 1822, has obliterated a sizeable portion of the monument and extends almost as far as the inner rampart (see Newman 1997, figs 14 and 37). The church replaced one built in the fifteenth or sixteenth century (*ibid.*, 38–43), portions of which were reused in the modern building. A large lump of mortared stone in the graveyard to the south-west of the church may be part of the original tower. On the south side the outer rampart touches the edge of Rath na Ríogh.

The name of the site—*Ráith na Senad*—refers to the reputed, but unsubstantiated, holding of synods here by Patrick, Rúadán and Adomnán in 695 (Byrne 1973, 54, 158).

The excavation

Excavations under Professor Seán P. Ó Ríordáin began at the Rath of the Synods in June 1952 and continued

Fig. 1.1—The archaeological complex at Tara, Co. Meath.

Fig. 1.2—Vertical aerial view of the Hill of Tara before excavation (Air Corps V.211/143. 25.05.1952).

Fig. 1.3 (left)—Aerial view from north-west of the Rath of the Synods before excavation. Note the proximity of ditch 3 to the bank of Rath na Ríogh.

Fig. 1.4 (right)—Pre-excavation plan of the Rath of the Synods—a trivallate enclosure incorporating an earlier barrow—showing the main excavation cuttings, entrances, ditches and burials D, F, G and J/K.

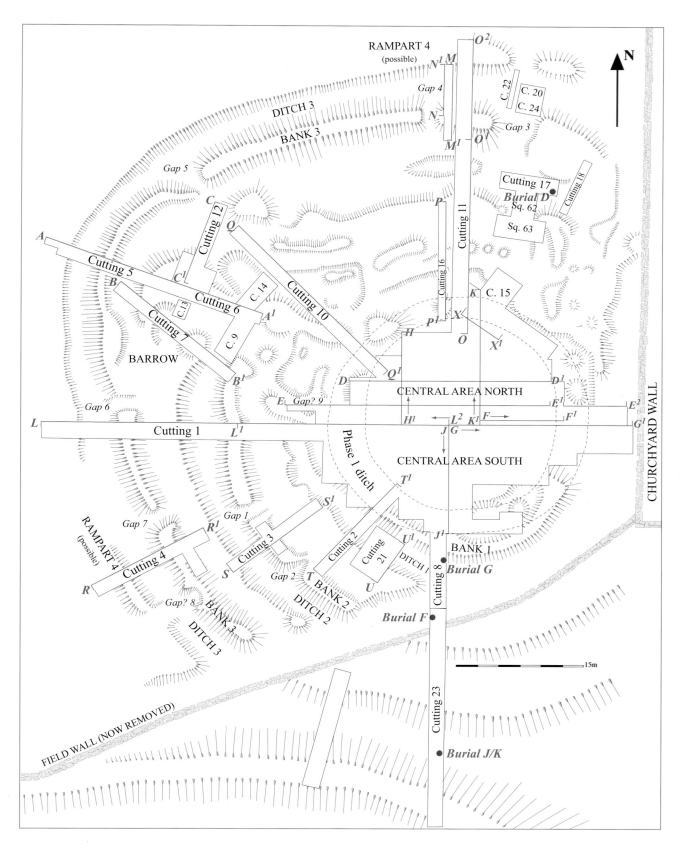

under his direction until 1953 (Ó Ríordáin 1954a). Subsequent excavations were carried out by Ó Ríordáin at the nearby passage tomb, the Mound of the Hostages, for two seasons, 1955–6 (O'Sullivan 2005). After his untimely death in 1957, excavation continued under the direction of Ruadhrí de Valera, his successor as Professor of Celtic Archaeology at University College Dublin.

Following a long association with the Lough Gur area in County Limerick, where he carried out over twenty excavations (Ó Ríordáin 1951; 1954b; Ó Ríordáin and Ó h-Iceadha 1955), Ó Ríordáin had planned a substantial campaign at Tara. He had chosen the Rath of the Synods as the starting-point principally because it was known to have suffered considerable disturbance in the period 1899–1902, when a misguided investigation was conducted by a group called the British-Israelites (see below). The initial aim of Ó Ríordáin's excavation was to determine the extent of the British-Israelite damage to the site, as well as the nature and date of the site itself. He also intended this excavation to provide a guide to the general soil conditions, level of preservation and stratigraphical sequences on the hilltop. A logical arrangement of the areas and cuttings to be investigated was laid out, and this is preserved in the pre-excavation survey of the site. The process of excavation appears to have involved the meticulous stratigraphic assessment of the central area of the site, within the inner rampart of the ringfort, and a more selective excavation of the areas extending across the outer ramparts. The latter strategy included the initial rapid excavation of cutting 1 on the west side of the site (Figs 1.4, 1.6, 1.7 and 1.9) to the old ground surface, except where features were clearly preserved; above-subsoil features were thus largely recorded through sections and descriptions.

The excavations excited a considerable amount of public interest, not all of it favourably disposed to the 'unstudied interference with the ancient features' (*The Irish Times* letter column, 4 May 1952). There was a lively debate in the press, including contributions from Maud Gonne, who, together with Arthur Griffith, Eoin MacNeill, Seán T. Ó Ceallaigh (in 1952 the president of Ireland) and others, had been instrumental in bringing the British-Israelite destruction to an end. The excavations were formally started by the taoiseach,

Eamon de Valera, who 'turned the first sod' on 21 June 1952 at a ceremony attended by a large number of distinguished visitors (Frontispiece).

Excavation layout

The excavation took place in two seasons over nine weeks in 1952 (Monday 23 June to Friday 22 August) and a further five weeks in 1953 (Monday 6 July to Friday 28 August). Work concentrated on the central part of the enclosure, which was gridded in a series of 3m squares (Fig. 1.8). Major cuttings, generally 1.5m wide, extended from this area across the visible earthworks to the north (cutting 11), west (cutting 1, 1952) and south (cutting 8, continued by cutting 23, 1953) (Figs 1.4 and 1.8). Cutting 23 extends beyond the Rath of the Synods across the northern ramparts of Rath na Ríogh (Fig. 1.4). Another cutting, no. 24 (1953), is shown on the overall site survey to the west, extending over the outer earthwork of the enclosure and across the outer bank of Rath na Ríogh (see below). To the east the excavation was restricted by the adjacent graveyard and on this side there was a rectangular extension to the grid. Another cutting was extended to the north-west (cutting 10, 1952) and further cuttings were opened across the earthworks in the south-west (cuttings 2, 3 and 21) as well as square 62 (1953, abutting cutting 17) (Fig. 1.4).

In the north-west quadrant (cuttings 14, 15, 17, 18, 20, 22 and 24, all 1953) cuttings were made across the barrow. The central area of the enclosure and part of the barrow, including a substantial portion of the interior, had suffered considerable disturbance and damage during the illicit 1899–1902 campaign (Figs 1.5 and 1.8). The barrow was investigated in 1952 by means of a transect (cuttings 5 and 6) and by subsidiary cuttings (nos 7, 12 and 13), while the intersection between the third rampart of the enclosure and the barrow was also excavated (cuttings 9 and 14). The eastern side of the ringfort is severely truncated by the adjacent churchyard (St Patrick's Church; Figs 1.4, 1.6 and 1.7).

The British-Israelite investigation

A considerable area of the Rath of the Synods was investigated between 1899 and 1902 by the British-

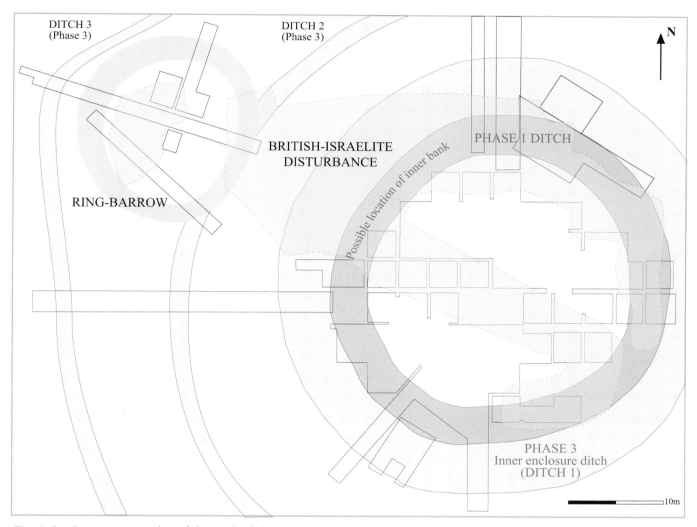

DITCH 3
(Phase 3)

DITCH 2
(Phase 3)

N

BRITISH-ISRAELITE
DISTURBANCE

Possible location of inner bank

PHASE 1 DITCH

RING-BARROW

PHASE 3
Inner enclosure ditch
(DITCH 1)

10m

Fig. 1.5—Pre-excavation plan of the Rath of the Synods, showing the main excavation sections, the phase 1 ditch, the outlying phase 3 burials and the British-Israelite destruction.

Israelites (Fig. 1.5; see Carew 2003; Bhreathnach 1995a, 28; Macalister 1931, 39–43), when intermittent work was carried out in a misguided attempt to find the Ark of the Covenant. West of the centre of the site a large irregular area, measuring *c.* 22m north-west/south-east by 16m north-east/south-west, was removed (see Figs 1.5 and 1.8). Extending from this, a wide ditch was cut through the centre of the enclosure; it ran north-west/south-east across the site, widening from 5m at the south-east to 7m at the north-west. Another spur of this ditch curved across the northern centre of the site, almost meeting the terminal of the first section on the eastern side. Two smaller openings were also made, one

at the north-east and the other on the western side in the centre of the barrow. These cuttings all penetrated to, and into, the old ground surface and totally removed all archaeological material.

The digging was conducted by Walton Adams and Charles Groom under the general auspices of the British-Israel Association of London and commenced in May or early June 1899 (this account relies largely on Carew's (2003) extensive research). Although the Ark of the Covenant appears to have been the primary target of this work, other interests, including the grave of Princess Tea Tephi, the most widely accepted resting-place of the Covenant, had been frequently discussed by members of

7

Fig. 1.6 (above)—Aerial view of the site from west at the beginning of the excavation. The mound is in the left foreground, with cutting 1 opened in the foreground. The outer ditch and bank are clearly defined in the foreground and to the left (north).

Fig. 1.7 (left)—Aerial view of the site during excavation, looking north. The Mound of the Hostages and the rampart of Rath na Ríogh are in the foreground, with the Banqueting Hall in the background and St Patrick's Church to the right.

the British–Israel Association and the Freemasons in the various plans to excavate at Tara. Tea appears to be a medieval invention and was described as the daughter of a pharaoh and wife of Eirimón, son of the eponymous Milesius (Míl) of the Spanish Milesian invaders of Ireland (Bhreathnach 1995a, 69; 1995b); in some British-Israelite writing Míl was equated with the prophet Jeremiah, and it was suggested that Tea may have arrived from Thebes in the company of a group of Hebrews. The grave was reputed to be covered by a small mound between the *Forad* and *Tech Cormaic* (Newman 1997, 78, fig. 33), on the hill summit to the south of the Rath of the Synods. Permission to excavate in this area was refused, however, by the landowner, John Francis Stanley (2nd Earl Russell), whereas the landlord of the Rath of the Synods, Gustavus Villiers Briscoe, himself a Freemason, was an enthusiastic supporter of the venture. While the prime movers in this enterprise appear to have been the Reverend Denis Hanan, rector of Tipperary and the first president of the British-Israel Association of Ireland, and Richard H. McDonald from Portlaw, Co. Waterford, neither of these gentlemen appears to have been directly connected to the efforts of Adams and Groom. The work at Tara quickly came to public attention, and one consequence was the temporary cessation of work under pressure from the Board of Works. Subsequent developments revealed that the Board had no authority to prevent the digging and, indeed, Briscoe received a public apology and monetary compensation in September 1899. Excavations may have been resumed for a short period in July 1899 and again in the spring of 1900, but on these occasions the work was directed by Briscoe himself and neither Adams nor Groom appears to have been involved. While there was some negative coverage in the newspapers, most of this, and the concerns of bodies such as the Royal Society of Antiquaries of Ireland, the Royal Irish Academy and the Board of Works, seems to have focused principally on the perceived unscientific nature of the digging.

Following a visit to the site in December 1900, Arthur Griffith, the editor of the *United Irishman*, and Maud Gonne began a more vociferous campaign against the investigations. Articles in the *United Irishman* and other publications criticised not only the work at Tara but also prominent organisations, such as the Academy

and the Antiquaries, for not being more forthright in halting the destruction. By June 1902, when Groom returned to recommence his digging, even previously sympathetic observers, such as Reverend John Healy, rector of Kells, were clearly concerned at the lack of archaeological or scientific control. Pressure was, however, being brought to bear on Patrick Boylan, Briscoe's tenant on that part of the hill. Amongst those involved in these behind-the-scenes efforts were Robert Cochrane, inspector of ancient and national monuments in the Board of Works and honorary general secretary of the Royal Society of Antiquaries of Ireland, and Edward Percival Wright, president of the Society. They corresponded with Boylan and with the British-Israel Association of Ireland, urging them to halt the work. While Captain John Fielding, honorary secretary of the Association, denied its involvement, he and Hanan were also prominent members of the London Association, which was the principal supporter of the enterprise, and both had hosted visits to the investigation by British members in April 1902. It may be, as Carew (2003, 83–4) has suggested, that they too were disillusioned by the lack of expert involvement and, perhaps, by the absence of a more significant role for the Irish branch. Certainly, both continued to believe that Groom and Briscoe were digging in the wrong location.

Gradually the weight of public and media attention appears to have worn down the resolve of Briscoe and Groom to continue, and the will of Boylan to permit ongoing work. It was, however, the intervention of formidable literary figures that finally tipped the balance. In June 1902 W. B. Yeats, George Moore, Douglas Hyde and Arthur Griffith visited the site while work was being directed by Briscoe and Groom, and were briefly menaced by one of Briscoe's employees with a gun. A letter to *The Times* by Hyde, Moore and Yeats (27 June 1902) appears to mark a significant point in the campaign, and subsequently the writer T. W. Rolleston persuaded Boylan to withdraw permission. While part of Rolleston's successful intervention was the promise that the Royal Society of Antiquaries would take over the excavation, the Society had not been party to this pledge and both refused to become involved and deplored Rolleston's role in the process.

While the digging at Tara had aroused considerable

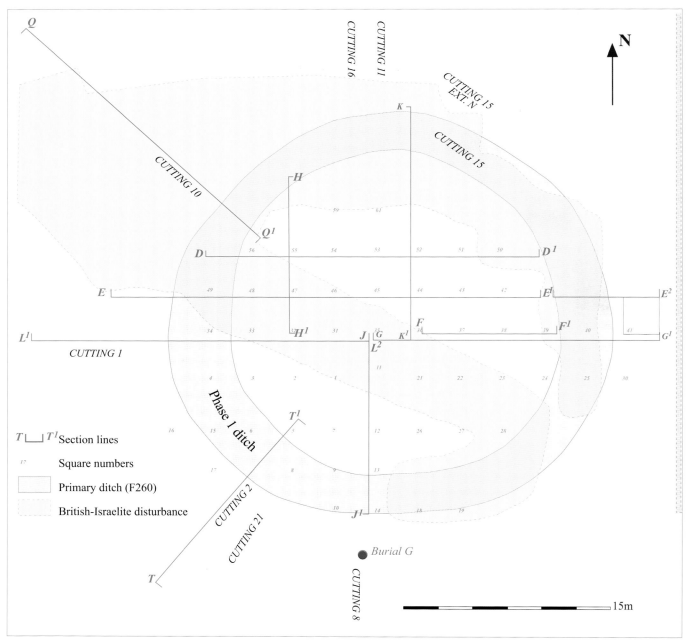

Fig. 1.8—Central area of the Rath of the Synods with the excavation grid, sections, British-Israelite disturbance and the phase 1 ditch.

Fig. 1.9—View from west of cutting 1 extending from the west side of the site across the ringfort ramparts into the centre of the site. The spoil has been deposited on the north edge of the cutting. The figure in the centre foreground is standing in the excavated base of ditch 3, phase 3, while behind is another person in ditch 2. On the left the figures are standing on the (unexcavated) summit of banks 3 and 2 respectively. A narrow sondage is visible along the north side of the cutting. This was intended to determine the nature of the soil sequence, including subsoil development, as well as confirming the precise level of the old ground surface. These narrow sondages are a feature of the excavation of the outer cuttings, including those across the rampart of Rath na Ríogh. The excavation of the central area is under way in the right background.

debate, in particular the negative campaign spearheaded by those with both a nationalist and anti-establishment position, other groups, such as nationalist political representatives, and the cultural bodies, such as the Academy, the Antiquaries, the Board of Works and the Dublin Museum of Science and Art (frequently referred to—erroneously at the time—as the National Museum), played a very restricted role. It may be, as Carew (2003) has suggested, that there was a general fascination with the excavations and the possibilities of what might be

unearthed. Certainly it is a fact that many prominent members of these organisations were Freemasons, including Cochrane, Hanan, McDonald and Fielding, as well as the archaeologist Thomas J. Westropp.

During this investigation several artefacts are rumoured to have been recovered. No record of these survives (Carew 2003), with the exception of a small cache or hoard of Roman coins found in 1900 (see Appendix E).

Outline sequence of activity at the Rath of the Synods

Four principal phases of activity were identified during the excavation. The earliest (phase 1) is represented by a large ditched enclosure of unknown date, which was followed, probably in the developed Iron Age, by a series of circular ritual enclosures. The third phase consists of funerary activity, including a barrow on the north-west side of the site and an unenclosed flat cemetery in the centre. The burials appear to date from *c.* the first to the second century AD. The final phase is the large residential enclosure and associated domestic and industrial activity probably dating from the third century AD.

The excavation archive

The original archive, finds and samples, as well as computer discs of this report and databases of the finds and samples (Windows 95: Microsoft Word 7.0 and Works 4.0), are deposited in the National Museum of Ireland.

All of the finds in this report retain their original excavation number with the prefix E615. The prefix, however, is omitted on the find illustrations. An asterisk * before the find number indicates that it is not illustrated, and a find number which is <u>underlined</u> means that the object cannot be located.

The find drawings were executed during the original excavation and some were mounted for publication; others were drawn, often without sections, on the site excavation cards. The most important finds have been redrawn in the Department of Archaeology, University

Fig. 1.10—Visitors to Tara in 1953: (from left) Gay McCarron, Mortimer Wheeler, Maire McDermott, Ó Ríordáin and Hugh Kearney.

College Dublin, by Ursula Mattenberger. All of the bone objects are missing, having possibly been removed for analysis.

The original archive consisted of a comprehensive card index for most of the finds, notebooks covering both seasons, and field drawings, including a pre-excavation survey of the monument. It was not possible to discover several important site drawings although some plans and sections had been prepared from these for publication. Regrettably, the nature of the permatrace used at the time rendered it vulnerable to long-term degradation. As a result, all of these inked drawings had become reduced to small fragments as little as a few square millimetres in area. While it was possible to avail of some of the drawings, or portions of them, in writing this report, others were beyond restoration. Since further information had been added in the form of pencil notes, most of them in Ó Ríordáin's own hand, it may be that some detail, especially relating to the sections, has been irretrievably lost. Where possible, individual feature numbers have been allocated.

The human remains, other than some small quantities of cremation which are in the National Museum of Ireland, have not been located, and the report relies on identifications made in the 1950s.

The archives also contain the following: a soil report by S. Graham Brade Burk, dated Canterbury, Kent, 14 July 1952; a mollusc report by A. W. Stelfox, submitted to the Royal Irish Academy, 18 August 1952; a glass report by D. B. Harden, submitted to the British Academy, dated 16 December 1953, as well as an undated bead report; a bead report by Peggy Piggott, dated 18 October 1954; a coin report by Harold Mattingly, dated Cambridge, 17 August 1953 (see p. 46); an undated and unsigned geology report; a preliminary report and list of discarded animal bones by Ó Ríordáin (Appendix F); and correspondence with and reports from specialists in Britain concerning the Roman pottery. Some of this pottery is now missing and their analysis of the missing sherds is given in Appendix G.

Dating

As the excavations were conducted in the era before the development of radiocarbon dating there were no samples taken that were tied down to the type of specific stratigraphical location required for useful dating. All of the surviving samples were scrutinised for suitable dating material but three principal difficulties were encountered with these. Some bulk samples, from the fill of trench A, for example (see Chapter 2), consisted of burnt mature oak that was considered inappropriate for dating; in some instances these, and other smaller samples, did not retain sufficiently specific labelling to convincingly associate them with any particular context. Other more suitable dating material, for example the inhumation burials and the bone pins, could not be located and, indeed, remain 'at large'. The initial research for this publication took place in the late 1980s and at that time it was not possible to date cremated bone; in any case, the whereabouts of the cremations were unknown, although it was apparent that some had been sent to Stockholm for analysis. Some of the inhumations (burials D and H) were subsequently identified in the National Museum of Ireland when part of the National Collection was transferred to Collins Barracks, and these have been sent for dating (Appendix J). Prior to publication, in consultation with the external reader, it was determined that some form of chronological framework was required for publication. The samples were therefore reassessed and, accepting the limitations outlined above, fifteen were selected and submitted (Appendix J).

Author's acknowledgements

The completion of this publication has been a long process and many people have been involved in its finalisation over the years. Five people deserve special mention for their contributions. Throughout the process Seamus Caulfield provided insight and advice while acting as an erudite sounding-board for the interpretation of the material. During the 1980s Noel Dunne carried out a considerable amount of work disentangling the site plans and notes, as well as the samples and finds. Subsequently, Caroline Velzian Donaghy brought order and clarity to the archive, and in particular the finds catalogue, as well as providing enormous energy and support for the writing process. In the final stages of production Kim Rice managed the compilation processes as well as the complex realisation of the radiocarbon dating and the finds cata-

Fig. 1.11—Ó Ríordáin with some of the workmen from the Rath of the Synods site.

logue. In the end-game leading up to this publication Muiris O'Sullivan offered constant encouragement and advice while also dealing with issues of funding and organisation.

Successive heads of department in the Department (now School) of Archaeology, University College Dublin—George Eogan, Barry Raftery, Gabriel Cooney and Muiris O'Sullivan—were instrumental in providing funding and support for this project: I am very grateful for their persistence and encouragement. It is my pleasure to record thanks to many colleagues, especially Seamus Caulfield, Barry Raftery, Muiris O'Sullivan, Edel Bhreathnach, Raghnall Ó Floinn, Helen Roche, Tom Condit, Richard Warner, Sarah Cross and George Eogan, for fruitful discussion and helpful advice. The expertise on Roman material provided by Lindsay Allason-Jones, Museum of Antiquities, University of Newcastle upon Tyne, was invaluable, particularly in view of the scarcity of this type of material in Ireland (Appendix A). My special thanks to Edward Bourke, Jeremy Evans, Lorna O'Donnell and Fiona Dillon for their work on the glass vessels, the Roman pottery and the flint (Appendices C, G and D).

Final drawings for the publication were undertaken by Ursula Mattenberger, Maeve Maher, Mark Woods, Rob Carney and Mary Cuthbert. The late Albert Glaholm, Department of Archaeology, University College Dublin, was of great assistance in the early stages of production, and the final product owes much to the work of his successors David Jennings, Conor McDermott and Rob Sands.

These excavations, as with Ó Ríordáin's campaign at Lough Gur (which was completed with a final season in 1954), were to become an important training ground for a number of distinguished future archaeologists. Among those who worked on the site were George Eogan, Breandán Ó Ríordáin, Marcus Ó hEocaide, Patrick Healy (who also drew some of the artefacts for publication) and Etienne Rynne. Throughout his campaign Ó Ríordáin was assisted by the late Maire MacDermott (later de Paor), who undertook much of the assessment of the excava-

tions, both in the field and in subsequent research. Supervision on the excavations was also provided by Gabriel McCarron and Hugh Kearney, and in the 1953 season geological expertise was provided by Jimmy Brindley. The workmen (Fig. 1.11) came from the Tara/Navan area, with the exception of Michael Dwyer, Pallas, Co. Limerick, who had worked for several seasons at Lough Gur (Dwyer 1988). Some of the publication drawings were prepared by Bepi Gaidoni, who also worked on the site.

The excavation was visited by several illustrious contemporaries, including Christopher Hawkes (August 1953), Vere Gordon Childe, Mortimer Wheeler and Martha Stromberg (July 1953) (Fig. 1.10), as well as Ciarán MacMathuna. Hawkes visited the site for several days in August 1953 and provided valuable parallels for the Roman material, which was a complete novelty at that time in Ireland.

CHAPTER 2

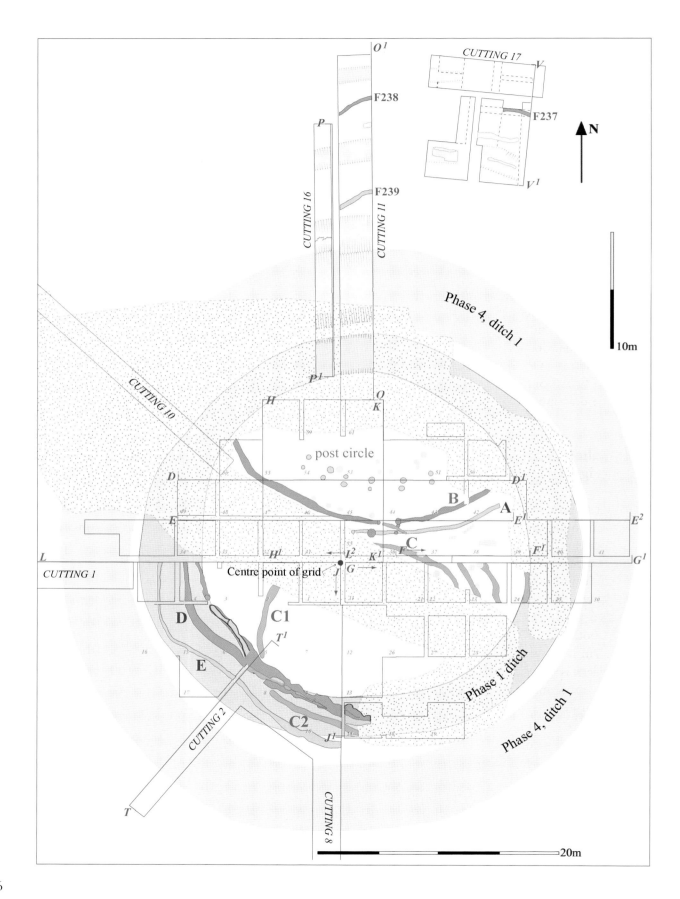

CUTTING 17

V

F238

F237

F239

CUTTING 16

CUTTING 11

V¹

N

O¹

P

Phase 4, ditch 1

10m

CUTTING 10

P¹

H

O

K

post circle

D

D¹

B

A

E

E¹

E²

C

L

H¹

F

F¹

G¹

CUTTING 1

Centre point of grid

J

G

K¹

D

C1

E

T¹

Phase 1 ditch

C2

CUTTING 2

J¹

Phase 4, ditch 1

T

CUTTING 8

20m

16

PHASES 1 AND 2: THE IRON AGE

Outline of sequence

The features associated with these phases all underlie the residential enclosure and consist of a ditch and several narrow curvilinear trenches (all of which had been truncated by British-Israelite destruction, see Fig. 1.8), as well as pits and post-holes forming a series of enclosures (Figs 2.1 and 2.5). The burial cluster (phase 3 cemetery, Fig. 3.5) intruded onto the line of three of these enclosing features, and burial B overlay trench A (see below). The finds from phase 2 are dealt with together between the descriptions and the discussion.

Phase 1: the primary ditched enclosure (F260) (Figs 2.2 and 2.4)

The earliest feature on the site consists of a partly rock-cut ditch enclosing an internal area measuring 26.5m (north–south) by 23m (east–west) and having maximum external dimensions of 32m (north–south) by 27.5m (east–west). It was sectioned on the northern, southern, eastern and western sides, and some short portions were excavated to the south-west and north-east. The ditch has a flat-bottomed to gently U-shaped section. It averages 1.7m in depth, with the lower 0.9–1.25m cut into the shale; it is up to 2m in depth on the western side but appears to be only 1.3m deep on the eastern side. The width varies from 4.7m to 3.9m and averages 4.4m. The fill consists of dark brown gravelly earth with a considerable number of small angular pieces of shale, which seem to have been derived from the original construction of the ditch.

There is no indication in the archive of any

Fig. 2.1—General plan of the phase 1 and 2 enclosures.

interpretation of the history or date of the ditch fill. The ditch may have been associated with a substantial inner and/or outer bank, or it might have provided material for a low internal mound. The sections are not particularly instructive in this regard, although those on the western and south-western sides (Fig. 2.2: L^1–L^2 and T^1–T^2; see also Fig. 2.3) show a very stony basal fill: this might indicate a primary slip consisting of shaly material derived from the lower ditch and piled onto the top or sides of a bank. On the south-eastern side (Fig. 4.4: G–G^1) there is a very distinct thin layer of stony material across the mid-point of the ditch fill, and its configuration, thickest on the eastern edge and tailing off towards the western (inner) side, might suggest slip from an external bank. This layer appears to occupy a similar position to a fill break shown on the western side of the site (Fig. 2.2: L^1–L^2) and what appears to be a sod layer that developed over this level of the ditch fill indicated on the south-east side (Fig. 2.2: T^1–T^2). On the basis of this evidence it seems reasonable to suggest that the lower part of the ditch gradually filled up, and at some point the erosion or collapse stabilised and a sod layer developed over the ditch. It may be that the remainder of the putative bank was levelled into the ditch to prepare the site for the phase 2 enclosures, although there is no detailed stratigraphic evidence to either prove or disprove this hypothesis.

No original gap or entrance was found in the excavated parts of the enclosure, whose function is unknown. It had completely silted up, or had been deliberately backfilled and levelled, prior to the construction of the palisade trenches (below), since three of these (trenches D–F) had been dug into the upper fill. No features within the enclosure could definitely be ascribed to this period, nor were there apparently any finds directly associated with it. A small amount of

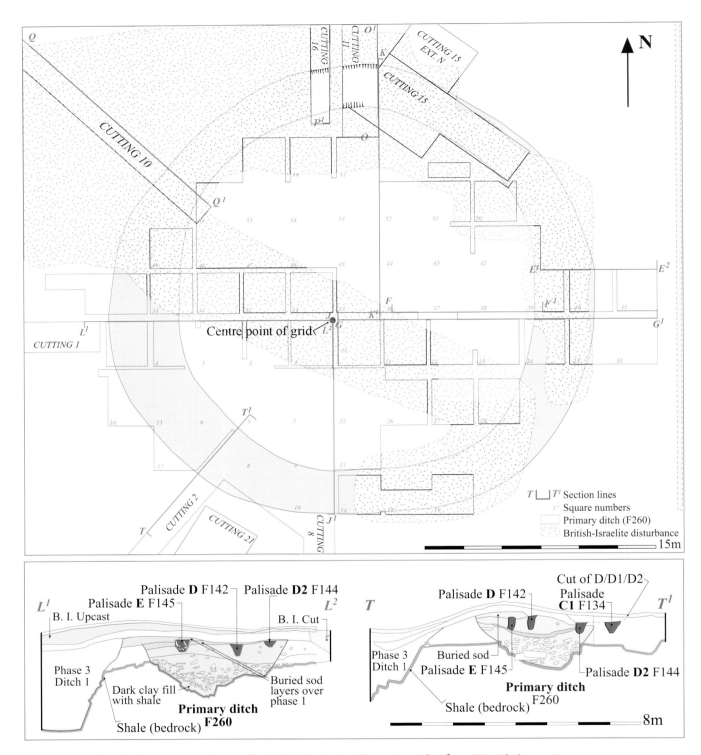

Fig. 2.2—Plan of phase 1 pre-enclosure ditch (F260) (top) with sections L¹–L² and T–T¹ (bottom).

charcoal and some fragments of cremated bone (not identified) came from the ditch fill, however.

Phase 1: discussion

Only small sections of the primary enclosure (F260) were excavated, and none produced any definitive dating evidence. It appears to have been almost circular, with internal measurements of *c.* 23m by 26m. A gradual period of silting and collapse, possibly derived from an external bank, may have been succeeded by deliberate levelling in preparation for the phase 2 activity. Given the range of Bronze Age and Iron Age monuments on the Hill of Tara (Newman 1997; O'Sullivan 2005), it is probable that this was a ritual or funerary site, possibly a barrow or a small embanked enclosure, perhaps similar to Rath Gráinne.

Phase 2: the palisade enclosures

A series of narrow, curved trenches were identified within the central part of the site (Figs 2.1–2.7). Despite the British-Israelite destruction and limited excavation in the area to the north of the primary enclosure, it was possible to identify a series of circular palisade enclosures as well as a circle of posts. Although a general sequence of construction is postulated, only limited comparative dating was identifiable. The stratigraphic evidence (Fig. 2.2: L[1]–L[2] and T–T[1]; see also Fig. 2.3) suggests that the palisade trenches were cut directly into what has been suggested (above) to have been material backfilled into the upper ditch in preparation for phase 2 construction.

Enclosures A/B

Trench A (F101) (Figs 2.1, 2.5–2.6)
This is a narrow palisade trench that curves across the northern part of the site from north-east to west. The excavated portion is 12m long, 0.3–0.4m wide (0.35m on average) and 0.59–0.64m deep. Towards the western side it turns slightly to the south, but the area beyond this was heavily disturbed. If it is part of a circular enclosure it would have had a diameter of *c.* 30m. At the eastern end the trench is clearly identified in the boulder clay, but to the west it only appears beneath the level of the overlying

features of both trench B and the later cemetery (see Chapter 3). The upper level of the trench must have been removed during the construction of these features; trench A is therefore the earliest on this part of the site and was superseded by trench B. The fill consists of charcoal-flecked stony soil, and some of the stones may have been set vertically as packing for posts. The sides and base of the trench are considerably fire-reddened.

Trench B (F100) (Figs 2.1, 2.5–2.7)
This is a narrow palisade trench that curves across the northern part of the centre of the site, forming part of an enclosure with its centre to the north. The excavated portion is 21.5m long and appears to consist of about one-fifth of a circular enclosure *c.* 27m in diameter. The trench has an average width of 0.5m but varies from 0.25m to 0.6m. At the eastern end it is concentric to, and 1m to the north of, trench A. In the area between 2.75m and 5.3m from its eastern side the trench follows a slightly erratic path, kinking to the north before resuming a more regular curve. Burial B (see Chapter 3) occurs just at this point and the head of this burial clearly extended over the southern lip of the trench. To the west of this irregular section the two trenches are within 0.5m of each other. At a point 2m from its western end, however, trench A turns slightly to the south. At this point, where it is truncated by the modern disturbance, it is again 1m outside trench B but there is no indication that it resumes a concentric course since the relevant area is entirely disturbed. Some individual post-holes within the trench fill were referred to in the field notes but not described.

Several apparently contemporary post-holes (F123, F125–6, F129–31) occur along the inner edge of the trench to the west of the entrance (below). These may form part of this enclosure or another, now poorly defined example, like the post-hole enclosure (below).

Entrance feature (Fig. 2.5)
Towards the centre of the excavated area trench B (F100) is terminated at the east by a substantial post-hole (F98). Although not on the original ground-plan, the finalised plan of the area prepared under Ó Ríordáin's supervision also shows a post-hole (F103) terminating the western section, indicating a 1m-wide gap between the two

Fig. 2.3—The palisade trenches cut into the primary ditched enclosure on the west side of the site (see section L¹–L²).

Fig. 2.4—Cutting 15 and cutting 15 extension, showing the partly rock-cut phase 1 ditch as well as British-Israelite destruction.

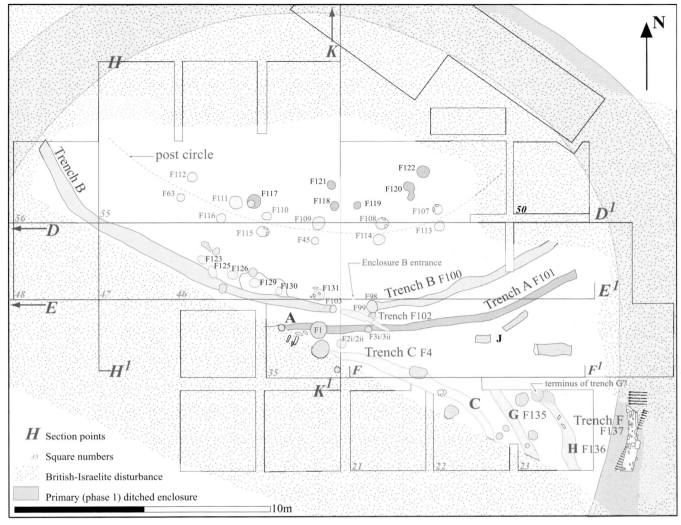

Fig. 2.5—Detailed plan of the phase 2 enclosure complex A–B.

portions of the trench. This appears to be an original entrance feature. To the south of the entrance two parallel lines of post-holes and pits (F2i, F2ii and F99, F3i, F3ii) appear to continue the feature with a narrow passage *c.* 0.78m wide and extending *c.* 1.2m to the south of the trench line. The upper fill of these features and of pit F1, which overlies trench A (F101) immediately to the west, contains habitation debris from phase 4. Beneath this (but not in F1) is a sterile layer of yellow clay with a basal layer of hard, fire-reddened earth containing small quantities of animal bone (not identified), very similar in composition to the fill of trench A.

Post circle (Figs 2.1 and 2.5)

A concentric enclosure consisting of a double line of substantial post-holes occurs to the north of and *c.* 2m inside trench B (F100); this would have had a diameter of up to 24m. The post-holes are 0.35–0.66m deep. They occur 0.2–0.4m apart, in pairs: F107/113, F108/114, F109/45, F110/115, F111/116 and F112/63. The distance between the pairs averages 2m (range 1.6–2.25m). The outer line is continued to the west by post-hole F63. One of the post-holes of the phase 4 house (F27 below) was apparently cut into the south-eastern edge of a matching feature, F112.

The post circle occurs within enclosure B. The curve

21

Trench B

F111/116 F21

F20

F114 F108

Burial E Burial H F120

Burial C

Trench A Trench B

Fig. 2.6—Central area north. The palisade enclosure complex from west. Trench B (F100) is fully excavated. The eastern end of trench A (F101) in the centre foreground is also excavated, but the later features associated with both the phase 3 burials and the phase 4 occupation still overlie it in the right centre. The phase 3 burials C, D and H are in the centre with, beyond, the phase 4 structure F20.

Fig. 2.7—Central area north. Palisade enclosure complex from the north-west. Trench B (F100) is fully excavated. In front of trench B is the position of the phase 4 house (F20) (centre). Although not identified on the site plans (or elsewhere in the archive), there may be a large circular house defined on the north side (at left) by possible concentric arced trenches (arrowed).

of the post-hole line matches that of trench B, and the outer post line is between 1.73m and 2.13m to the north with an average separation of 1.96m, suggesting a roughly equal distance between the post pairs and the trench. Other post-holes (F117–22) occur at the same level within this area. These may belong to the post-hole enclosure or to another, possibly associated, feature of broadly the same period. The post-holes here differ from the post- and stake-hole complex of phase 4 (see Chapter 4), as they are larger and several are stone-lined (F107–8, F111 and F115). The only possible pattern is that F117–20 and F122 appear to form an arc and might represent another post circle with a slightly different centre.

Summary
There is no unequivocal evidence as to whether the activity represented by trenches A and B and the post circle belongs to one or more phases. Nevertheless, a possible sequence is suggested, beginning with an enclosure represented by trench A. The nature of the fill suggests that the enclosure was made up of posts, or possibly upright planks, set into the trench and destroyed by fire, although individual post-holes within the trench were not recorded. Subsequently a second enclosure, represented primarily by trench B, was erected. This was up to 27m in diameter and followed closely the perimeter of trench A; this fact alone suggests that the interval between the destruction of enclosure A and the construction of enclosure B was short. The post circle, which could be up to 24m in diameter, may be contemporary with enclosure B since the intervals between the post pairs and those between the curve of the posts and trench B are similar. Other features, such as the remaining large post-holes of phase 2, in this area are impossible to analyse in relation to the enclosures themselves, but the possibility of other, less well-preserved post circles cannot be discounted.

Enclosure C (Figs 2.1, 2.5 and 2.9)

This occurs to the south of enclosure complex A/B. The northern part is represented by trench C (F4), which curves in an opposing direction from trench B. The surviving portion is 7.5m long, 0.26–0.52m wide and 0.18–0.27m deep. Although following a reasonably regular curve, it has a slight southward kink roughly midway along its excavated length. The trench follows a curve that appears to be continued to the south-west by trench C1 (F134) to form an enclosure about 16.5m in diameter. Trench C1 curves from north to south and formed the south-western side of the enclosure; the main portion is 5.5m long, 0.43m in average width and 0.8–1.1m deep. The lowermost portion of the trench is cut into the underlying shale.

The fill is heavily oxidised and is clearly indicated at the old ground level as a red burnt band that contained a large quantity of charcoal and burnt bone (not identified). Close to the base of the trench towards the northern end (not more closely located) fragments of bone, apparently human, were found under some large stones, and the area around and immediately above the deposit was especially heavily burnt. Enclosure C appears to continue with trench C2 (F139) on the south. Although the area between C1 and C2 was cut through by trench D (F142, see below), there seems to be an original entrance, 2.44m wide, formed by terminals at the south of C1 and the north of C2. Trench C2 is 7m long, 0.39–0.47m wide and 0.37–0.8m deep and is truncated at the eastern end by the British-Israelite destruction.

At some stage the south-west side of enclosure C was altered: trench C2 became defunct and was replaced by F140, an extension of C1, which cut across and narrowed the original entrance and extended to the north and west of trench C2 (Figs 2.1 and 2.2: T–T[1]). Another modification to this portion of the enclosure is represented by trench D1 (F143), which extends in a south-eastward curve from trench C1 on the northern side of F140. This trench is entirely rock-cut and underlies trench D, which cuts across the line of F143. Although its edges are irregular, it seems to form a curve similar to that of C1. Trench F143 is 4.33m long, 0.42–0.71m wide and 0.7–1.4m in depth below the boulder clay. There is no indication of whether F141 is earlier or later than F140 but its clear junction with trench C1 shows that it was later than the latter feature.

Trenches G (F135) and H (F136)
Two short sections of trenches (trench G, F135, and trench H, F136) occur to the east of trench C and are

apparently concentric with it (Figs 2.5 and 4.4: F–F[1], G–G[1]). Trench G is 0.8m east of C and trench H is a further 1–1.25m east of G. These are slighter features than trench C but their position suggests that they are contemporary and form outer elements of the enclosure on the east side; they do not, however, appear to be replicated on the south-west side of the site, although this area was severely disturbed by the elements of enclosure D. On the site plans trench H appears to be terminated by a pit or large post-hole: although not referred to in the archive, this may represent a terminus forming one side of an entrance feature. Another short section of trench, F102, follows the curve of trench C on the northern side (Fig. 2.5). Although much narrower, this may be a continuation of trench G. F102 lies across the entrance to enclosure B and may be truncated by it, suggesting that it is earlier. F102 may cut across the enclosure B entrance, however, and block it deliberately. Trench A clearly underlies F102 and is therefore an earlier feature.

Summary

Enclosure C appears to consist of a circle with a flattened southern side, 16.5m in diameter and enclosed by a single palisade trench (F4, F134, F139, F140) with an entrance gap on the south-west side. On the north-east side the trench is reflected by two outer concentric circles (trench G, F135, and trench H, F136) that may not have extended beyond the south-east quadrant. The innermost (trench G, F135) appears to be continued to the north by another short trench, F102. The enclosure was later modified to extend it to the south outside its original perimeter (F140), and this may have involved the relocation of the entrance to the southern side. Another modification (D1, F143), either later or earlier than the previous one, involved redefining the southern side on a line inside that of the original circle.

Trench F (Figs 2.1, 2.5 and 4.4: G–G[1])

A short section of a trench (F137), 1.4m long by 0.45m wide and 0.52m deep, occurs on the eastern edge of the undisturbed portion of the site, cut into the upper fill of the phase 1 ditch. The edges of the trench are nearly vertical and the western end is lined with vertical shale slabs. Small fragments of burnt bone (not identified)

came from the surface of the boulder clay on the western lip of the trench and the binding of a bronze dagger chape (161, see below) came from the base of the trench.

Trench J (F138) (Figs 2.1 and 2.5)

This is a short section of a linear feature between trenches A and B, discovered at the same level as trench B. It appears to be cut by the grave (F6) of burial W and should therefore date from phase 2. It is also cut by pit F159, which belongs to phase 4 (see Chapter 4). The trench is 2.08m long, 0.28m wide and deepens from 0.12m at the west to 0.32m at the east.

Enclosure D (Figs 2.1–2.3 and 2.9–2.10)

This is later than enclosure C. It is defined on the southern side of the site by trench D (F142), which extends from the western side of the central area in a south-easterly curve. The excavated portion in this area is 15m long, 0.4m in average width and 0.4m in average depth. If circular, the enclosure would have been about 40m in diameter (Fig. 2.10). Two modifications to the perimeter of the enclosure were noted in this area. First, the line of trench D appears to have been cut through the outer, i.e. southern, edge of an earlier trench (D1, F143). This was shallower than trench D. The surviving identifiable portion is 0.45m wide, 0.4m deep and runs for about 10m along the south-eastern edge of trench D. At a later stage the line of enclosure D was altered to run inside the original perimeter on the western and south-western sides. This modification is marked by trench D2 (F144), which joined with D (F142) at the point where the earlier trench (D1) began. Trench D2 runs for 7.9m to the north-west of this point and averages 0.4m in width with a depth of 0.2–0.55m.

The fill of these three features consists of dark earth with a considerable quantity of charcoal and fragments of animal bone (none identified), and finds. Trench D in particular shows evidence of intense *in situ* burning, with a charcoal-rich fill containing 'a great many bones'. The nature of the fill, apparently representing pockets of charcoal and bone, in combination with stone packing indicates that the trenches supported posts.

To the north-east, beyond the area of British-Israelite disturbance, another short section of trench, trench K

Fig. 2.8—Central area north. Palisade enclosure complex from south.

(F146), appears to continue the curve of either enclosure D or D1 (Fig. 2.8; see below). The trench is 3m long, 0.6–1.3m wide (narrowing to the north, perhaps as a result of the destruction of the upper levels) and 1.2–1.3m deep. Stone packing occurs in the upper levels, and the lowermost portion of the trench is cut into the underlying shale. Since this trench occurs immediately inside the inner ditch of the later phase 4 enclosure it is more likely to be a continuation of enclosure D.

Enclosure E (F145) (Figs 2.1–2.2: L^1–L^2, T–T^1, and Figs 2.9–2.10)

The south-west side of this enclosure is represented by the curving trench E (F145), which occurs 0.8–1.8m outside enclosure D. Despite the variation in the distance between them, trench E follows a path similar to that of trench D and could be a contemporary or near-contemporary feature. It appears that enclosure E would have been *c.* 42m in diameter, if circular. The surviving portion of the trench in this area is 20.5m long, 0.3–0.7m wide and 0.25–0.6m deep. It is shallowest towards the north-west end, but in this area several post-holes were identified in the base and these are up to

Table 2.1—Finds from phases 1 and 2; detailed descriptions (and a list of samples) are presented in Appendix A (*not illustrated; <u>underlining</u> indicates that the object cannot be located).

	E no.	Object	Context		E no.	Object	Context
Copper alloy	E615:149	Type 1 penannular ear-ring	Trench C (F4)	**Iron**	*E615:6	Penannular strip	Trench D1 (F143)
	E615:161	Dagger chape binding	Trench F (F137)		*E615:16	Square-sectioned stem	Sq. 9
					*E615:61	Staple	Trench E (F145)
Amber	*E615:62a	Small fragment	Trench D or D2		*E615:62a	Fragments	Trench D or D2 (F142/144)
					*E615:77	Pointed stem with E615:75	Trench D (F142)
Glass	E615:2	Glass setting	Trench D (F142)		*E615:82	Pin or nail stem	Trench D (F142)
	E615:116	Half of blue cylindrical bead	Trench C (F4)		*E615:90	Round-sectioned nail or pin	Trench D (F142)
					*E615:110	Very corroded bar	Trench D (F142)
Fired clay	*E615:54	Elliptical ball	Trench D (F142)		*E615:111	Stem and fragments	Trench B (F100)
					*E615:113	Circular-sectioned nail/pin	Trench D (F142)
Stone	E615:26b	Part of sandstone bowl rim	Trench D1 (F143)		*E615:144	Fragmented corroded ring	Trench B (F100)
	*E615:60	Disc-shaped pebble	Trench E (F145)				
	*E615:75	30 pebbles, game? (see E615:75)	Trench D (F142)				
	E615:121	Flint (see Appendix D)	Trench C (F4)				
	*E615:255	Circular flat palette	Trench A (F101)				
	*E615:258	Gaming piece/rubbing stone?	Trench A (F101)				
	*E615:259	Gaming piece/rubbing stone?	Trench D (F142)				
	*E615:275	Three gaming pieces/rubbing stones?	Trench D2 (F144)				

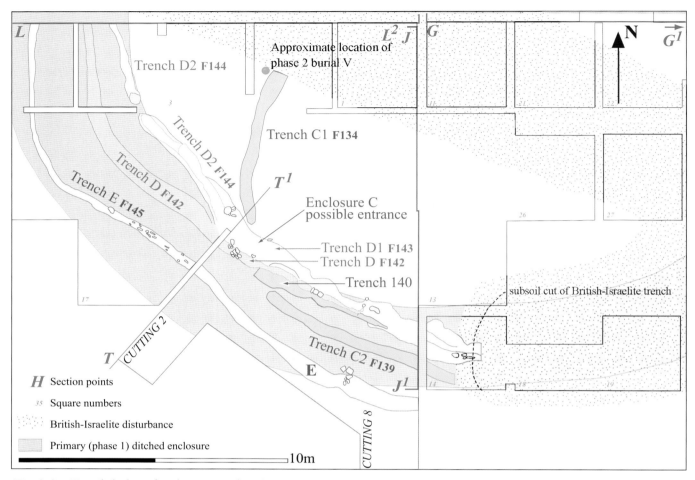

Fig. 2.9—Detailed plan of enclosure complex C–D.

0.5m deep. While some small post-holes, perhaps designed to hold the base of posts in position, were identified at the eastern end, it appears that in the latter area the posts were set into a continuous bedding trench. Packing stones were noted in several places in the trench and the fill was dark, charcoal-flecked soil. There were no finds, other than animal bone (not identified), in the trench, which is sealed under the inner bank of the later residential enclosure.

Other trenches

Another palisade trench, F237, was identified beneath bank 2 of the later residential enclosure (cutting 17, sqs 62, 63 extension east; Figs 2.1, 2.10, 4.6 and 4.7: O–O^1) and sealed by a buried sod layer. This was also identified in cutting 11 (F238; Figs 2.1, 2.10, 4.6 and 4.7: O–O^1). This trench runs north-eastward across the northern side of the

site and follows a very different curve to that of the enclosing features of the phase 4 enclosure. To the south of F237 is another trench (F239; Figs 4.6 and 4.7: O–O^1) that appears to follow the same curve. It may represent the northern side of enclosures A and B (Fig. 2.10).

Finds from phase 2 (Fig. 2.11)

Detailed descriptions (and a list of samples) are presented in Appendix A.

A small quantity of finds came from phase 2 (Table 2.1; Appendix A). The most interesting are a copper-alloy type 1 penannular ear-ring (E615:149, Fig. 2.11; Allason-

Fig. 2.10—Schematic sequence of enclosures, phase 1. Inset: comparison of the south-west perimeters of enclosures B–E.

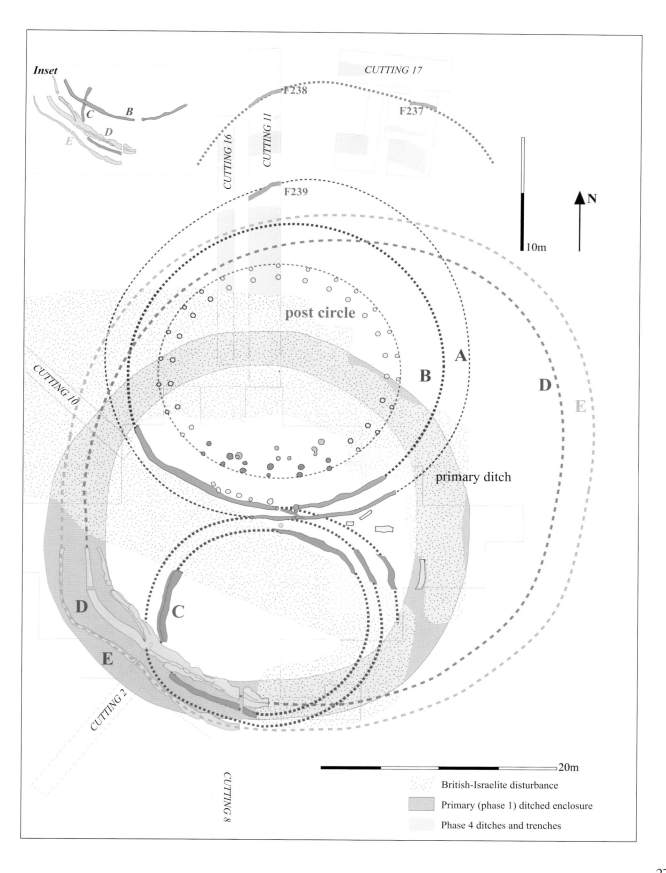

Inset

CUTTING 17

F238

F237

CUTTING 16

CUTTING 11

F239

post circle

A

B

D

E

CUTTING 10

primary ditch

D

C

E

CUTTING 2

CUTTING 8

20m

British-Israelite disturbance

Primary (phase 1) ditched enclosure

Phase 4 ditches and trenches

10m

N

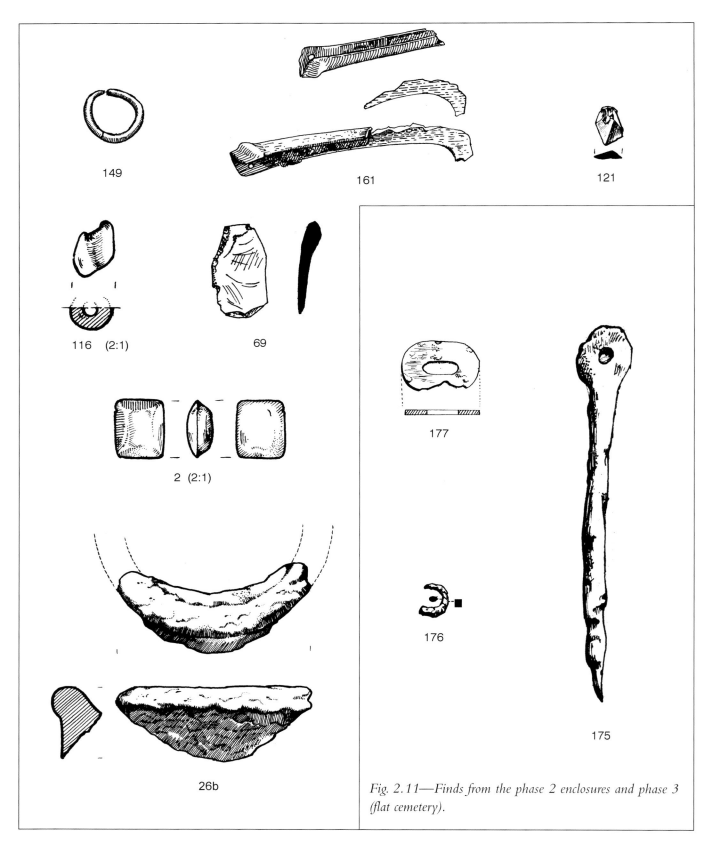

149

161

121

116 (2:1)

69

177

2 (2:1)

176

26b

175

Fig. 2.11—Finds from the phase 2 enclosures and phase 3 (flat cemetery).

Jones 1989, 2–3), similar to those from Feerwore, Co. Galway (J. Raftery 1944, fig. 4:29), and from a burial at Knowth, Co. Meath (Eogan 1974, fig. 31:188), and part of a bronze dagger chape (E615:161, Fig. 2.11). Amongst the iron objects is a pointed stem (★E615:77) found with 30 water-rolled pebbles (★E615:75) bearing signs of wear from rubbing: these items may be part of a gaming set. Caches of worn, non-local pebbles were also found in a burial at Knowth, Co. Meath (Eogan 1974, 76–8, fig. 32), at Uisneach, Co. Westmeath (Macalister and Praeger 1928–9), and in the Iron Age phase 1 at Millockstown, Co. Louth (C. Manning 1986). A similar, but uncontexted, stem (★E615:94) was also found with similarly worn pebbles (see Appendix H). There are a number of other possible gaming pieces or rubbing stones (★E615:258, ★E615:259 and ★E615:275) from phase 2.

A setting of green/blue glass (E615:2, Fig. 2.11 and Pl. 1) and half of a blue bead with a slanting cylindrical shape (E615:116, Fig. 2.11) also came from the trench fills. A roughly circular flat stone palette with one well-polished face (★E615:255) came from trench A (F101). Traces of iron staining suggest that this palette was held in an iron frame; it may have been used for mixing ointments and pigments. Part of the slightly out-turned rim of a dressed sandstone bowl (E615:26b, Fig 2.11) came from trench D1 (F143): signs of burning suggest that it may be part of a lamp.

Phase 2: discussion

A reasonably well-defined sequence is represented by the palisade enclosures (Figs 2.1, 2.5, 2.9 and 2.10). The earliest stage is represented by the construction of enclosure A on the northern side. This appears to be about 30m in diameter and would have cut across the earlier ditch, although evidence for this was not produced through excavation. A part of the northern edge of this enclosure appears to be represented by F239. Next is enclosure C, to the south of and partly overlapping A, which is about 16.5m in diameter with an entrance on the south-west side. This side of the feature was remodelled, putting the new entrance slightly further to the south. The relative positions of enclosures

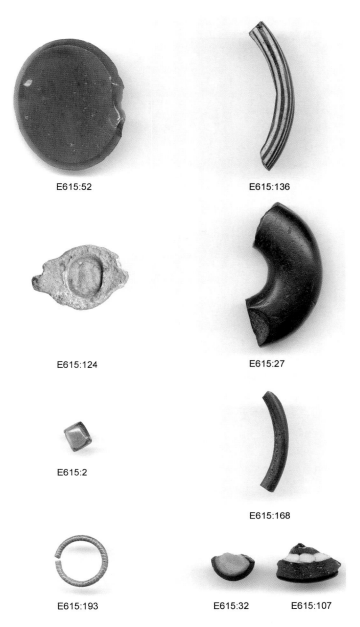

E615:52

E615:136

E615:124

E615:27

E615:2

E615:168

E615:193

E615:32   E615:107

Pl. 1—Collection of small finds from the site.

B, D and E are not clear, and B, with a possible inner ring of paired posts, could have occurred entirely within either D or E, so there may not have been a physical overlap in the trenches.

The palisades appear to have consisted of closely spaced, but not apparently contiguous, posts set into individual post-sockets within the trenches. These were up to 1.1m deep and could have supported posts over 2.5m in height. The trench and post-holes in enclosure

D were larger than those of the other enclosures. Many of the identified post-holes in all of the enclosures were much shallower, however, and the palisades may have been less substantial than this. The post-holes of the post circle were more substantial than those of the palisade trenches and appear to have contained larger, if not necessarily higher, posts.

There is no indication of the nature of the activity that took place within the palisade enclosures. Apart from the post ring in enclosure B and several other post-holes within it, no other features could definitely be assigned to this phase. Some cremated bone was found in the trenches and some of that from trench A was identified as 'human'. Whether it represented formal burial or an element of funerary activity associated with other ritual is not known.

An interesting, although unexplained, feature of enclosures B–E is the distinct flattening along the south-western side (see Fig. 2.10: inset); indeed, on enclosures D and E there is a slight incurvation along this part of the perimeter. While the enclosure B and C entrances are in this general area, there is no direct evidence for similarly located breaks in D–E. Nevertheless, the flattened façades in this area indicate a strong element of referencing between these four enclosures (this portion of enclosure A had been completely removed).

There was considerable evidence for burning in, and along the sides and edges of, trenches A, C and D. This, together with the charcoal from the fill, suggests that they were destroyed by fire. Given the apparent sequence in the enclosures, it is possible that enclosures A and C were deliberately burnt in order to make way for enclosure B and the remodelled enclosure C. Similarly, the removal of enclosure D may have facilitated the construction of the final palisade, E.

Unfortunately, later activity, including the phase 4 enclosure and the British-Israelite investigations, severely compromised the phase 2 enclosures on the northern side of the site in particular. Within the excavated area this has certainly removed enclosures A–E and the post circle on the north-west side, but there is potentially undisturbed evidence for all six enclosures as well as the possible relationships between them on the north-east side (Fig. 2.10). Palisades F237 and F238 are certainly

stratigraphically early and are sealed beneath bank 2 of the phase 4 enclosure. They do not appear to form part of the other phase 2 enclosures, but their combined suggested curvature may indicate the presence of another enclosure on the northern side of the excavation (see Figs 2.10 and 4.6).

Comparative sites

The closest comparisons for the phase 2 monuments at the Rath of the Synods are at Dún Ailinne, Co. Kildare (Wailes 1970; 1976; 1990), where four major phases of construction were recognised, at site B, Emain Macha, Co. Armagh (Lynn 1986; Waterman 1997), which had three principal phases, and at Raffin, Co. Meath (Newman 1993a; 1993b; Fig. 2.12).

Following a series of perhaps intermittent episodes of activity beginning in the Neolithic, two principal building phases are represented at Emain Macha B (Lynn 1986, figs 2 and 3). In the first there is a ditched enclosure, 47m in internal diameter, with its entrance on the east side. Within this is a complex sequence of figure-of-eight structures, each consisting of a larger circle (diameter 18–20m) with a smaller one (diameter *c.* 10–14m) attached to the southern side. Both are defined by slot-trenches. The larger structures have funnel-shaped passages extending from the entrance, which faces slightly south of east. Simple entrances in the smaller enclosures face slightly north of east. A very similar arrangement occurs at Dún Ailinne, where both circles are larger (diameters *c.* 30m and 17m respectively) ('rose' phase; Wailes 1990, 12–13, figs 2–3; Lynn 1991, 51–3, fig. 1A). The entrances to both circles face slightly north of east.

While there are problems with the sequence at the Rath of the Synods, the juxtaposition of enclosures A/B (with a diameter of *c.* 40m) and enclosure C (diameter 16.5m) immediately to the south is remarkably similar to the figure-of-eight arrangements at both Emain Macha and Dún Ailinne (Fig. 2.12). The first phase of the smaller of the Rath of the Synods structures has a south-west-facing entrance. The gap in trench B seems, if it is contemporary, to have provided access to enclosure C via the small corridor defined by two lines of posts extending for *c.* 3m between the enclosures (Fig. 2.5, enclosure B entrance). There is no evidence for another

Dún Ailinne, Co. Kildare
Summit area

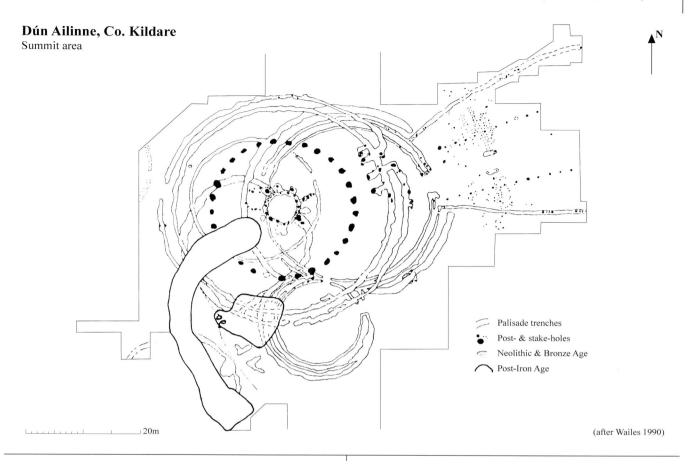

Palisade trenches
Post- & stake-holes
Neolithic & Bronze Age
Post-Iron Age

20m

(after Wailes 1990)

Navan Fort Site B, Co. Armagh
Pre-mound late Bronze Age wall slots

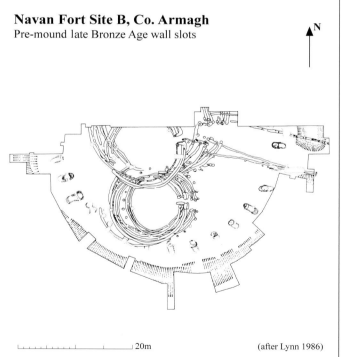

20m

(after Lynn 1986)

Raffin Fort, Co. Meath

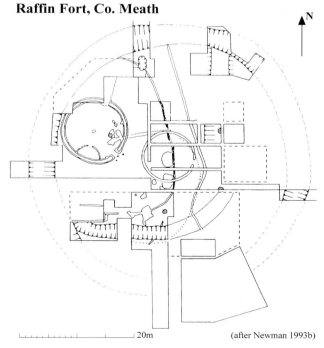

20m

(after Newman 1993b)

Fig. 2.12—Comparative sites for the phase 2 enclosures.

entrance but only the southern arc of enclosure B was excavated.

The presence of the primary enclosing ditch at the Rath of the Synods is reminiscent of the situation at Emain Macha B, where an enclosure ditch 47m in diameter was large enough to encompass the figure-of-eight structures. At Tara, however, the primary ditched enclosure pre-dates the slot-trenches of all the enclosures.

At Raffin, Co. Meath (Newman 1993a, 23), a substantial enclosure, *c.* 40m in internal diameter, defined by a ditch and external bank, comes at the end of a sequence of ceremonial activity on the summit of the drumlin. Centrally placed within this is a circular structure defined by a slot-trench with a diameter of 9m, surrounded by a ring of six substantial free-standing posts, 21m in diameter. This phase yielded a radiocarbon date of 30 cal. BC–cal. AD 670. This ring of posts can be compared to the double circle within enclosure B at the Rath of the Synods, which has a diameter of *c.* 24m. There is a ring of large posts within the ditch at Emain Macha B phase 2 (diameter 39m) and phase 4 (diameter 40m), which defined the large structure. A post circle (diameter 25m) also occurs inside the 'mauve' phase enclosure at Dún Ailinne.

A ditched enclosure (internal diameter *c.* 27m) with an external bank also occurs at Emain Macha A and, while there is no clear evidence for dating, it may be a ritual circle broadly contemporary with site B (Lynn 1986, 12–13, fig. 1). Underlying it were three concentric slot-trench circles (diameter 16.6–20.3m), with the trenches used sequentially in the same manner as those at site B.

Clearly a range of elements were in use either singly or in combination at these ceremonial centres. Ditches, with or without evidence for associated banks, occur at the Rath of the Synods, Emain Macha A and B, and Raffin. Only at Raffin, however, is there secure evidence to place this feature firmly in the Iron Age. The stratigraphic evidence shows that the primary ditched enclosure at the Rath of the Synods pre-dates the slot-trench enclosures on the southern side of the site (C, D and E) but could be earlier than those on the northern side (A and B). The fact that it had apparently been deliberately backfilled prior to the construction of C, D

and E suggests that its life-span was short and that it was removed to prepare the site for the other circles. No evidence survived to indicate whether it had an associated bank such as the external ones at Raffin and Emain Macha A.

At Uisneach, another important complex of sites in County Westmeath, a 'conjoined ringfort' that was excavated in the 1920s (Macalister and Praeger 1928–9, 87–91, pl. III) overlay an interesting earlier feature (Donaghy and Grogan 1997). This consists of a penannular ditched enclosure (diameter 48m) with evidence of an external bank or wall of stone. Traces of an outer ditch occurred on the northern side, and what appears to have been a slot-trench was found on the southern side at about the same distance from the main ditch. Two substantial pits or post-pits flanked the entrance on the inside. The 'conjoined ringfort' itself shows that in certain areas construction of the banks and ditches was achieved by modifying an earlier monument. Taking into consideration the structure of the underlying ditch and some evidence from the finds, the Uisneach monument could well be part of the Iron Age series under discussion.

Structures represented by slot-trenches occurred on all of the sites under discussion. The most striking comparisons are between the figure-of-eight arrangements at Emain Macha B (phase 3), Dún Ailinne ('rose' phase) and the potential example comprising enclosures A/B and C at the Rath of the Synods (Figs 2.8, 2.10 and 2.12; Table 2.2). All three consist of larger structures on the north, apparently attached, or very closely related, to smaller enclosures on the southern side. The absence of evidence for internal features, other than the large double post circle within enclosure B at Tara, suggests that none of these enclosures were roofed. Those at Dún Ailinne and the Rath of the Synods are very similar in size, but the Emain Macha examples are somewhat smaller. At Dún Ailinne and Emain Macha each of the enclosures consists of three concentric slots, which at Emain Macha are shown to have a sequential use. This sequence was evidenced at the single enclosure forming the first phase of activity at Emain Macha. The Dún Ailinne slots appear to have been contemporary.

While less coherent than the other two sites, it can be suggested that both enclosure A/B and enclosure C at the Rath of the Synods were made up of three elements. The trench defining enclosure A was earlier than that of enclosure B. As suggested earlier, the post circle within B could be earlier, later or contemporary with B. Three concentric slots appear to form the north-eastern perimeter of enclosure C. A sequence was also evident between enclosure B and the later trench F102, which appears to form the middle element in enclosure C. While the stratigraphical evidence is by no means clear-cut, it is possible that the complex of enclosures formed by A, B and C at the Rath of the Synods represents a figure-of-eight arrangement with a sequential construction involving three elements in both the northern (enclosures A/B) and southern (enclosure C) components.

A pair of concentric slots also supported the main enclosing elements at the final phase of Emain Macha A and in the late Bronze Age structure at Raffin. These enclosures, with internal diameters of 13m and 10m respectively, contained internal posts and could have been roofed.

The final stages of Iron Age ceremonial building at Emain Macha and Dún Ailinne are represented by large elaborate enclosures (Lynn 1986; 1991; Wailes 1990). The stratigraphic evidence suggests that at the Rath of the Synods an equivalent phase consisted of two concentric slot-trenches (enclosures D and E), each encircling an area c. 40–42m in diameter. Part of the innermost of these, trench D, appears to have been modified, including the redigging of the trench itself and the addition of a new element (F144) on the south-western side. In combination, therefore, there is again an indication that enclosure D/E was made up of three components that were used sequentially (see Figs 2.9 and 2.10).

Dating

The parallels for the enclosures cited above suggest that this phase of the Rath of the Synods should date from before c. 100 BC. There are very few artefacts from this phase and none is closely datable. The bronze ear-ring (E615:149, Fig. 2.11) from trench C can be compared with two from a probably first- to second-century AD burial at Knowth (Eogan 1974, fig. 31), as well as with

one from Feerwore (J. Raftery 1944, fig. 4:29). The portion of a bronze chape binding (E615:161, Fig. 2.11) from trench F, whose position within the enclosure complex is itself unclear, is of ultimate La Tène type (B. Raftery, pers. comm.) and may date from as late as the first or second century AD. The chape and the striated ear-ring are of types that have a much longer currency, however, extending back to the final centuries BC. In this regard it is important to note the chape's similarity to two pieces (E615:138 and E615:217, Fig. 4.10), which indeed could be from the same artefact, from the phase 4 habitation (Chapter 4): this casts further doubt on the association of the chape with the phase 2 activity.

The possible gaming sets represented by the cache of small pebbles with areas of scratching and rubbing (*E615:75) and a possible iron pointer (*E615:77) from trench D, two individual pebbles from trenches D (*E615:259) and A (*E615:258) and three other pebbles found together in trench D2 are similar to those from the Iron Age burials at Knowth (Eogan 1974, fig. 32), as well as possible examples from phase 1 at Millockstown (C. Manning 1986, 161–2) and from Uisneach (Macalister and Praeger 1928–9; Donaghy and Grogan 1997). A more elaborate version, in bone with detachable pins, came from the same Knowth burial, together with a parallelepiped bone die (Eogan 1974, fig. 31) similar to examples from Newgrange (Carson and O'Kelly 1977, pl. 8a). Other examples from phase 4 or disturbed contexts at the Rath of the Synods (below) include two pebbles with a small pointed iron implement (*E615:94a and b), two quartz pebbles with fragments of iron (*E615:18c), a group of 65 pebbles (*E615:46) found together, a pair (*E615:38) and a single find (*E615:257).

The stone palette (*E615:255), the stone bowl fragment (E615:26, Fig. 2.11), the glass bead (E615:116, Fig. 2.11) and setting (E615:2, Fig. 2.11 and Pl. 1), the possible iron scabbard mount (*E615:6) and most of the iron pieces are not closely datable. The five iron pin shafts (or possible nails) are apparently unique; while there are only five, their average length (42.8mm) is significantly less than that of 53mm for the nails from phase 4 (Chapter 4; Fig. 4.12). Three are from trench D, one is from a post-hole close to trench D and the fifth is from trench B. It is possible that they indicate a structural feature of the palisade itself, such as horizontal planking, or perhaps some form of entrance feature on the southern side of the enclosure, the area within which the earlier entrance to enclosure C had been located.

As already noted, the comparisons with Emain Macha, Dún Ailinne, Uisneach and Raffin suggest that a general date of before 100 BC, but possibly as late as the first century AD, is probable for the Rath of the Synods enclosures. This accords well with the evidence from the subsequent burial phase, which appears to begin some time during the first century AD into the second century AD (Chapter 3).

Although no firmly datable finds came from phase 1, the chape binding, scabbard mount and gaming pieces indicate an Iron Age horizon with parallels at Knowth, Millockstown, Feerwore and Uisneach (above). In view of the very solid evidence for the termination of this phase of activity at Emain Macha, it is probable that the Rath of the Synods enclosures date from the period around 100 BC or very soon after.

Table 2.2—Comparison of Iron Age ceremonial structures (diameter and orientation).

Slot-trench enclosure	North structure diameters (m)	South structure diameters (m)	Entrance orientation
Dún Ailinne, 'rose' phase	29, 31, 35	15, 17, 18	ENE–ENE
Emain Macha B, phase 3	18, 19, 20	10, 13, 14	ESE–ENE
Rath of the Synods, A/B, C	35, 40	14, 15, 16	SW
Dún Ailinne, 'mauve' phase	37, 42		ENE
Emain Macha B, phase 4	37, 40		?
Rath of the Synods, D, E	c. 40, 42		?
OTHER STRUCTURES			
Emain Macha B, primary	16, 18, 20		?
Emain Macha B, secondary	13, 16		E
Raffin, late Bronze Age	10, 12		SE
Raffin, Iron Age	9		E
POST CIRCLES			
Rath of the Synods, B	24		
Dún Ailinne, 'mauve'	26		
Emain Macha, phase 3 enclosure	39		
Emain Macha B, phase 3 structure	40		
DITCHED ENCLOSURES			
Rath of the Synods	c. 25 by 30		?
Emain Macha A	21		?
Emain Macha B, phase 3	48		W?
Raffin	40		SE?
Uisneach	48		ENE

CHAPTER 3

Fig. 3.1—Aerial view of the site from south-east at the beginning of the excavation. The excavation of the barrow (centre background) is under way; both cutting 1 and the central area south have been fully opened. The palisade trenches of the enclosure complex C/D/E are visible curving across the southern side of the site.

PHASE 3: THE IRON AGE BURIALS

Introduction

Two areas on the site were used for burial in the late prehistoric period: a barrow on the north-west side and a flat cemetery centred on the eastern side of the phase 2 enclosures. While at least some of the burials in the flat cemetery are clearly later than phase 2, there is no stratigraphic relationship between that phase and the barrow. Both burial areas are, however, treated here for convenience, and it is in any case probable that they belong to a single funerary phase at the Rath of the Synods.

Phase 3 burials: the barrow

Introduction (Figs 1.2, 3.1–3.4)
This feature is on the north-west side of the site between ramparts 3 and 4 of the later residential enclosure, which respects it. It was visible prior to excavation as a small irregular mound measuring *c.* 12m north-west/south-east by 10.5m north-east/south-west, and there was evidence of interference in the form of scoops and hollows in the surface. The layout of the cuttings through the barrow is described on page 6.

The primary phase (Figs 3.1–3.4)
The barrow is surrounded by a V-sectioned ditch, from *c.* 2.6m to 3m wide and from *c.* 1.4–1.6m to 2m in overall depth. The base of the ditch is cut into the underlying bedrock to a depth of between 0.8m and 1.15m. The material from the ditch was used to construct the barrow, which rested on the undisturbed natural sod (Fig. 3.3: A–A^1). This primary phase of the barrow has maximum dimensions of 14.9m north-west/south-east by 16.5m north-east/south-west and survives to a height of 0.85m. It has a substantial stone

core consisting of an upper capping of both large blocks (up to 0.6m by 0.45m) and smaller stones overlying a compact clay layer containing small stones, and may originally have been up to 14m in diameter. The stones, particularly the larger ones, appear to have been derived from the base of the ditch. A reasonably well-preserved portion of the core, measuring 11m north-west/south-east by 8m north-east/south-west and 0.55m in maximum height, survived immediately east and north-east of the centre of the barrow (Figs 3.2–3.3), and another part survives on the south-east side. These portions extend to within 1m and 3m respectively of the inner edge of the ditch. On the eastern side the undisturbed edge of the core is 4m from the inner lip of the ditch. The undisturbed element of the overlying barrow consists of a 0.2–0.6m-thick layer of compacted yellow/brown clay and small stones. The barrow contained five primary cremations (burials L, M, R, S and T; see below).

The sections show evidence of some silting in the base of the ditch in the form of a basal layer of 'sticky fill' (Fig. 3.3: A–A^1) containing a considerable amount of loose stone. The presence of snail shells associated with burial Q (a cremation deposited on a small ledge on the inner edge of the rock-cut lower section of the ditch on the south-east side, see below; Fig. 3.3: B–B^1) suggests that the ditch was an open feature for at least a short period after its construction. Animal bones (not identified), including an 'ox head', were found close to the bottom of the ditch on the south-east side. Most of the animal bones from the excavation, other than some small quantities in the samples, were discarded, but a list of animal bones from the Rath of the Synods, in Ó Ríordáin's handwriting (Appendix F), contains the following observation:

'A large number of bones occurred in the ditch of

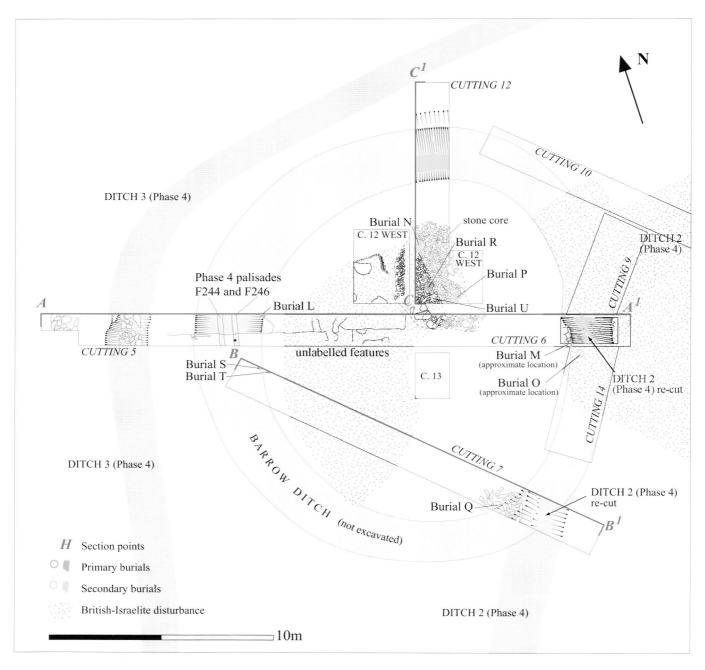

the mound (barrow) and to a lesser degree scattered through the mound. The dog fragments occurred only in the mound and below the old turf line.'

The secondary phase (Figs 3.2–3.4)

The primary barrow appears to have been extensively remodelled by levelling off the top and spreading the material, resulting in a more extensive but slighter feature up to 19m in diameter (Fig. 3.2). While this overlay and reached beyond the ditch on the western and northern sides, it does not appear to have extended over the eastern part of the site. The outer edge of the barrow, including the ditch fill, was removed in this area during the 1899–1902 investigations (Fig. 3.3: A–A[1], east side). The profile of the secondary mound mirrors the ditch below and slopes up beyond its outer edge (Fig. 3.3: A–A[1], west side), giving it the appearance of a low mound with a wide shallow ditch and slight outer bank.

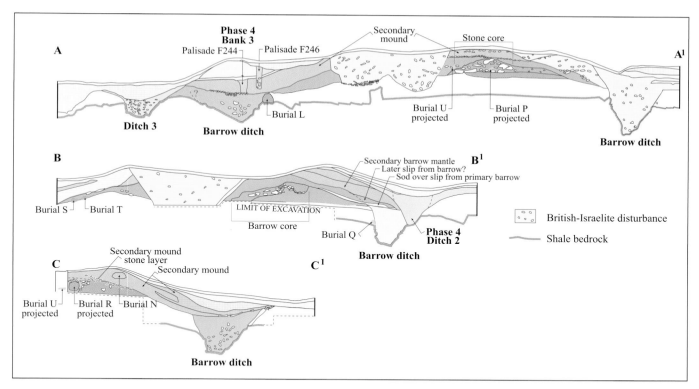

Fig. 3.2 (left)—Plan of barrow. Location of burials L–U. Although cuttings 9 and 14 are shown on the overall site plans, they may not have been fully excavated.

Fig. 3.3 (above)—Sections (A–A¹, B–B¹, C–C¹) across the barrow and ramparts 3 and 4 of the residential enclosure.

The sections indicate that this layer is made up of material virtually indistinguishable from the primary barrow.

The secondary mound was covered by a 0.2m-thick natural sod layer (Fig. 3.4), apart from an area in the centre, over the core, where this horizon was marked by a layer of small stones and pebbles (Fig. 3.3: C–C¹). The presence and depth of this sod indicate a considerable period during which the barrow was left unaltered. Subsequent disturbance was caused during a later period, when the barrow became a renewed focus for burial (see below). Other evidence of interference consists of a pit (no. 1) cut into the core on the south-east edge (Fig. 3.3: B–B¹).

Later use

Three episodes of disturbance to the barrow were identified (Fig. 3.3). The first is a period during which

burials were placed on, or inserted into, the secondary mound. During the formation of the overlying sod an apparently unprotected cremation, burial O (Fig. 3.2), was deposited directly over the ditch. Subsequently an outer mantle of earth, up to 0.65m deep, was added to the mound on the north side after the formation of the sod layer. This extended beyond the outer line of the ditch in a uniform horizon 0.15m thick and was cut into near the crest of the barrow to facilitate the insertion of a cremation, burial N (Fig. 3.3: C–C¹).

Subsequent interference

The second episode of alteration is represented by the apparent insertion of a cremation, burial P, and an inhumation burial (U, see below) into the stone core immediately to the north and east respectively of the centre of the barrow. This is clearly indicated by the absence of the natural sod layer over the cairn at this point (Fig. 3.3: A–A¹) and by the interference to one of the primary cremations (burial R), part of which was found mixed through burial U. The surface of the barrow over the core in this area is marked by a thin horizon of small pebbles.

The final ancient episode of disturbance is

represented by the digging of ditches 2 and 3 of the phase 4 enclosure (see below). On the western side, ditch 3 cut obliquely through the sod layer and the underlying spread of the secondary mound (Fig. 3.3: A–A[1]). Bank 3 of the phase 4 enclosure had been erected in part over the secondary mound (Fig. 3.3: A–A[1]). On the south-east side, the construction of ditch 2 completely removed the primary ditch of the barrow and cut through the outer edge of the earlier disturbed material (Fig. 3.3: B–B[1]).

The most recent, and most extensive, damage was caused during the 1899–1902 British-Israelite investigation (Figs 1.5 and 3.2). This consists of a large, irregular pit, cut through the central western part of the barrow, which measured 11.5m north–south by 3–6m east–west and was between 1.6m and 1.8m deep. The eastern side of the barrow had also been cut into, and in this area part of the ditch had been emptied (Fig. 3.3: A–A[1], east). The butts of two posts representing a modern fence running roughly east–west across the site had also been driven into the upper surface of the barrow.

The burials

Ten burials came from the barrow, with five cremation burials (L, M, R, S, T) associated with the primary phase. Burials O and Q were found in the fill of the ditch. Two cremations, burials N and P, and a single inhumation (U) had been inserted into the secondary phase of the mound. Unless otherwise stated, there are no grave-goods associated with the burials. Some of the burials were identified at the time of excavation by Professor J. Keenan, then of the Department of Anatomy, University College Dublin, but unfortunately their present location is not known. Others, now in the National Museum of Ireland, were also identified at that time by Nils-Gustaf Gejvall, Stockholm.

Primary burials

Burial L (Figs 3.2 and 3.3: A–A[1]). Cremation deposit covering an area of 0.46m (east–west) by 0.35m (north–south) and 0.4m deep, resting on the edge of, and at least partly sealed by, the barrow. It occurred beside a natural hollow in the rock immediately inside the western edge of the ditch. Young adult.

Burial M (Fig. 3.2). Cremation deposit 0.15m deep resting on small flat stones arranged in an irregular V-sectioned setting. Some of the bones had spilled out on the western side, where they rested on shingly shale. The remainder of the deposit rested on and was covered by 'sticky yellowish clay'. Two small shale slabs partly covered the deposit on the eastern side. While the sod layer over the secondary mound appears to have been cut above burial M and some of the fill above it was identified as 'disturbed black clay, filled with animal bones' (not identified), the burial itself seems to have been deposited on or in the undisturbed sod layer beneath the primary barrow. Not identified. Cutting 9, north-west corner; depth 1.79m.

Burial Q (Figs 3.2 and 3.3: B–B[1]). Cremation deposit (not identified) from the ditch on the south-east side of the barrow. The deposit rested on a ledge of rock on the inner edge of the ditch at a depth of 1m under the natural sod layer covering the primary barrow. Numerous small snail shells were found with the burial, suggesting that the deposit was exposed for some period. The shells were identified by A. W. Stelfox (18 August 1952) as land molluscs from a freshwater shallow pool or the marshy edge of a pool that would be dry in summer.

Burial R (Figs 3.2 and 3.3: A–A[1]). Cremation deposit from among the large stones of the upper level of the core. Part of the burial underlies an inhumation (U, see below) whose insertion caused some disruption of the cremation. The burial covered an area of 0.8m by 0.5m and formed a pocket in the stone core 0.4m deep. Not identified.

Burial S (Figs 3.2 and 3.3: B–B[1]). Unprotected cremation deposit *c.* 2m from the western edge of the barrow and immediately beneath the natural sod layer over the barrow. The deposit formed a small patch of bone and compact grey clay 0.31m in diameter and 0.15m deep. Not identified.

Burial T (Figs 3.2 and 3.3: B–B[1]). Unprotected cremation deposit 0.15m east of burial S and immediately beneath the natural sod layer over the barrow. The deposit formed a small patch 0.25m in diameter and 0.1m deep.

Fig. 3.4—Cutting 5, north face of cutting, showing sod layers over secondary mound (bottom) and overlying this material levelled from the barrow (top). The sod layer over the levelled barrow seals a palisade trench (F244). Bank 3 and its internal revetting palisade (F245) overlie the second sod layer. Spoil from the 1899–1902 campaign overlies the inner portion of bank 3.

Identified by Nils-Gustaf Gejvall, Stockholm (manuscript dated 6 July 1954), as an 'adult'.

Secondary burials
Burial N (Figs 3.2 and 3.3: C–C^1). Cremation deposit, 0.15m by 0.15m, resting on an area of burnt clay on the northern side of the barrow at a depth of 0.45m. The mantle of earth added on this side over the sod layer of the secondary phase had been cut through, and the burial occurred at a high level within the fill and contained some animal bone. Not identified.

Burial O (Fig. 3.2). Unprotected cremation deposit *c.* 1m south-east of burial M within the secondary natural sod layer over the line of the ditch. The burial lay on a small heap of stones and covered an area of about 0.22m by 0.15m, the main portion resting on a flat stone. Not identified.

Burial P (Figs 3.2 and 3.3: A–A^1). Cremation scatter in the upper level of the stone core about 2m south-east of

the centre of the barrow. The material covered a narrow band *c.* 3.9m by 0.25m by 0.1m deep but concentrated within a smaller area, 1.7m long. The deposit occurred within the body of the core at a depth of 0.45m below the barrow surface. The natural sod layer over the barrow was disturbed in the area immediately above the burial and the deposit could be a later intrusion despite its dispersed nature. Some small snail shells (of the same type as those from burial Q above) were found with the burial. Not identified.

Burial U (Figs 3.2 and 3.3: A–A^1 and C–C^1). Crouched inhumation over the centre of the barrow. The body lay on its right side (facing west) with the hands in front of the face and appears to have been aligned north-north-east to south-south-west. The lower portion of the body had suffered considerable disturbance. There was an upright stone behind the back of the skeleton, possibly to prop the body on its side. The burial does not appear to have been identified but seems to be that of an adult. Some cremated bones (weight 39.72g) derived from burial R were found mixed through the stones in the upper level of the core immediately beneath burial U. 'A considerable amount of animal bone lay around and under' the burial. Not identified.

Other human bone from the barrow
Cremated bone was also found above the barrow on the western side. It formed a loose scatter covering an area *c.* 2–3m long. The origin of this material is unknown. Two pieces of human skull and some human teeth came from the vicinity of the barrow and may have been derived from disturbed burials:

Skull fragment; cutting 10, 0.0m N, 0.4m W; depth 1m; in shaly clay overlying shale bedrock.

S156, skull fragment; cutting 9, disturbed; no further information.

Two human teeth; cutting 6, stiff yellow clay, 9.65m W, 0.62m from N edge of cutting.

Finds from the barrow
Detailed descriptions (and a list of samples) are presented in Appendix A.

A small quantity of material came from the barrow area. A piece of cut antler (★E615:114) came from the primary silt of the ditch and a struck flint flake (★E615:28) was incorporated into the secondary mantle of the mound, while a small ball of either yellow ironstone or haematite (★E615:70a, Appendix G) may be Romano-British. The remaining material, including a corroded iron blade (★E615:83) and green glass fragments (★E615:70b, ★E615:86), appear to be of post-medieval date.

Phase 3 burials: the flat cemetery (Fig. 3.5)

The flat cemetery overlies the area of phase 1 and 2 activity. All of the earlier features, however, were sealed by a sterile layer of yellow clay by the time the cemetery came into use. The origin of this layer is uncertain although it could represent a natural sod formation.

A small cluster of seven burials occurred within an area measuring 6m north–south by 4m east–west. Five of these were inhumations (B, C, E, H and I) and two were cremations (V and W). The cemetery does not appear to have been formally delimited. It may originally have been more extensive, since an outlying cremation (burial A) occurred 10m to the east and the cluster is bounded immediately to the north-east, and at a greater remove to the east, by the British-Israelite disturbance.

Burial B (Figs 3.5, 3.6, 3.7 and 3.8)
Inhumation, limbs flexed, probably crouched burial, in pit F7. The pit was 0.35m deep and measured 1.08m in maximum length (north–south) by 0.6m (east–west); a thin shale slab formed its north-west side. The burial was in a matrix of charcoal-rich earth containing burnt animal bone, which may have been derived from the habitation layer (F8) overlying the pit. Most of the skeleton was present in the grave although the skull was crushed and portions of the lower limbs were missing; the north-eastern end of the pit had cut into trench B (Chapter 2). An iron bolt was found in the top level of the pit fill over the skeleton; no other information is available, nor can the object now be located. The burial is that of a child aged 10–12. Sq. 37, at a point centred on 7.1m E, 2.5m N; depth 1m.

Table 3.1—Finds from the phase 3 barrow; detailed descriptions (and a list of samples) are presented in Appendix A (★not illustrated; <u>underlining</u> indicates that the object cannot be located).

	E no.	Object	Context		E no.	Object	Context
Iron	★E615:83	Corroded blade	Cutting 12	**Glass**	★E615:70b	Green glass fragment	Cutting 13
					★E615:86	Green glass fragment	Cutting 12, S ext.
Ceramic	★E615:70a	Small ball of yellow ironstone/haematite	Cutting 13, S ext.				
				Bone	<u>★E615:114</u>	Cut antler	Cutting 9, base of ditch
Stone	★E615:28	Struck flint flake	Cutting 5				
	★E615:84	Disc-shaped whetstone?	Cutting 13				

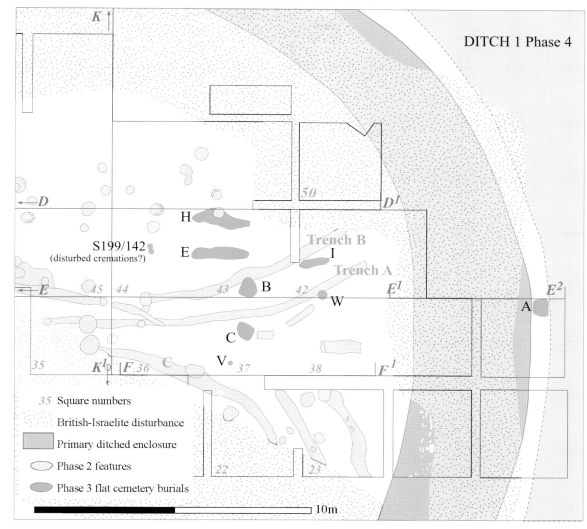

DITCH 1 Phase 4

S199/142
(disturbed cremations?)

Trench B

Trench A

35 Square numbers

British-Israelite disturbance

Primary ditched enclosure

Phase 2 features

Phase 3 flat cemetery burials

10m

Fig. 3.5—Top:
plan of phase 3
cemetery.
Bottom: (left)
burials H, E, B
and C in situ,
showing phase 2
post-pits
(F106–8,
F114, F119)
and phase 4
paving; (right)
burials C, B and
E in situ.

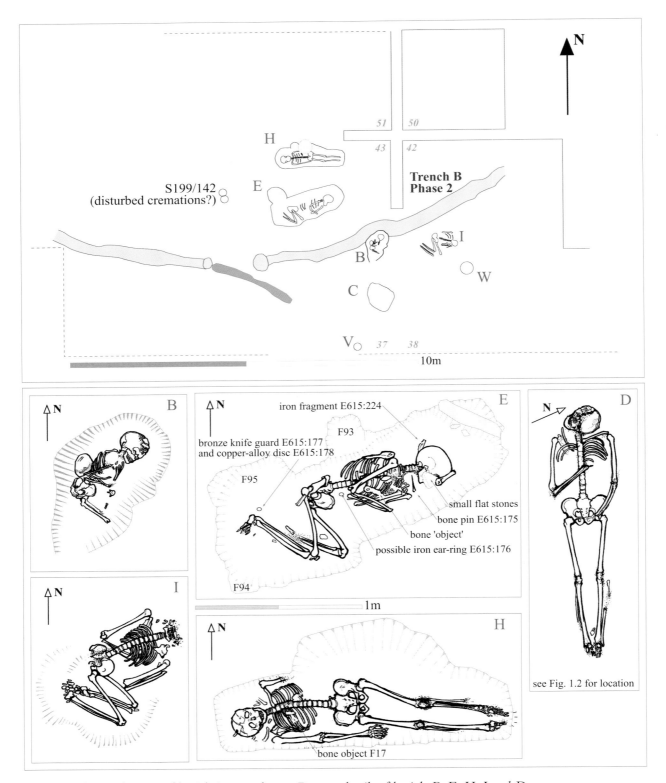

Fig. 3.6—Burials. Top: location of burials in central area. Bottom: details of burials B, E, H, I and D.

Burial C (Figs 3.5 and 3.7)

Disturbed and poorly preserved inhumation burial lying within a sub-oval pit. The crushed remains of the skull were separated by *c.* 0.4m from fragments of longbones, probably human, in very poor condition. Sq. 37, 7.6m E, 1.9m N; depth 0.5m.

Burial E (Figs 3.5, 3.6, 3.7 and 3.9)

A crouched inhumation with grave-goods (see below) contained in pit F97 (1.97m east-north-east/west-south-west by 0.43m north-north-west/south-south-east by 0.43m deep). The body lay on its left side, facing south-east and orientated east-north-east/west-south-west. The knees were tightly flexed and raised above the level of the remainder of the body. The right arm was flexed across the chest, with the hand resting against the south side of the pit; the left arm was sharply flexed with the hand resting on the chest immediately below the neck. Two small flat stones are shown overlying the face (see Figs 3.6 and 3.9) but it is not known whether these represent a deliberate arrangement or a fortuitous aspect of the grave fill. The fill of the pit consisted of charcoal-rich earth with two cremated human bones (S136, not identified) and some animal bones (not identified but one of these appears to overlie the skull: see Figs 3.6 and 3.9). A pit (F95) and two post-holes (F93–94) were cut through the northern side of the burial pit from the habitation level of phase 4. The individual was an adult but there was no further identification. Sqs 43/44 at a point centred 4.6m N, 6.6m E.

Burial E grave-goods (Figs 2.11, 3.6 and 3.7)
The archive, including original field drawings, suggests that there were a small number of grave-goods with this

Fig. 3.7—Overview of burials B, C, E and H. Phase 3 cemetery (looking west).

Fig. 3.8—Burial B, phase 3 cemetery (looking south).

burial. Apart from a bone pin, ★<u>E615:224</u>, and an otherwise unidentified bone 'object' (both now missing), however, the evidence for the contexts of the other objects is not completely convincing. In particular, the knife guard (E615:177, Fig. 2.11), the possible coin (★E615:178), an iron fragment (E615:224, Fig. 2.11) and part of a possible bronze pin (★E615:218) appear to have come from the pit fill and were not directly associated with the burial: it is probable that these represent residual phase 1 or 2 material accidentally incorporated into the grave.

Copper alloy

E615:177 (Fig. 2.11), flat elliptical perforated knife guard, 20.3mm x 14.3mm x 1mm, perforation 10mm x 4.9mm to receive the tang; from fill of pit over abdomen area, found with E615:176 (Fig. 2.11).

★<u>E615:178</u>, small circular copper-alloy disc, possibly a coin; from fill, over feet. The object is now lost. The following letter, however, is in the archives of the excavation.

Fitzwilliam Museum,
Cambridge.

17.8.53

Dear Dr. Ó Ríordáin,
I have kept your bits for some days & have had several tries at them, but cannot report much success.
(1) The bits of silver. I cannot convince myself that they are from a coin—though, of course, they might be. If any coin is in question, I should think it a silver penny—not a Roman siliqua.
(2) The bronze. I'm inclined to think it is a coin—early fourth century Roman at a guess. But after much gentle prodding with knife and brush, the edge began to break, and application of acid failed to reveal any type. I kept applying a glass to detect any faint traces & think that we must conclude that the corrosion has gone too far. I can promise that nothing was missed as I was cleaning it.
I am really sorry that we have not had more luck,
Yours sincerely,
Harold Mattingly.

Fig. 3.9—Burial E, phase 3 cemetery (looking west).

(The silver bits referred to are ★E615:191, phase 3 below).

★E615:218, possible pin fragment, small length of bronze with round section; one end broken, the other hooked with extremity of hook broken; L 5mm, D 1–1.5mm; *c.* 9.15m E, 4.5m N; depth 1m; charcoal fill of pit over skull.

Iron

E615:176 (Fig. 2.11), incomplete U-shaped object with tapering round section, possibly an ear-ring; T 2.5–4mm, int. D *c.* 10mm; 4cm above abdominal region.

★E615:224, poorly preserved object; sketch on excavation card shows a tapering object, above and touching skull.

Bone

E615:175, perforated bone pin from the neck of burial E, now lost; L *c.* 103mm, W 1–14mm, with the oval perforation in the expanded round head, terminus pointed, no section on drawing. The location at the neck might indicate a type of clothing pin if not a shroud-pin.

The original drawing of the burial (Fig. 3.6) shows what appears to be a waisted bone artefact perforated at one end and labelled 'bone object'. There is no other record of this item.

Burial H (Figs 3.5, 3.6, 3.7 and 3.10) (Appendix J)

An extended inhumation contained in an oval pit, F96 (1.97m by 0.6m by 0.32m deep), and aligned west–east. The body lay on its back with the head at a higher level and tilted slightly to the right; the right arm was extended by the side with the hand resting palm upwards and tightly gripped. Only the upper portion of the left arm, which was also extended by the side, survived, the lower portion having been removed by the digging of two post-holes (F68–9) of the later habitation level (phase 4, below). The pit fill contained a considerable quantity of charcoal, animal bone and fragments of cremated bone (not identified), while the basal layer consisted of 'sticky' clay containing further animal bone. Animal bones were apparently used to support and flank the head, while part of an animal jaw lay on the right-hand side of the chest. The individual was an adult, possibly male. Sqs 43/4, at a point centred on 5.9m N, 6.8m E.

Grave-goods
★E615:260, bone object, found on the right ribs near the vertebrae. No further information.

Burial I (Figs 3.5 and 3.6)

A crouched inhumation aligned north-east/south-west. This lay on a 'stony layer' apparently resting on the boulder clay and was covered by a layer of redeposited clay; there was no surviving indication of a grave, although the plan of the burial (Fig. 3.6) shows a cut around the west and south sides of the skeleton. The upper portion of the body lay on its chest, with the right arm across the left shoulder. The upper left arm lay under the left side, with the lower arm across the abdomen. The lower part of the body lay on the left hip but the pelvis and right hip were twisted and lay upwards. The legs were sharply flexed, with the right lying over the lower portion of the left. The body was apparently that of an adult but was not further identified. Sqs 37/42–3, at a point centred on 3.45m N, 8.8m E.

Sample
S125, charcoal. Sq. 43/42, pit, F158 under baulk, around burial I.

'*Sqs 43/42/37 baulk, around Burial I, one good-sized dog (or wolf) fragment of shed antler of red deer, several pigs, one horse tooth, several ox of various age. Some bone burnt.*' Transcription of Ó Ríordáin's field notes; the reference to 'several pigs' probably indicates a few bones representing more than one animal. These bones were not retained.

Burial V (Figs 3.5 and 3.6)

Cremation: a considerable quantity of cremated bone was found on and in the immediate vicinity of a large earthfast boulder. No further information. Sq. 37, 0.4m N, 9m E; depth 0.4–0.55m.

Burial W (Figs 3.5 and 3.6)

Cremation contained in an oval pit, F6 (0.75m north-west/south-east by 0.63m north-east/south-west and 0.41m deep), with a U-shaped section. The top of the pit was partly sealed by four small flagstones. The fill contained charcoal and cremated bone 'in considerable quantity' but the cremation was not further identified. At the base of the pit was a thick concentration of charcoal, which appeared to be the remnant of a vertical post. Sq. 38, at a point centred on 1.3m N, 8.8m E; depth 0.65m.

Other possible human remains (Figs 3.5 and 3.6)

S199: Fragments of cremated bone, tooth and charcoal found with fragments of amber or glass (★E65:142). Sq. 44, edge of black area, *c.* 3.9m N, *c.* 4.4m E; depth 0.7m.

S142: *c.* 70 fragments of cremated bone found with E615:170a–c, an iron stem and pebble (Fig. 4.13) and a pivot for a buckle (Fig. 4.11). Sq. 44, stony habitation level.

Two small collections of cremated bone in the NMI are labelled as coming from Sq. 2:

S168, two human bones, and cremated bone, near charcoal, 'rib removed for identification'. Sq. 2, pit.

S185, human cremation. Sq. 2.

Other burials from the Rath of the Synods

Other burials from various parts of the Rath of the Synods are dealt with here for convenience. Unless

Fig. 3.10—Burial H, phase 3 cemetery (looking north-west).

otherwise stated, no grave-goods are associated with the burials.

Burial A (Fig. 3.5)

This occurred 10m to the east of the cemetery and may be an outlier. It was an apparently unprotected cremation lying on the boulder clay at the outer edge of ditch 1 of the phase 4 residential enclosure. Adult female, under middle age, 1,385.6g. Identification by Nils-Gustaf Gejvall, Stockholm (manuscript dated 6 July 1954). Sq. 40, 3.2m N, 17.9m E; depth 0.35m.

Burial D (Fig. 3.6) (Appendix J)

Extended inhumation aligned west-north-west/east-south-east. The skeleton lay on its back with the head to the north. The feet were close together and the right arm was bent inwards so that the hand lay over the lower chest. Both hands (bones decayed?) were missing. The head is twisted so that the lower jaw rests on the right shoulder and the head looks over the shoulder. Male? Cutting 17, 30.2m N, 10.8m E; depth 0.5m.

Burial F

Cremation. Possibly under the bank of phase 4 rampart

2, immediately south of modern field wall. Cutting 23, east side, immediately under humus layer, 882.05g (in three separate bags in NMI: 429.07g + 39.72g + 413.26g). No further information.

Burial G

Cremation, 147.38g. Cutting 23, east side. No further information.

Burial J/K

Inhumation. This was discovered during Ó Ríordáin's excavations in the fill of the enclosing ditch of Rath na Ríogh (Roche 2002, 23, fig. 3). No further information.

Burial F107 (Fig. 3.5)

Inhumation. This was discovered in the lower fill (F107) of the enclosing ditch of Rath na Ríogh during the 1997 excavations (Roche 2002, 45). It consists of a small collection of human bone, possibly disturbed, that came from an adolescent or young adult (Ó Donnabháin 2002, 123, no. 122).

Burial F105

Inhumation. This was discovered on the surface of a lower fill (F103) of the enclosing ditch of Rath na Ríogh during the 1997 excavations; some dog bones appear to have accompanied the burial (Roche 2002, 45). The remains are those of a child of about six months of age (Ó Donnabháin 2002, 123, no. 124).

Disturbed burial F15/103

Inhumation. Fragmentary remains of probably the same individual came from fill layers F15 and F103 of the enclosing Rath na Ríogh ditch during the 1997 excavations (Roche 2002, 45). The remains may be those of a young adult male (Ó Donnabháin 2002, 123–4, nos 57 and 163).

Burial at the Rath of the Synods: discussion

All of the burials, including those from the barrow, are discussed here. At least 22 burials were identified at the Rath of the Synods, although cremated and unburnt

human bone was found in several other locations (Fig. 3.5). Two cemeteries are recognised, one associated with the barrow at the north-eastern edge of the site (Fig. 3.1), the other an apparently unmarked group of seven burials in the central area. Despite the presence of the barrow and the burial cluster, burial evidently occurred over a wide area on this relatively level shoulder of the hill adjacent to Rath na Ríogh. Indeed, it is possible, given the number of funerary monuments recognised at Tara (Newman 1997, 153–4, fig. 108), that a substantial part of the hilltop was considered an appropriate area for burial.

Within the unprotected cemetery seven burials (B, C, E, H, I, V and W) occur in an area 5m in maximum dimensions (Fig. 3.5). Another, burial A (10m to the east), occurs in the vicinity and may form part of the original cemetery; the area between the focal area and burials A and G has been severely damaged by the early twentieth-century investigation. The relationship of the single burial (D, extended inhumation) 25m to the north-east is difficult to assess. The rite and orientation (west-north-west/east-south-east), however, suggest that it could be contemporary. Four other burials—G (cremation) 19m to the south-west, F (cremation) c. 8m south of G, and J/K and F105 in the ditch fill of Rath na Ríogh, a further 15m to the south—suggest that the flat cemetery may originally have been more extensive and was disturbed by the residential enclosure. If burials J/K and F105 are contemporary with the other burials, then it indicates that the period of funerary activity post-dates the hilltop enclosure of Rath na Ríogh. The ditch was dug during the second or first century BC; burial F105 was sealed by a layer of slip (F108) that produced a date of cal. AD 67–289 and was deposited on the upper surface of layer F102, which was dated to 193–95 cal. BC (Roche 2002, 56, table 1).

The barrow and flat cemetery offer an interesting contrast in what appear to be contemporary burial practices (see below). Other than the central mound covering the primary burials in the barrow, little emphasis was placed on providing formal delineation of the individual burials. One of the primary burials (M) was found on an irregular V-shaped setting of flat stones and was partly covered by two small flagstones. The other burials within the mound, including the secondary crouched inhumation, appear to be simple deposits without settings, pits or covering features. While five of the burials within the flat cemetery (B, C, E, H and W) were contained in pits, two others (V and A) appear to have been unprotected. Burial V, a cremation, lay partly on a large earthfast boulder. The only deliberate marker may have been the timber post set in the base of the pit containing cremation burial W, although burial I, a crouched inhumation, was apparently covered by a layer of earth, possibly the remnant of a small mound.

Dating

No clearly datable grave-goods were found with any of the burials. The nature of the grave-goods, however, including iron and copper-alloy objects from burial E, the general paucity of artefacts and the mixture of cremations with both crouched and extended inhumations suggest a date late in the Iron Age, possibly in the first or second century AD (O'Brien 1990; 1992, 131). Fourteen of the burials are cremations, there are four crouched and two extended inhumations, and the placement of the two other inhumations could not be determined. While the burials are considered to be a generally homogeneous group, it is conceivable that some of the isolated and unaccompanied cremations could be of Bronze Age or even Neolithic date.

The dating of the Rath of the Synods burials is largely dependent on the somewhat generalised evidence available for Iron Age burials in Ireland. Nevertheless, what is relevant is that both cremations and crouched inhumations occur, and this suggests that the earlier burials date from the first century AD. If the burials from the ditch of Rath na Ríogh were contemporary, then the date range for these would extend from c. 100 BC to the late first or second century AD. The introduction of extended inhumations seems to have occurred in the second century, and it is probable, therefore, that burial continued into this period at the Rath of the Synods.

Contemporary background and comparative sites

Research on burials of this period, of which only a small number have been identified in Ireland, has shown that there is a very considerable diversity in rite, context and association (B. Raftery 1981; O'Brien 1992; Cooney and Grogan 1994, 199–200). Nevertheless, the research suggests that there is a general sequence beginning with cremations, followed by crouched inhumations and then extended burials (O'Brien 1992, 131–3). The gradual alteration in burial rite appears to have been influenced from Britain during the first two centuries AD. The first-century change came under the influence of the late Iron Age custom of crouched burial, and the second-century change through changes in Roman funerary practice from exclusively cremation to increasing emphasis on extended inhumation (B. Raftery 1981, 200; O'Brien 1992, 131). This general sequence appears to hold at the Rath of the Synods, although only three specific pieces of evidence can be offered to support such a development. One of the final burials in the barrow was also the only inhumation (burial U, crouched), while cremated bones in the grave-pits of burials H and E (extended inhumations) suggest the possibility that earlier burials had been disturbed. It is probable that the relatively small number of burials and the close clustering of seventeen of them in two locations indicate a reasonably short period of funerary activity on the site, perhaps spanning the first and second centuries AD.

The barrow, consisting of a mound with a stone core, c. 14m by 16.5m and surrounded by a ditch 2.6–3m wide and up to 2m deep, is comparable to tumuli 2 and 3 at Cush, Co. Limerick (Ó Ríordáin 1940), both of which produced single cremations. Although there was no surviving evidence for an external bank, the Rath of the Synods barrow has similarities with the ring-barrows at Grannagh and Oranbeg, Co. Galway, excavated by Etienne Rynne (B. Raftery 1981, 180; 1983, figs 154–5; 1994). The Grannagh mound had a stone core and burials occurred in the ditch. The mound at Seskin, Co. Kilkenny, also appears to have had an irregular stone core (B. Raftery 1981, 7–8), while at Furness, Co. Kildare, a kerbed mound with a stone core covered three cremations (Grogan 1983–4). Cremations also occurred in the ditches surrounding Carbury Hill A, Co. Kildare (Willmot 1938, 130–5), and Carrowjames 8, Co. Mayo (J. Raftery 1938–9; 1940–1).

Unprotected cemeteries do not appear to be a feature of Iron Age funerary practice in Ireland, although individual graves or clusters of burials without grave-goods are extremely difficult to date and could belong to a wide range of periods (e.g. B. Raftery 1981, 191). Some clustering of Iron Age burials can be observed on the southern side of the main mound at Knowth, where eight burials occur in an area *c.* 20m in diameter (Eogan 1974, fig. 28). Another cluster occurs on the northern side, where seven burials occur within an area measuring 50m. The general picture, however, is similar to that at the Rath of the Synods in that burial occurred throughout the level ground on the northern, western and southern sides of the main mound.

None of the Knowth burials had identified coverings although some were contained in pits. Many were found either in or close to the small passage tombs of the Neolithic cemetery, which may have offered a measure of protection. This was also the case at Kiltierney, Co. Fermanagh (Daniels and Williams 1977), where nineteen small mounds clustered around the earlier passage tomb. Within the embanked enclosure at Carbury Hill B, Co. Kildare (Willmot 1938, 135–40), cremations and inhumations occurred in pits without further covering.

Broadly contemporary burials have been excavated at several sites in the region. At Knowth a mixture of 34 crouched and extended inhumations occurred around the perimeter of the main mound in the passage tomb cemetery (Eogan 1968; 1974). These are contemporary with the late Iron Age phase of settlement. Although the grave-goods do not provide parallels with the Tara burials, a small number of finds from the Rath of the Synods are similar to the Knowth grave-goods. Among these are the bronze ear-ring (E615:149, Fig. 2.11) from phase 2, striated bronze rings (E615:134, Fig. 4.10; E615:193, Fig. 4.10 and Pl. 1) and the glass pinhead (E615:216, Fig. 4.13) found in the later habitation layers. Similar striated rings came from burial 2 at Knowth, which also produced two plain rings (Eogan 1968, 367–8, fig. 37: 2). Two small ear-rings came from burials 10 and 11 at Knowth (Eogan 1974, fig. 31). The striated bracelet (E615:195, Fig. 4.15) from the phase 4 occupation can be paralleled by those from Oranbeg and Lisnacrogher, Co. Antrim (B. Raftery 1983, figs 155 and 150). The uncontexted Tara stone cone (B. Raftery 1981; 1983, 230, fig. 185) has close parallels in the two examples from burial 1 at Knowth (Eogan 1968, 366, fig.

37: 1). Stone cones also come from Feerwore and from a disturbed context at Millockstown (C. Manning 1986, fig. 14: 26).

Conclusions

Little can be said, in the absence of detailed anatomical analysis, about the nature of the society using the site for burial. While the identified burials represent the remains of eight adults and one child, only two of the fourteen cremations (burial L and burial B, a child) have been identified. The variation in the burial rite and the general paucity of grave-goods are in keeping with the evidence for Iron Age burial practice in Ireland.

O'Brien (1992, 131) has pointed out the similarities of some elements of the burials at Knowth, Newgrange, Oranbeg and Grannagh, Co. Galway, and site A, Carbury Hill. These burials form an interesting contrast with the at least broadly contemporary funerary activity at the Rath of the Synods. While the burial rite amongst the inhumations, crouched, flexed and extended, appears to reflect the range of burial customs in the late Iron Age in Ireland, the comparative poverty of the Tara Iron Age burials contrasts with the wealth of some examples from Knowth, Grannagh and Oranbeg in particular.

At the Rath of the Synods only five burials, E, H, I, U and possibly B, contained grave-goods. In burial H the head appeared to have been supported on, and flanked by, animal bone, and a bone object was apparently found in the rib area. The crouched inhumation, U, inserted into the barrow also appears to have been accompanied by animal bone. These and the animal bone in the grave-pit of burial E and in possible association with burial I may represent food offerings in the Roman manner (O'Brien 1992, 132). Only burial E, with its possible collection of artefacts, the knife guard, pin and coin or disc of copper alloy, the possible iron ear-ring and pin, the bone pin and the animal bone, stands out as relatively prestigious. As pointed out earlier, however, there is considerable doubt about the context of several of these objects (see p. 46).

The barrow itself was of importance in this regard, but in general it appears that the community represented by the burials was not of particularly high social standing. It may be, therefore, that this interpretation places too much emphasis on the grave-goods. The Hill of Tara itself was a high-status location, and the position of the unprotected cemetery within the earlier ritual enclosures may suggest a quite different assessment of the Rath of the Synods group.

The barrow appears to form part of a continuum of burial monuments on the hilltop, some of the earlier ones being of similar form; certainly burial was a major element of activity at Tara since the Neolithic, with the adjacent Mound of the Hostages passage tomb (O'Sullivan 2005). Whatever the status of those interred here in the Iron Age, the burials form an important link in the ongoing story of Tara as a place of major ritual agglomeration.

Clearly the burials pre-date the construction and occupation of the residential enclosure. The barrow was carefully and deliberately incorporated into the enclosure, which necessitated the flattening of the curve of the middle rampart and the creation of a corresponding bulge in the line of the outer rampart. Although some disturbance of burials within the inner enclosure is apparent, three of the inhumations, which were contained in very shallow graves, remained largely undamaged, suggesting that some time had elapsed between the burial phase and the construction of the residential site.

CHAPTER 4

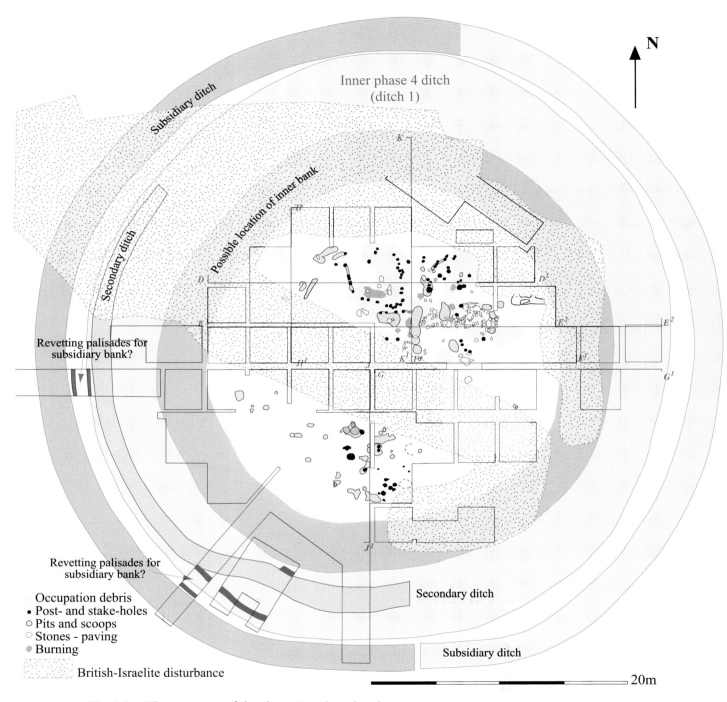

N

Subsidiary ditch

Inner phase 4 ditch
(ditch 1)

Secondary ditch

Possible location of inner bank

Revetting palisades for
subsidiary bank?

Revetting palisades for
subsidiary bank?

Occupation debris
• Post- and stake-holes
○ Pits and scoops
◌ Stones - paving
● Burning

British-Israelite disturbance

Secondary ditch

Subsidiary ditch

20m

Fig. 4.1—The inner area of the phase 4 residential enclosure.

PHASE 4: THE RESIDENTIAL ENCLOSURE

Introduction

The Rath of the Synods was originally constructed as a trivallate enclosure with maximum external dimensions of 83m from north to south; at a later stage, possibly after the main ramparts had fallen into disrepair, a fourth enclosing element was added. On the eastern side the graveyard of the modern church intrudes on the two outer ramparts, and on the north-west side the outer rampart swings outward to incorporate the barrow (see above). Apart from the latter anomaly, the enclosure appears to have been roughly circular. Before excavation (Figs 1.2–1.7) the main features of the site were identifiable as standing earthworks, although considerable disturbance was visible on the surface, particularly in the central and north-western areas. As noted earlier, the central part of the site, within the inner rampart, was extensively excavated, and cuttings were extended from this area to the north, north-west, west, south-west and south to establish the relationship between the ramparts and between the enclosure and the barrow.

The central enclosure (Fig. 4.1)

An extensive spread of domestic activity occurred within the central enclosure. This was divided by the British-Israelite disturbance and is described below under the headings of the northern and southern areas for convenience. The habitation layer occurred throughout the undisturbed portions of the central area and in two places it could be traced running up to, but not under, bank 1 (see below).

Northern area (Figs 4.1 and 4.2)

This was truncated on the northern and southern sides by the late nineteenth/early twentieth-century interference, leaving a roughly oval area measuring 24m north-west/south-east by 8m north-east/south-west relatively undisturbed. Only on the eastern side was it possible to determine the relationship between the phase 4 activity and the surrounding bank and ditch, and it appears that the habitation layer (F8 below) ran up to the edge of bank 1.

Throughout this area the habitation layer was sealed by a layer of sod 0.3–0.35m deep, which in some areas was sealed beneath upcast from the British-Israelite disturbance (see for example Fig. 4.4: D–D^1; Fig. 4.5: K–K^1). Beneath this there was a discontinuous horizon of dark, charcoal-rich earth averaging less than 0.1m in depth but reaching up to 0.2m in some places. The most continuous evidence for this layer was in the eastern area, where two extensive spreads (F8 and F16) (Figs 4.2 and 4.4: D–D^1) produced evidence for paving, cobbling, pits, post-holes and fire-reddened patches. Two concentrations of post-holes and narrow slot-trenches occur in the central part of the northern area (house F20 and post-hole complex F66, Fig. 4.2). While both of these features appear to represent structures, only F20 provided a discernible house outline. Although any of the features cut into the subsoil (and this includes most of the pits and post-holes) could belong to activity of phase 2 or phase 3, several of these (e.g. F62, F22, F68–9, F93–5) cut into either the phase 2 trenches or the phase 3 burials, and the majority appear to be associated with the domestic activity of phase 3.

House (F20) (Figs 2.7 and 4.2)

This occurs towards the western side of the northern area and consists of a substantial part of a rectangular or subrectangular structure measuring *c.* 3.9m (north–south) by 3.5m (east–west) internally. On the western side the house is defined by a slot-trench (F21)

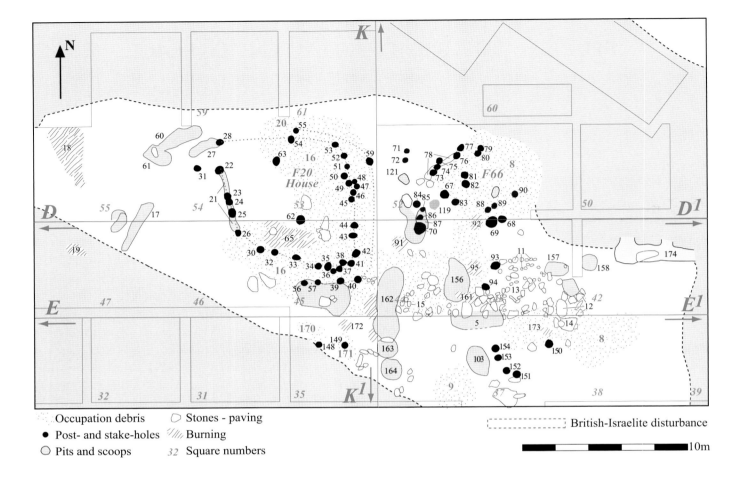

Occupation debris   ▢ Stones - paving

● Post- and stake-holes   ▨ Burning

○ Pits and scoops   *32* Square numbers

British-Israelite disturbance

10m

Fig. 4.2 (above)—Plan of phase 4: the northern area of the inner enclosure.

Fig. 4.3 (right)—Plan of phase 4: the southern area of the inner enclosure.

containing five post-holes (F22–6). Another short slot (F27) 0.5m to the north contains a single post-hole (F28) at the eastern end. On the southern and eastern sides the house is defined by a line of post- and stake-holes forming a more or less single line, although in some places, and on the eastern side in particular, the line consists of two or even three post-holes. These are 0.15m in average diameter and 0.12–0.26m deep, although some of those within the western slot are up to 0.48m in depth. There is a suggestion of a double-skinned wall indicated by a possible outer line of posts on the eastern and southern sides (F39, F40, F45, F59, F55, F56 and F57). On the north-west side a single post-hole (F31) is set opposite the terminal post-hole (F22) in the slot-trench. The juxtaposition of post-holes F22 and F31 with the slot-trench (F21) is suggestive of an entrance because of the thickness of the wall (0.83–1.18m). The only internal features are two median post-holes (F62 and F63), a fire-reddened area towards the southern end

of the house (F65), possibly a fireplace, and some stake-holes (F29, F30, F32–3, F58, F64) that occur mainly around the internal perimeter. The post- and stake-holes of the house contained a dark fill with fragments of burnt bone (not identified).

To the north-west of the house are two conjoined pits (F60–1, Fig. 4.2). Although apparently at the same level, their relationship to the house is uncertain. The dark layer (F16) that appears to coincide with the external edge of the house on the eastern side may represent the floor level, or at least an associated spread of habitation debris (Fig. 4.4: D–D[1]).

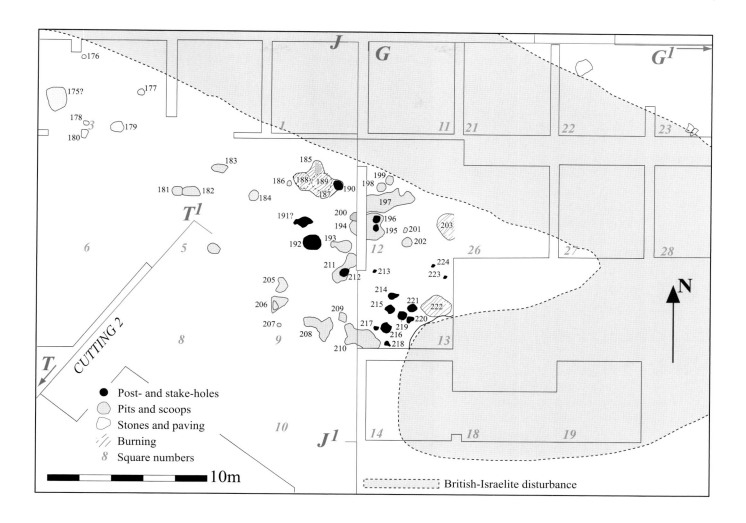

Post- and stake-hole complex (F66) (Fig. 4.2)

This occurs in the area to the east of the house and consists of a series of post- (F67–70) and stake-holes (F71–7, F79–90), a slot-trench (F78) and two small fire-reddened areas (F91, F92). The complex covers an area of 3.5m by 2.75m, and partly underlies the main habitation layer F8 on the eastern side. The clustering of the features appears to represent the foundations of a possibly rectangular structure but it is not possible to determine the exact size or nature of the building. Part of one wall may be indicated by the slot-trench, in which there are five well-defined stake-holes (F73–7), while lines of stakes (F84–6) and a post-hole (F70) on the western side and stake-holes (F89–90) on the southern side might represent two other walls.

Other features (Figs 4.2 and 4.5: K–K[1])

To the south of the post-hole complex is an extensive but discontinuous floor horizon made up of paving (F12–15) and cobbling (F11), which is in part embedded in and in part underlying the main habitation layer (F8) in this area. This covers an area of 5.7m (east–west) by 2.4m (north–south). F11 consists of closely spaced small stones forming an irregular cobbled area measuring 2m by 1.5m. To the east some larger stones formed a limited (1.25m by 1m) area of paving (F12). Further patches of flat stones (F13–15), some of them clearly disturbed to the east, west and south-west, suggest a single, more extensive floor level in this area covering c. 6m by 2.5m. Mostly underlying this floor level is a patch of dark, charcoal-rich material (F8) measuring 6.5m (east–west) by 2–3m (north–south)—part of the wider spread of habitation material in this area. This included dark

Table 4.1—Finds from the inner phase 4 enclosure, northern area; detailed descriptions (and a list of samples) are presented in Appendices A, C (glass vessels) and D (flint and chert) (*not illustrated; underlining indicates that the object cannot be located).

	E no.	Object	Context		E no.	Object	Context
Silver	*E615:191	Fragments with inscription or design in relief, coin?	Sqs 44/65	**Iron**	*E615:126b	Pin stem?	Sq. 42 (F174)
					E615:133	Chisel?	Sq. 42
Copper alloy	E615:125	Half ring of penannular brooch	Sq. 55		E615:135a, b	(a) ring, (b) awl	Sq. 52
					*E615:152	(a) socket	Sq. 52
	E615:126a	Part of pin	Sq. 42		*E615:156	Blade fragment	Sq. 44
	E615:134	Ring	Sq. 42		*E615:158	Rod—fine tool?	Sq. 47
	E615:138	Moulding strip—chape?	Sq. 37		E615:160	Plate	Sq. 37
	E615:193	Striated ring	Sqs 36/37		E615:164	Stud with trefoil head	Sq. 45
	*E615:212	Mirror fragment?	Sqs 38/42		E615:165a–c	(a) stem, (b) blade, (c) stem	Sq. 52
	E615:217	Moulding strip—chape?	Sq. 35		E615:167	Type 1 barrel padlock	Sq. 37
	E615:220	Pin shank/penannular brooch?	Sq. 43		E615:170a	Buckle pivot bar	Sq. 44, disturbed S142?
					*E615:170b	Stem	Sq. 44, disturbed S142?
Lead alloy	E615:124	Seal	Sq. 42		*E615:180	Strip	Sq. 36
Glass beads	E615:130a	Blue spherical translucent	Sq. 52		*E615:190	Tanged chisel?	Sq. 52
	E615:130b	Translucent blue	Sq. 52		*E615:240a	Metalworking pan?	Sqs 44/45
	E615:131	Squared opaque blue	Sq. 55		*E615:240b	Stem and fragments	Sqs 44/45
	E615:132	Opaque turquoise	Sq. 42				
	E615:168	Part ultramarine bracelet	Sq. 43	**Nails**	E615:128	Nail, pyramid head	Sq. 42
	E615:182	Blue spherical	Sqs 36/37		E615:139a–b	Nails	Sq. 55
	E615:204	Green spherical	Sqs 46/54		E615:147a–b	Nail and stem	Sq. 54 (F16)
	E615:214	Blue glass waste	Sq. 52		E615:148	Nail, pyramid head	Sq. 37 (F5)
	E615:216	Blue pinhead	Sqs 37/43		E615:153	Stem of E615:148	Sq. 37 (F5)
					*E615:155	7 stems	Sq. 53
Glass vessels	E615:140	Rim sherd of Roman bowl	Sq. 38		E615:159a–b	Nail and stem	Sq. 36
	*E615:145	3 fragments	Sq. 53		E615:166a–d	Stem, nail, staple, blade	Sq. 37
	*E615:151	Bowl fragment	Sq. 42		E615:173	Nail	Sq. 37 (F16)
	E615:154	9 cone beaker rim/body sherds	Sq. 52		*E615:181a–b	Nails	Sqs 37/43 (F5)
	*E615:200	Fragment	Sq. 55		*E615:188a	Nail with *E615:188b	Sq. 52
					*E615:199	Nail	Sq. 53
Ceramic	E615:127	Spindle-whorl/Roman sherd	Sq. 52		*E615:223b	Stem	Sq. 59
	E615:137	Sherd of Roman flagon	Sq. 47		*E615:230	Stem	Sq. 45 (F16)
	E615:146	12 sherds Samian ware	Sq. 53 (F16)		E615:235	Nail	Sqs 37/43 (F5)
	E615:165d	Sherd Samian ware	Sq. 52 with E615:165a				
	*E615:188b	Crucible rim sherd	Sq. 52 with E615:188a	**Flint**	E615:18	Struck flake	Sq. 36
					E615:135c	Flake	Sq. 52
Stone	E615:170c	Water-rolled disc	Sq. 44		E615:184a, *b	Struck flakes	Sq. 53
	*E615:272	2 quartz pebbles	Sq. 52		*E615:271	Chert flake	Sq. 54
					*E615:273	Chert flake	Sq. 44
Antler	*E615:112	Stem	Cutting 10		*E615:274	Small chert flakes	Sq. 54 (F16)

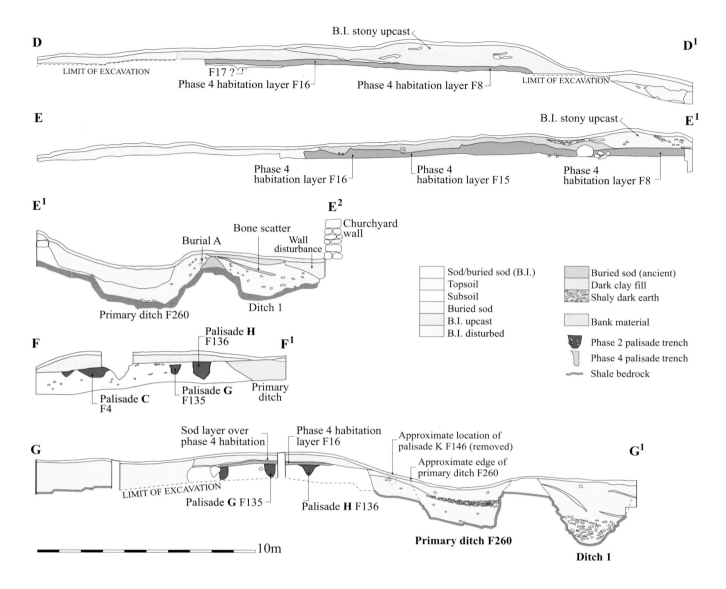

Fig. 4.4—Sections across the Rath of the Synods (D–D¹, E–E¹, F–F¹, E¹–E², G–G¹).

patches of well-defined habitation debris (F9i, F9ii, F170–1), pits (F1, F103, F156–8, F160, F162–4), postholes (F93–4, F147–54) and fire-reddened areas and patches (F172, F161, F173). This area produced several objects.

F5 is an ash pit (Fig. 4.2). It measured 0.86m (east–west) by 0.62m (north–south) with a basal fill of dark, charcoal-rich earth. Animal bone and finds E615:181a, E615:181b and E615:235 (a large, possibly Roman, nail) came from this layer near the base of the pit. The upper fill consisted of a 0.15m-deep layer of grey, charcoal-flecked ash.

F174 is a section of trench with dark, charcoal-rich fill containing a considerable quantity of animal bone (not identified). A portion of a bronze pin (E615:126a, Fig. 4.10) and an iron rod (E615:126b) came from the upper fill towards the eastern end.

F162–4/F1 are shallow scoops, 0.2–0.3m deep, with a fill of habitation debris and small stones (Figs 4.2 and 4.5: K–K¹), joined at the southern end by a deeper pit, F1, with a similar fill. This cut into the top of trench A (F101). The southern side of F1 appears to have been cut

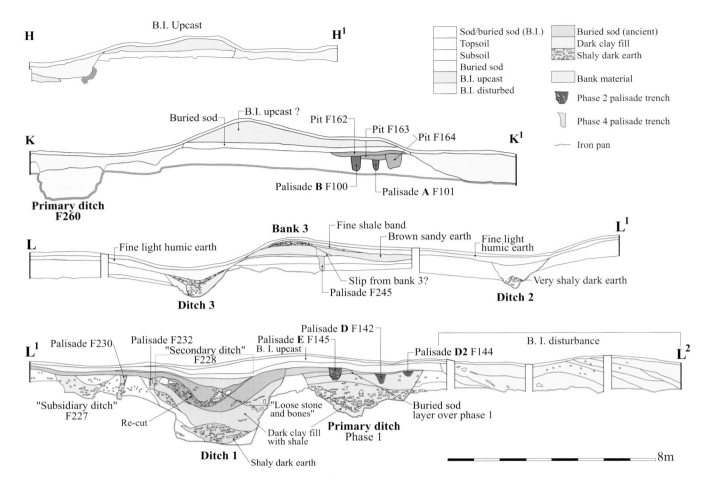

Fig. 4.5—Sections across the Rath of the Synods (H–H[1], K–K[1], L–L[1], L[1]–L[2]).

by another pit, F164, which cut through trench C (F4) of phase 1. A fragment of copper-alloy sheet moulding (E615:217, Fig. 4.10) came from the fill of F163.

F138/159/F10 occur on the south-east side of the habitation in the northern area (not illustrated). F10 is an irregular scoop filled with habitation debris, beneath which a short trench (F138, see Chapter 3) had been cut by grave-pit F6 of burial W (see Chapter 3) and another pit, F159. The latter appeared at the same level as F6 and although it did not contain any evidence for burial it may also belong to phase 2.

Finds from phase 4 inner enclosure, northern area (habitation layer) (Figs 4.10–14 and Pls 1–4).
Detailed descriptions (and a list of samples) are presented in Appendices A, C (glass vessels), D (flint and chert) and G (pottery).

A wide range of material came from this area. This can be broadly divided into three groups: material imported from the Roman world, objects that may have been manufactured locally but are copies of types more common in the Roman world, and a small number of native, late Iron Age, artefacts, some of which may be derived from earlier phases of activity. Amongst the imported items is a small quantity of pottery, including thirteen sherds of south Gaulish *terra sigillata* (E615:146, Fig. 4.16 and Pl. 3; E615:165d, Pl. 2), a rim sherd from a first/second-century AD flagon (E615:137, Fig. 4.13 and Pl. 2), and a spindle-whorl made from a worn, undiagnostic sherd (E615:127, Fig. 4.13 and Pl. 2). There are fourteen sherds from at least five Roman glass vessels (E615:145, E615:151, E615:154, E615:200, Fig. 4.14), including a rim sherd from a mould-blown bowl (E615:140, Fig. 4.14). Amongst the other Roman

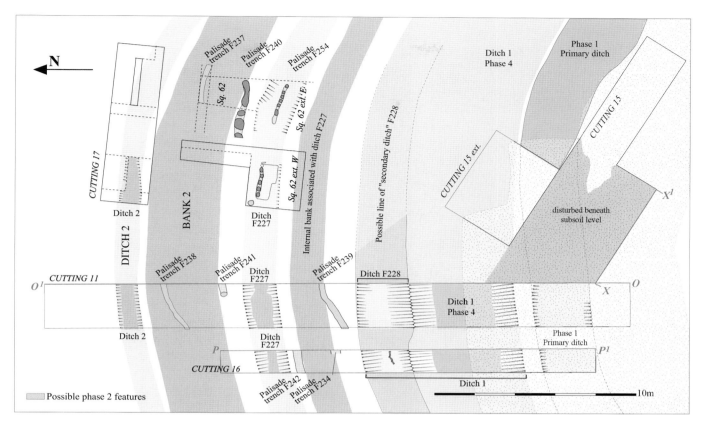

Fig. 4.6—The phase 4 residential enclosure, north side. Plan of cuttings 11, 16 and 17, and squares 63 and 64.

imports are an oval lead seal with the raised impression of a bird (E615:124, Pl. 1), a possible copper-alloy mirror fragment (★E615:212), a type 1a iron barrel padlock (Donaghy 1991), and several glass beads (including E615:130b, E615:131, E615:132, E615:182 and E615:204, Fig. 4.13).

The second group includes several large iron nails, such as the pyramid-headed (E615:128, E615:148/153, E615:235, Fig. 4.12) and ball-headed (E615:159a, E615:173, Fig. 4.12) examples (type 1; W. H. Manning 1985), as well as several smaller or fragmentary nails (E615:139a, Fig. 4.12; ★E615:181a–b, ★E615:199); these are discussed in more detail in Chapter 5. The third group, of native artefacts, includes some—such as the striated penannular copper-alloy ring (E615:193, Fig. 4.10 and Pl. 1), fragments of the copper-alloy binding strips from a chape (E615:217, Fig. 4.10) and part of an ultramarine glass bracelet (E615:168, Fig. 4.10 and Pl. 1)—that may be derived from the phase 3 activity. Other items of significance include part of the ring of a type E

or Ei (Fowler 1960) penannular brooch with a zoomorphic terminal (E615:125, Fig. 4.10), and part of a cast, probably ring-headed, pin (E615:126a, Fig. 4.10). There are several simple domestic iron tools such as chisels (E615:133, Fig. 4.11; ★E615:190), awls (E615:135b, Fig. 4.11) and blades (★E615:156, ★E615:165b, E615:166d, Fig. 4.12).

None of the objects is closely datable, but a broad range from the second to the fourth century AD encompasses all of the probable dates for this material.

Southern area (Fig. 4.3)

The undisturbed area to the south of the British-Israelite disturbance measures *c.* 20m by 9m but part of this had been covered by upcast and dumps of soil from that activity. Within this, features were recognised only as they cut into the boulder clay, and the stratigraphical sequence in this area was less clearly defined. The undisturbed stratigraphy was a very thin sod layer, 0.2–0.25m thick, and a thin horizon of topsoil covering

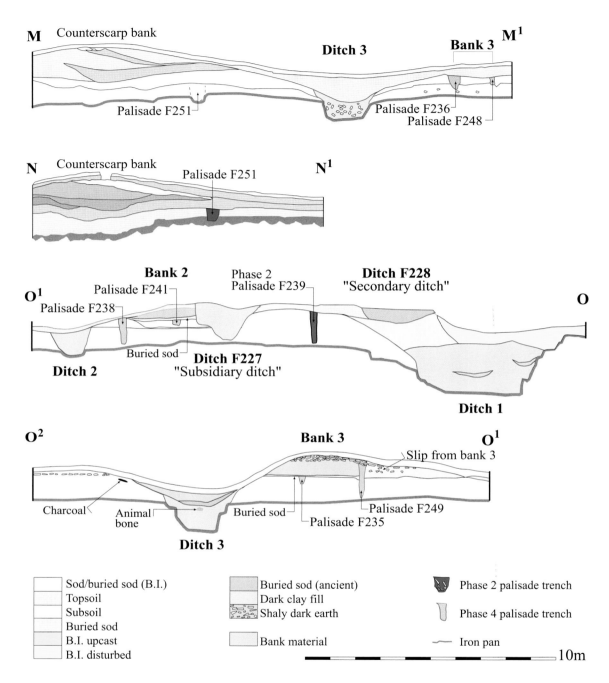

Fig. 4.7 (above)—Sections across the Rath of the Synods (M–M¹, N–N¹, O–O¹, O¹–O²).

Fig. 4.8 (right)—Sections across the Rath of the Synods (P–P¹, Q–Q¹, R–R¹, S–S¹).

the features over most of the area. The phase 2 palisade trenches (nos C1, C2, D1, D3, F134, F139, F142, F143, F145) have already been discussed (Chapter 2). The remaining features consist of pits, post- and stake-holes and fireplaces. There were fewer of these than in the northern area and the area also produced fewer finds, indicating that it was less intensively used.

There is some slight indication of a sequence of

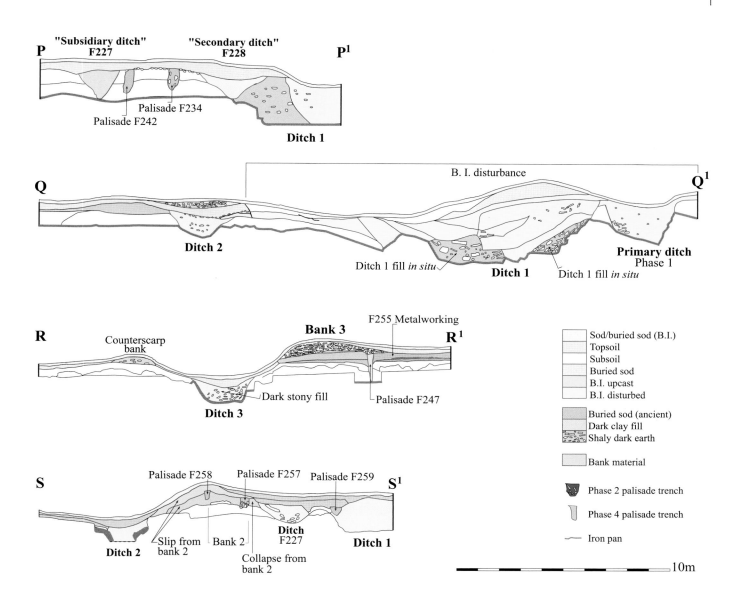

activity. In the middle of this area (Fig. 4.3) a fireplace (F187) overlies two post-holes (F188–9) and is in turn cut by another post-hole (F190). A little to the south-east of this two post- or stake-holes (F195–6) appear to have been cut into pits F194 and F200 respectively, while to the south a post-hole (F212) seems to intrude on pit F211. The features in this area appear to cluster around the three fireplaces (F187, F203, F222) and could represent three structures although no clear indication of ground-plans was discernible. The apparent arcs of post-holes (e.g. F220, F221, F224 and F214–16, F223), including one with four large post-holes (F190–2, F212), may be entirely fortuitous. Some of the features

(e.g. F213–21, F223–4) appear to be the truncated bases of stake- or post-holes.

Finds from the southern area
Detailed descriptions (and a list of samples) are presented in Appendices A and D (flint and chert).

Only a small quantity of material came from the southern area. This consists of a copper-alloy strip (E615:213a, Fig. 4.13), part of an iron nail (*E615:81), an iron stem (*E615:213b), a struck flint flake (E615:37, Fig. 4.13) and a fragment of copper-alloy waste (S133) from the charcoal- and slag-rich area in the south end of sq. 10.

The ramparts

Introduction

The site was originally constructed as a trivallate enclosure but was modified at a later stage with the addition of a fourth enclosing element (Fig. 4.1). The ramparts are substantially preserved on the northern, western and southern sides but had been removed on the eastern side by the graveyard attached to the early nineteenth-century church. The inner two ramparts enclose circular areas, 26m and 50m in diameter respectively. The outer rampart extends out on the north-west side to encompass the earlier barrow but appears otherwise to have been circular and about 67m in internal diameter. Each of the three main ramparts consists of two elements, a bank and an external ditch. An additional ditch (F227) occurred between ramparts 1 and 2 and appears to post-date both of those features.

The ramparts (Figs 1.3 and 1.4) are numbered from the interior outwards, and the inner bank and ditch (bank 1, ditch 1) make up rampart 1. This rampart enclosed an area 26m in diameter. Between this and rampart 2 (bank 2, ditch 2) there is a subsidiary ditch (F227), which was traced from the north-east to the south-west of the site and may originally have been a complete circuit. The outer enclosing feature is rampart 3 (bank 3, ditch 3), and possible entrances were identified on the northern and western sides in bank 3 (see below; Fig. 1.4).

A level area or berm occurs between each of the ramparts. These are described in the discussion below.

Rampart 1
Bank 1 (Fig. 4.9: T–T^1)
Only slight evidence for this feature survives, owing in part to the disturbance caused by the British-Israelites, and the portion visible as a low bank before excavation (Figs 1.2 and 1.3) was not investigated. The only excavated portion of the bank was on the southern side, at the inner end of cutting 2.

Ditch 1 (Figs 1.4, 4.1, 4.4: E–E^1 and G–G^1, Fig. 4.5: L–L^1, Fig. 4.7: O–O^1, Fig. 4.8: Q–Q^1 and S–S^1, Fig. 4.9: T–T^1)
Six transects were made across ditch 1, cuttings 1 (Fig. 4.5: L–L^1), 2 (Fig. 4.9: T–T^1), 3 (Fig. 4.8: S–S^1), 8, 10 (Fig.

4.8: Q–Q^1) and 11 (Fig. 4.7: O–O^1). In addition, sections from the east side of the central enclosure (Fig. 4.4: E^1–E^2 and G–G^1; Fig. 4.7: O–O^1; Fig. 4.8: P–P^1) show the inner ditch. This description is based primarily on field notes as well as the plans and section profiles of cuttings 1, 2, 3 and 10. The ditch has an average width of 5.5m but varies considerably, from a maximum of 6.4m on the north-west side to 4.75m on the north. The ditch profile also varies but is mainly steep-sided with a flat bottom, the latter averaging 4m in width but up to 4.3m. The base of the ditch was cut to an average depth of 2.2m (2–2.55m), of which the bottom 1.3–2m is cut into the shale bedrock. The ditch fill varies in detail between the different sections but generally consists of a basal layer of very shaly material (small to medium pieces of shale) originally quarried from the ditch itself. This presumably made up part of the internal bank. On the north-west side a layer of large pieces of shale occurs against the outer edge of the ditch base and suggests a tumble of material that might have made up a revetment or low bank along the outer lip of the ditch (Fig. 4.8: Q–Q^1). Above the shaly layer is an amorphous layer described as 'dark clay fill' or 'yellow brown clay' which contained some animal bone, charcoal and pieces of shale. This material appears to have been a mixture of sod, topsoil, boulder clay and bedrock which made up the main body of the bank and which had slumped or washed back into the ditch. In some of the sections it contained lenses of shale or shaly earth that may represent separate collapse events. A thin horizon that occurs above this in most of the sections consists of 'sticky grey' earth and has the appearance of a sod formation over the primary ditch fill. The equivalent layer on the north-western side was 'fine brown sandy clay'.

It is clear from the size of the ditch that a very substantial bank occurred on the inner side. This could have averaged 5m in width and 2.5m in height. There is, as noted above, very little indication of a bank surviving other than as a pre-excavation feature, but the ditch fill appears to represent bank collapse, with the possibility of large amounts of material slumping into the ditch interposed between longer episodes of slip and silting represented by thinner lenses and horizons of clay and/or shale.

Activity overlying ditch 1 (Figs 4.6, 4.7: O–O[1], Fig. 4.8: P–P[1])

This is situated immediately north-east of the inner enclosure, but only the edge of the area suffered some disturbance at the beginning of the twentieth century (Fig. 1.5). The central feature is a roughly circular stone setting (F256), 1.15m in diameter, with apparently tightly packed stones up to 0.3m by 0.25m in size. The setting occurs within a 0.25m-deep spread of ash, charcoal-rich soil and burnt earth. The excavated part extends throughout cutting 15, extension north (Fig. 4.3), except on the southern side, where it was cut by the edge of the early twentieth-century disturbance. While the earth around the setting was heavily fire-reddened, neither the stones in F256 nor the earth between them showed signs of burning. The intensity of the burning around the setting, and the absence of burning on or within it, might suggest that it was used as a kiln. This possibility is supported by the presence of part of a crucible (E615:234 a–b; see Appendix A, Fig. 4.16) and other metalworking evidence from the feature.

Finds from rampart 1 (Figs 4.15 and 4.16; Pl. 2)
Detailed descriptions (and a list of samples) are presented in Appendices A, D and G.

Ditch 1 produced a small quantity of material (Table 2.2). Amongst the artefacts are part of a striated copper-alloy bracelet (E615:195, Fig. 4.15) and three rings, possibly ear-rings (E615:21a–c, Fig. 4.15). There are five sherds of Roman pottery (E615:10, E615:68, E615:174, E615:183a–b; Fig. 4.15 and Pl. 2) and a globular dark blue translucent bead (E615:71). Waste material from copper-alloy production came from the ditch fill in cutting 2 (see Appendix A and Chapter 5), and part of a crucible (E615:234a–b, Fig. 4.16) came from F256. At least 123.5kg of animal bone came from ditch 1 (Appendix F): according to Ó Ríordáin's notes, there 'was a concentration of ox jaw bones in the upper fill of the ditch. In cutting 1 these occurred in grey sticky soil just under the "pebbly" shale line (? 17.4mW depth: 0.62m). In cutting 8 they lay in the black fill on stones at a depth of 0.70–0.80m.' From Ó Ríordáin's general assessment of this material it is clear that cattle accounted for at least two thirds of the total, with pig by far the next most numerous; as he indicated (see Appendix F), there is remarkably little evidence for sheep, with only three bone fragments of this species identified on the entire site.

The incomplete shank of a copper-alloy pin came from bank 1.

*Table 4.2—Finds from the phase 4 rampart 1; detailed descriptions (and a list of samples) are presented in Appendices A, D and G (*not illustrated; <u>underlining</u> indicates that the object cannot be located).*

	E no.	Object	Context		E no.	Object	Context
Copper alloy	E615:66	Pin shank	Cutting 2, inside bank 1	**Iron**	*E615:11	Blade fragment	Cutting 2, ditch 1
					*E615:18d	Stem fragments	Cutting 1, ditch 1
	*E615:104	Fragments	Cutting 10, ditch 1		*E615:24b	Fragments	Cutting 1, ditch 1
	E615:195	Striated bracelet	Sq. 59 ext., ditch 1		*E615:64	5-sided stem	Cutting 8, ditch 1
	E615:21a–c	Rings or ear-rings	Cutting 2, ditch 1		*E615:78	Nail	Cutting 8, ext. S, ditch 1
					*<u>E615:192</u>	Stem	Sq. 59 ext., ditch 1
Glass	E615:71	Globular blue bead	Cutting 8				
				Stone	*E615:12	Flint flake	Cutting 1, ditch 1
Bone	*<u>E615:22</u>	Chipped bone?	Cutting 2, ditch 1		E615:18a–c	3 flint flakes, chert nodule	Cutting 1, ditch 1
	*<u>E615:29</u>	Bone point	Cutting 2, ditch 1		*E615:269	Chert	Cutting 1, ditch 1
					*E615:24c	Flint with E615:24b	Cutting 1, ditch 1
Ceramic	E615:10	Sherd Roman pottery	Cutting 1, ditch 1		*E615:24c	Flint	Cutting 1, ditch 1
	E615:68	Sherd Roman pottery	Cutting 10, ext. E, ditch 1				
	E615:174	Sherd Roman pottery	Cutting 15				
	E615:183a–b	2 sherds Roman pottery	Sq. 59 ext., ditch 1				
	E615:234a–b	Half crucible (Fig. 4.16)	Cutting 15, ext. N				

Rampart 2

Bank 2

This was visible as an intermittent feature on the west and south-west sides of the site prior to excavation (Fig. 1.4) and appeared as a spread of material 5–6m wide. The best-preserved segment occurs on the south-west side (cutting 3; Fig. 4.8: S–S^1), where it is 3.5m wide, 0.75m high and revetted internally by a palisade supported in a trench (F257). Apparently in this area the bank was surmounted by a palisade (trench F258), although this is the only segment with evidence for this feature. On the north-east side (cutting 17, sqs 62, 63 ext. east; Fig. 4.6) the bank is represented by a thin (0.4m) layer of redeposited boulder clay. The width is suggested by the presence of a palisade (F240), dug from the same level as ditch 2, 2m inside the ditch. In the same area the palisade (F241) in cutting 11 (Figs 4.6 and 4.7: O–O^1) is 2.5m inside the edge of the ditch.

Two gaps are visible in the bank in this area but neither was investigated. The more westerly of these (labelled 'possible entrance gap 1' on Fig. 1.4) is 1.6m wide. The northern side is represented by a simple terminal in the bank, but there is a distinct inwards projection to the bank on the southern side. The second gap (labelled 'possible entrance gap 2' on Fig. 1.4) appears to be funnelled, with inward projections to both bank terminals; it narrows inwards from c. 3m to c. 1m. It is not possible to determine whether either of these gaps is an original feature.

Ditch 2

This is a partly rock-cut ditch, 1.5–2m in width and up to 1.5m in depth (Fig. 4.6, Fig. 4.5: L–L^1, Fig. 4.7: O–O^1, Fig. 4.8: Q–Q^1 and S–S^1, Fig. 4.9: Z–Z^1). The profile is V-shaped to flat-bottomed. The fill appears as a homogeneous layer of 'dark stony' material, 'light brown with flecks of orange' or 'dark brown soil' and contained some animal bone (e.g. S114, 174–5).

Finds from rampart 2

Detailed descriptions (and a list of samples) are presented in Appendices A, C (glass vessels) and D (flint and chert).

The principal discoveries from this context consist of iron tools or possible tools, including two tanged chisels (E615:185, E615:189a) (Table 4.3). A quantity of animal bone came from the base of the ditch (S174–5; not specifically identified but see Appendix F).

Rampart 3

Bank 3

This is the best preserved of the enclosing banks and was clearly visible before excavation along the northern and western sides of the site (Figs 1.2–1.7). It appears to vary in width from 4.7m to 7m, but the excavated sections (cuttings 1, 4, 5, 11 and 23) show that originally it averaged c. 3m in width. On the north (cutting 11, Fig. 4.7: O^1–O^2) and south-west (cutting 4, Fig. 4.8: R–R^1) the bank is made up of two layers. The lower is of compact redeposited boulder clay while the upper is of shale chips. The inner face of the bank was revetted by a palisade contained in a trench up to 0.25m wide and 1.2m deep. The palisade trench (F245–9; Fig. 4.5: L–L^1, Fig. 3.3: A–A^1, Fig. 4.7: M–M^1 and O^1–O^2, Fig. 4.8: R–R^1, Fig. 4.9: Z–Z^1) is between 2.9m and 3.8m from the inner edge of ditch 3, showing that bank 3 averaged 3m in width. It appears that the palisade rotted in situ and the bank collapsed over the trench. In cutting 4 (Fig. 4.8: R–R^1) activity caused a build-up of material against the

Table 4.3—Finds from the phase 4 rampart 2. Detailed descriptions (and a list of samples) are presented in Appendices A, C (glass vessels) and D (flint and chert) (*not illustrated; underlining indicates that the object cannot be located).

	E no.	Object	Context		E no.	Object	Context
Copper alloy	E615:211	Sheet fragment	Sq. 62 E, F240, bank 2	**Iron**	*E615:185	Tanged chisel	Sq. 63 N, F240, bank 2
					E615:189a–c	(a) Tanged chisel, (b, c) stem	Cutting 21, bank 2
					*E615:205	Stem or tool?	Sq. 62, bank 2, F240
					*E615:215	Stem	Sq. 62, in bank 2
Stone	*E615:59a	Flint flake	Cutting 2, inside bank 2		*E615:242	Stem	Sq. 62 E, in bank 2
	*E615:14	Flint flake	Cutting 1, base of ditch 2				

E615:183a & b

E615:127

E615:165d

E615:35

E615:137

E615:150

E615:68

E615:174

E615:10

Pl. 2—Roman ceramics.

E615:146.4	E615:146.3	E615:146.2	E615:146.1
E615:146.8	E615:146.7	E615:146.6	E615:146.5
E615:146.12	E615:146.11	E615:146.10	E615:146.9

Pl. 3—Roman ceramics.

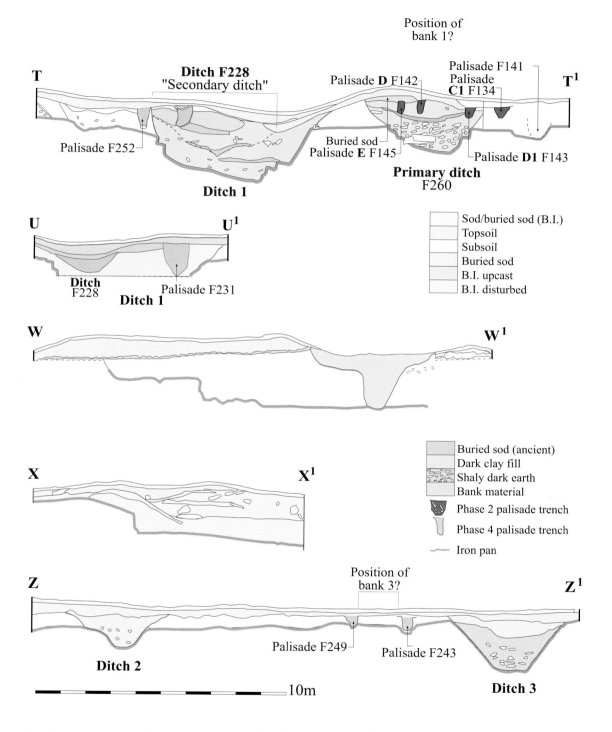

Fig. 4.9—Sections across the Rath of the Synods (T–T¹, U–U¹, W–W¹, X–X¹, Z–Z¹).

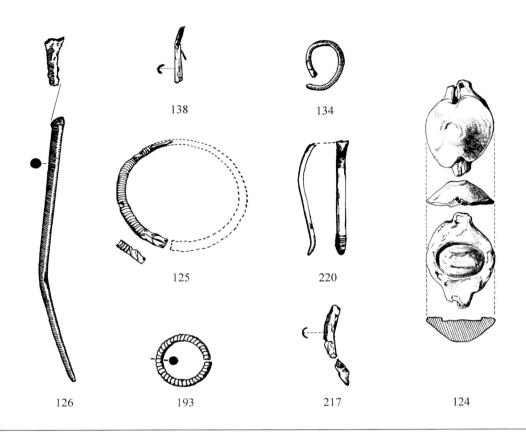

138

134

125

220

126

193

217

124

Fig. 4.10—Copper- and lead-alloy finds from the phase 4 enclosure, northern area (top); reconstruction of the use of the lead seal (124) for sealing documents (bottom).

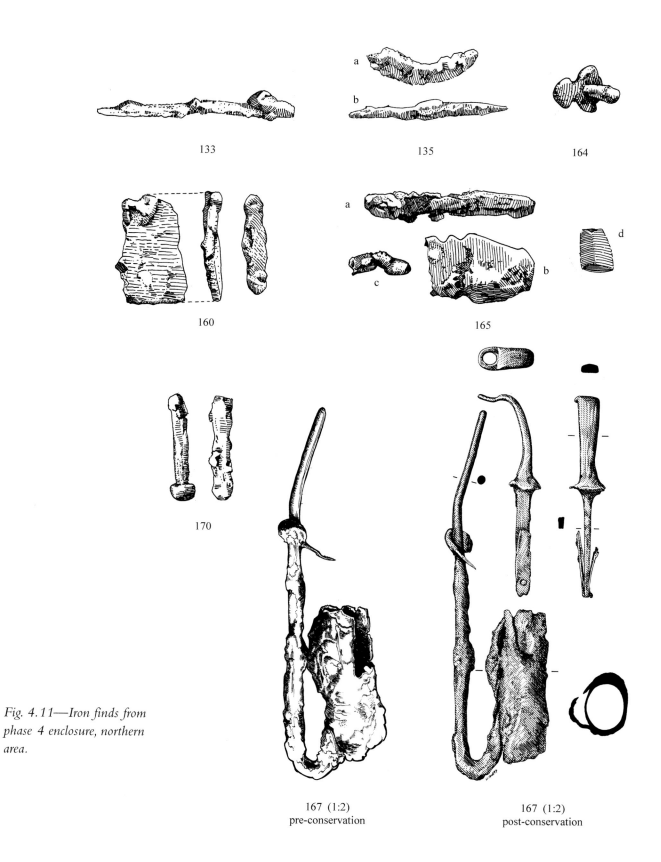

Fig. 4.11—Iron finds from phase 4 enclosure, northern area.

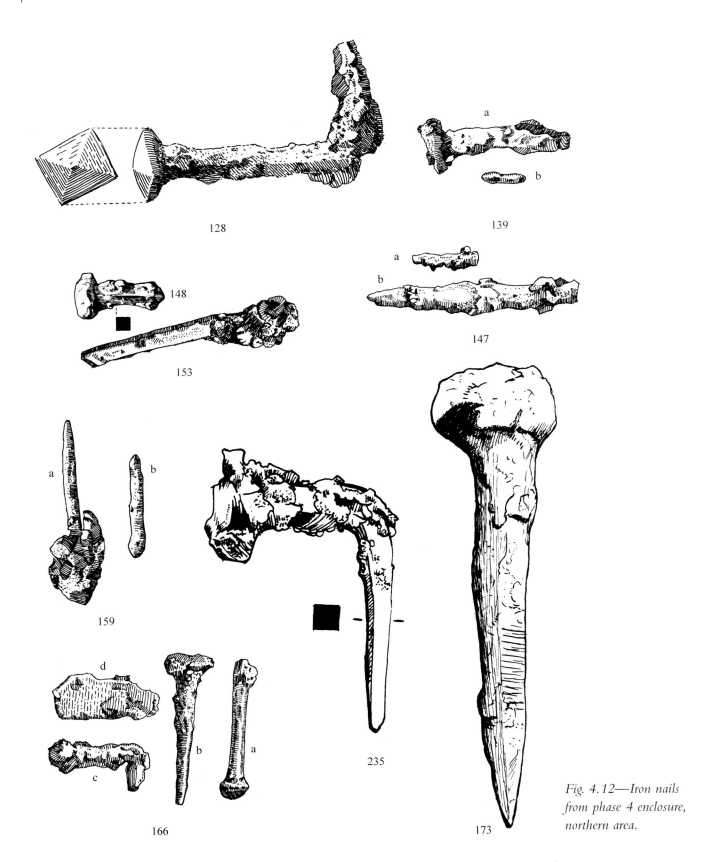

128

139
a
b

148

147
a
b

153

159
a
b

235

166
d
c
b
a

173

Fig. 4.12—Iron nails from phase 4 enclosure, northern area.

face of the palisade and the bank subsequently collapsed over this layer (see above). A similar palisade trench, F236, is clearly cut into bank 3 in cutting 24 (Fig. 4.7: M–M^1), however, and seems to indicate a palisade surmounting the bank. This palisade, whether contemporary with or earlier than bank 3, does not appear in the sections in either cutting 1 (Fig. 4.5: L–L^1) or cutting 4 (Fig. 4.8: R–R^1).

Activity within bank 3, south-west side (cutting 4)
Ironworking activity, perhaps of a limited nature, occurred immediately inside bank 3. The area, with maximum dimensions of 1.75m, consisted of a dark charcoal layer, 0.05m thick, that produced iron slag, charcoal and burnt clay (S10 and S11). This activity occurred on a sod layer on which bank 3 rested and therefore appears to be contemporary with the occupation of the site.

Entrances (Fig. 1.4)
Five gaps, three on the northern side and two on the western side (labelled 'possible entrance gaps 3–7' on Fig. 1.4), were identified in bank 3 on the pre-excavation survey but none were investigated. Of these, no. 5 at least appears to have been disturbed. No. 3 is a simple gap 2m in width. The gap on the north-west side (no. 4) narrows inwards from *c.* 4.5m to 1.5m and the eastern side is flanked by a simple terminal, while that on the western side narrows and curves inwards, giving the impression of an oblique entry to the enclosure. The south-western gap (no. 6), which is *c.* 2.2m wide, is similar to no. 2, although the bank of rampart 2 (see above) has a simple terminal on the northern side and an inward extension on the southern side. These two gaps are set almost opposite each other. In the absence of excavation none of these gaps can be shown to be original features. A more detailed assessment of the entrances is presented in the discussion below.

Finds from bank 3 area
The only artefacts from bank 3 (Appendix A) consist of a very corroded iron disc (★E615:41) and a fragment of chert (E615:44). A possible antler pick (★E615:276) and some unworked antler (★E615:277 and ★E615:280) came from the inner palisade, and iron slag (*c.* 860g,

E615:50) came from the area immediately inside the bank.

Ditch 3 (Fig. 3.3: A–A^1, Fig. 4.5: L–L^1, Fig. 4.7: M–M^1 and O^1–O^2, Fig. 4.8: R–R^1, Fig. 4.9: Z–Z^1)
This was visible as an almost continuous feature along the northern, western and southern perimeter of the site before excavation (Figs 1.2–1.7). The ditch is steep-sided, on average *c.* 2m wide and 1.5m deep, and cut into the underlying bedrock. In cutting 4 (Fig. 4.8: R–R^1) the sides are very gently curved but the central rock-cut portion is steep-sided. The fill consists of homogeneous dark shaly material. On the south-west side (cutting 25, Fig. 4.9: Z–Z^1) the ditch is 3m wide and is rock-cut for most of its 2m depth. The only apparent gap was on the south-western side (labelled 'possible entrance gap 8' on Fig. 1.4), where two well-defined terminals appear to flank an undug causeway.

Finds from ditch 3
There were no artefacts from the ditch but Ó Ríordáin's notes indicate that both cattle and pig bones came from the fill (Appendix F, cuttings 19 and 22; see also Appendix A).

Outer bank

In the pre-excavation survey (Figs 1.4–1.5) there appears to be an outer bank on the northern and south-western sides of the site. This is indicated by a slight feature, 1.5m wide and 0.2m high, on the outer lip of ditch 3 (cutting 4, Fig. 4.8: R–R^1). On the north side (cutting 24, Fig. 4.7: M–M^1 and N–N^1) this is a less clear but larger feature, 6.5m wide and *c.* 1m high, consisting of opposing sloping layers of dark, charcoal-flecked material. It is not certain that this is a bank. Apparently sealed beneath the inner edge of this feature is a palisade (F251, Fig. 4.7: M–M^1 and N–N^1) 0.4m wide and 0.8m deep.

Other enclosing features: trenches

Post-trench F235, F243–4, was noted beneath bank 3 on the north side in cutting 11 (Fig. 4.7: O–O^1), where it was sealed beneath a well-developed sod layer buried below the bank. It is 0.2m wide and 0.25m deep. The stratigraphy on the north-west (cutting 5, Fig. 1.4 and

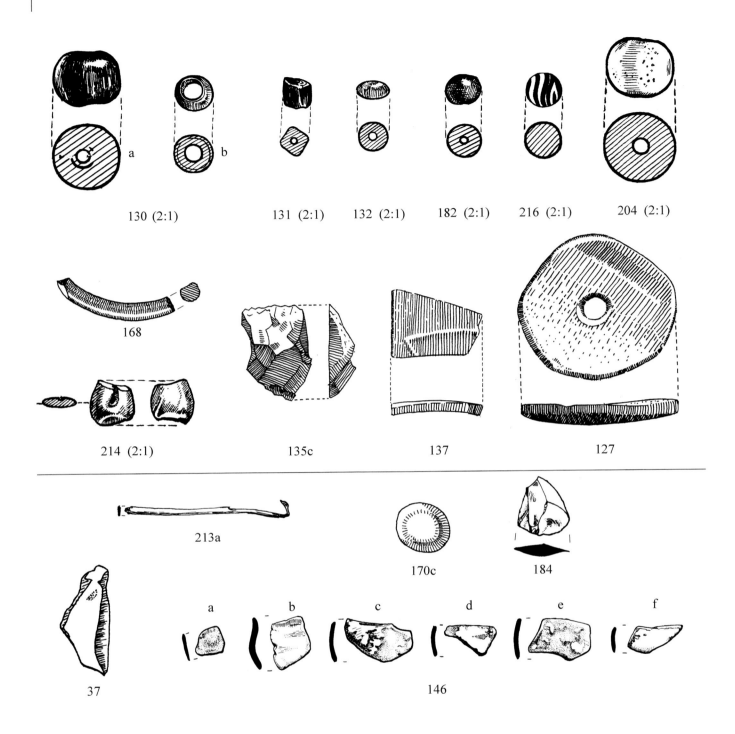

130 (2:1) 131 (2:1) 132 (2:1) 182 (2:1) 216 (2:1) 204 (2:1)

168

214 (2:1) 135c 137 127

213a

170c 184

37 146

a b c d e f

*Fig. 4.13—Finds from phase 4 enclosure: (top) northern
area, (bottom) southern area.*

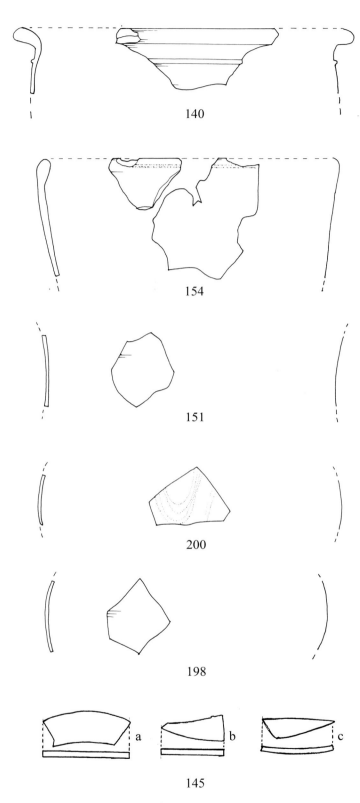

Fig. 4.14—Glass finds from phase 4 enclosure, northern area.

Fig. 3.3: A–A^1) and south-west (cutting 25, Fig. 4.9: Z–Z^1) sides is similar.

Two groups of features, consisting of narrow ditches and palisade trenches, were constructed between ramparts 1 and 2. One of these ('subsidiary ditch' F227) is later than rampart 2, while the other ('secondary ditch' F228) was dug at a stage after the primary ditches had silted up.

Subsidiary ditch (F227) (Figs 4.1 and 4.6)

This occurs between, and concentric to, ramparts 1 and 2. The ditch is 1.8–2.5m wide, with an average width of 2m. The profile varies considerably from V-shaped (Fig. 4.7: O–O^1, Fig. 4.8: P–P^1) to flat-bottomed (Fig. 4.8: S–S^1). It varies in depth from 0.9m to 1m, with the lower 0.4–0.5m cut into the shale bedrock. The fill appears to be generally homogeneous in each portion sectioned, but its nature varied from one area to another and was referred to as 'brown soil' (cutting 8), 'earth and some stones' (cutting 1) or 'dark fill' (cutting 11, Fig. 4.7: O–O^1, and cutting 16, Fig. 4.8: P–P^1). What may be a buried sod layer occurs over the ditch (and over the remnant of bank 2) in cutting 1. While the 'subsidiary ditch' and rampart 2 appear to be broadly contemporary, however, their relationship on the northern side of the site in cutting 11 (Fig. 4.7: O–O^1) suggests that F227 was cut through the inner edge of bank 2.

On the western side of the site the ditch is cut through the old sod line, which also runs beneath bank 2 and through which ditch 2 is cut (Fig. 4.5: L–L^1). A palisade trench—F232 in cutting 1 (Fig. 4.5: L^1–L^2), F242 in cutting 16 (Fig. 4.8: P–P^1) and F233 in cutting 8—occurs 0.3m inside the inner edge of ditch F227. It is 0.2m wide and 0.95m deep; the fill retains some packing stones, and this appears to be an associated feature. A sod layer overlying both F227 and F232 appears to have been cut by the 'secondary ditch' F228 (Fig. 4.5: L^1–L^2). On the south-west side the palisade is cut into the fill of ditch 1 in cutting 3, F259 (Fig. 4.8: S–S^1) and cutting 22.

The only surviving evidence for the associated bank observed during excavation was on the north-west side, where a deposit of 'yellow clay' (upcast boulder clay) was 3m wide and 0.5m in maximum height (cutting 10) (Fig. 4.8: Q–Q^1). There is no surface indication of an

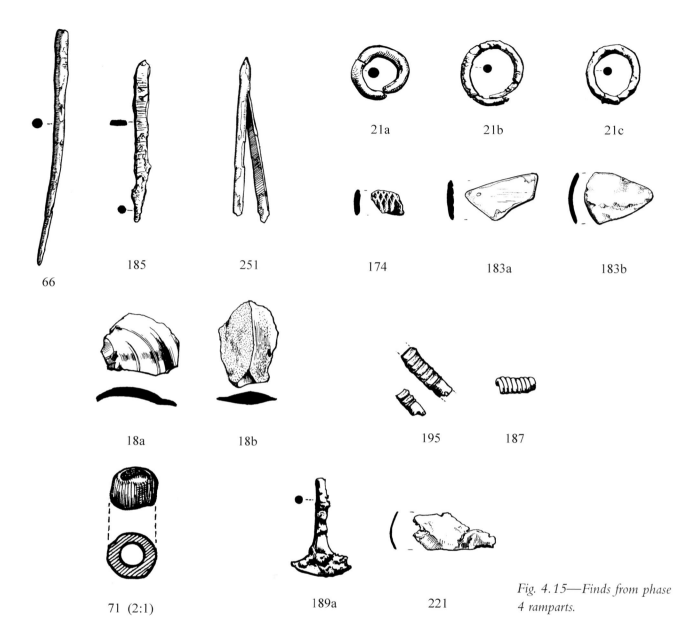

Fig. 4.15—Finds from phase 4 ramparts.

entrance gap, nor was evidence for one discovered during excavation.

Finds from the subsidiary ditch
There are two pieces of worked antler from the ditch (★E615:278 and ★E615:279; Appendix A).

Secondary ditch (F228) and palisade trench (F230/231/234/252) (Figs 4.1 and 4.6)

A shallow ditch (F228: 0.75–0.9m deep) was cut into the upper fill of ditch 1 at a considerably later stage when the ditch was almost completely silted up; it occurred towards the inner edge at a high level. It varied in width from 1.7m to 2.5m and appeared to average about 2m (Fig. 4.5: L–L^1, Fig. 4.7: O–O^1, Fig. 4.8: P–P^1, Fig. 4.9: U–U^1). The secondary ditch is identified in all the relevant sections and seems to have been a continuous feature around the site, concentric to the earlier ramparts. The upper fill consists of a 'dark layer with bone (animal)', and beneath this was a deeper layer of apparently similar material, 0.6–0.7m deep. Towards the base there was a considerable amount of animal bone,

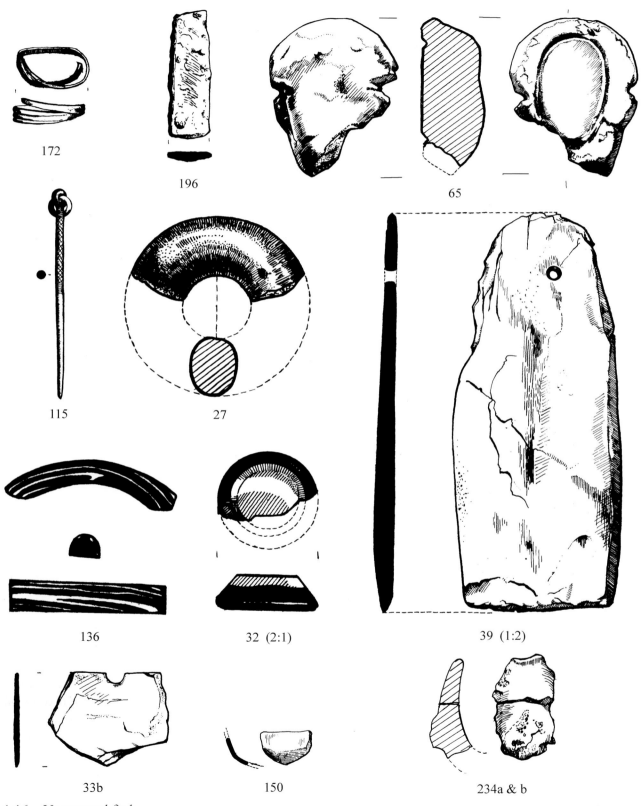

172

196

65

115

27

136

32 (2:1)

39 (1:2)

33b

150

234a & b

Fig. 4.16—Uncontexted finds.

which occurred in discrete pockets as well as spread out along the central line of the ditch *c.* 0.1–0.2m above the base. Where described or planned (in notebook sketches), the bones appear to be mainly jaw and limb bones, possibly of cattle (this observation is based solely on the size of the mandibles shown), with some complete or largely complete antlers. In view of the placement of the antler, it is possible that the skulls are those of deer. There was insufficient detail in the excavated cuttings to indicate the nature of these bones—i.e. whether they represent food debris dumped into the ditch or deposits of a more formal, possibly ritual, form. If these were deer carcases, and in particular heads, it may be that this material was dumped after the removal of antler associated with the antler-working noted on the north-eastern (sq. 63) and western (cuttings 9, 10 and 14) parts of the site. Nevertheless, Ó Ríordáin's notes (Appendix F) referring to this material seem to suggest that these were primarily cattle bones: 'Bones occurred all down through fill of (the) inner ditch. A remarkable feature was a concentration of ox jaw bones in the upper fill of the ditch. In cutting 1 these occurred in grey sticky soil just under the "pebbly" shale line (? 17.4mW, depth: 0.62m). In cutting 8 they lay in the black fill on stones at a depth of 0.70–0.80m.' A very large concentration of charcoal occurred in the fill of the ditch on the southern side in cutting 8 (S62–66). This is close to the copper-alloy-working area 8m to the north-west in cutting 2.

The most detailed section is in cutting 1 (Fig. 4.6: L^1–L^2). The primary collapse appears to be from the outer edge and consists of a wedge of loose stony clay and shale. The main fill is of brownish yellow clay with narrow upper bands of shaly soil and small chips of shale. Overlying the ditch and extending inwards over ditch 1 and outwards over the 'subsidiary' ditch (F227, above) is a well-defined sod layer buried beneath upcast from the British-Israelite disturbance. In this section ditch F228 appears to be cut from a higher level than the 'subsidiary ditch' (F227) and post-dates it.

A palisade trench runs concentric to the ditch and on average 1m outside it. It is identified in cutting 1 (F230, Fig. 4.5: L^1–L^2), cutting 2 (F252, Fig. 4.9: T–T^1), cutting 21 (F231, Fig. 4.9: U–U^1) and cutting 16 (F234, Figs 4.6 and 4.8: P–P^1). The trench is 0.25–0.5m wide and

0.45–1m deep. Packing stones occur throughout the apparently homogeneous fill and suggest that the trench held posts *c.* 0.3m in diameter, which may have been set edge to edge to form a continuous palisade. The trench is shown in all the sections as being cut from the same level as the ditch and seems to be a contemporary feature. In cutting 21 the section shows a large post-pit within the palisade slot (0.5m wide) set against the outer edge of the pit (F230, Fig. 4.5: L^1–L^2). On the south-west side (cutting 3, Fig. 4.8: S–S^1) a palisade trench (F259) was cut into the fill of ditch 1 along the outer edge, and this appears to continue into cutting 21 (F231, Fig. 4.9: U–U^1). It is not clear whether this is associated with F228 or the 'subsidiary ditch' F227.

Finds from the secondary ditch
Three significant artefacts—a glass fragment (★E615:198), possibly from the same Roman bowl as ★E615:200 from the northern area of the enclosure (see Appendix C, Table 4.1), a Roman fibula spring (E615:187, Fig. 4.15) and copper-alloy dividers (E615:251, Fig. 4.15)—came from the ditch fill (see Appendix A). Allason-Jones (Appendix A) notes that dividers are unusual in the Roman world and compares them to an example from Pompeii.

Later features
Two palisades post-dated the other enclosing features of the site. On the north-east side a palisade, F254 (Fig 4.6), identifiable over a length of 6m, was inserted into the fill of the 'subsidiary ditch' (F228). This appears to have consisted of individual posts about 0.2m apart without a trench. As it follows the line of the ditch it may represent a later enclosing feature in this area but was not identified in the adjacent cuttings (nos 11, 16 and 18).

Another palisade, supported in a trench, was identified on the south-west side (F253). This had been inserted into the fill of the 'secondary ditch' F228 (Fig. 4.9: T–T^1).

CHAPTER 5

PHASE 3: THE RESIDENTIAL ENCLOSURE: DISCUSSION

Introduction

The enclosure occupies the north-eastern edge of the level summit of the Hill of Tara, with sloping ground to the north and east but only very gentle slopes down (to the west) and uphill (to the south) (Fig. 1). The location of the site appears to have been deliberately chosen to occupy this level area, but its position necessitated avoiding the ditch of Rath na Ríogh to the south and accommodating the pre-existing barrow on the north-west side. The inner enclosure, represented principally by ditch 1, appears to respect the primary enclosure ditch (F260) despite the apparent time gap between the two structures. In fact the inner edge of ditch 1 respects it so closely that it must have been clearly visible at the time the residential site was constructed. This and the care taken to avoid Rath na Ríogh and the barrow suggest that the builders of the enclosure were aware of the importance of the site and planned the construction to minimise damage to existing features. By contrast, it is evident that the phase 3 burials were at least unmarked and possibly unknown at the time of the enclosure construction (see below).

Structure: the primary features

In its original form the Rath of the Synods is a trivallate site. It encloses a roughly circular area 22–26m in diameter and has maximum external dimensions of 80–88m (Table 5.1). The plan of the site is generally circular, particularly the maximum external appearance of the outer perimeters of the ditches (Newman 1997, fig. 37).

The internal areas defined by the banks tend to be slightly oval. Two later alterations were made to the site through the addition of a ditch ('subsidiary ditch' F227), which provided a fourth rampart, and the recutting of ditch 1 ('secondary' ditch F228).

The ramparts

The structure of the three ramparts, their relationship to each other and the (albeit sparse) stratigraphic evidence suggest that the three ramparts constitute a single constructional concept. The inner rampart, no. 1, is the most substantial, and although the ditch varied in size it averaged 5.5m in width and 2.2m in depth. The bank, of which very little survived in the excavation cuttings at least, may have had similar average dimensions. In combination the rampart would have been a formidable defensive feature. Ramparts 2 and 3 are similar to each other in size but slighter than rampart 1. The ditches average 2–3m in width and 1–1.5m in depth, and the banks appear to have been about 2.5–3.5m wide and may have been up to 1.5m high.

Revetting of the banks, in the form of slot-trenches to support palisades, is indicated along the inner face of banks 2 and 3. On the north side of the site bank 3

Table 5.1—Rath of the Synods: dimensions.

Internal area enclosed by:	N–S	E–W	Max. external dimensions (m)	N–S	E–W
Rampart 1	22	26	Ditch 1	41	41
Rampart 2	52	c. 48	Ditch 2	61	c. 62
Rampart 3	68	76	Ditch 3	c. 80	88

appears to have been surmounted by a palisade (F236), while on the south-west side a palisade ran along the top of bank 2 (F258). These features were not, however, noted in any other part of the site.

The berms

There is a slight berm between the ditch and bank of each rampart. The one between ditch 1 and the inner edge of bank 2 averages about 3m on the western side, expanding to *c.* 5.5m on the northern and southern sides. Apart from the outward bulge to accommodate the barrow, the berm between ditch 2 and bank 3 is consistently around 4m wide.

It seems that the placement of the original ramparts indicates an intention to maintain gaps of about 3–5m between them. Two constraints were intentionally introduced to this plan: the location of the site as close to Rath na Ríogh as possible while deliberately incorporating the barrow into the structure. On the south-west to north-west sides the gap between ramparts 1 and 2 (from the outside of ditch 1 to the inner edge of bank 2) averages 4m; on the north-west side this gradually widens to 12m. It appears to narrow again on the north-east side. The relationship between ramparts 2 and 3 seems to represent an attempt to maintain a constant distance between them (*c.* 4–5m) while extending rampart 3 outwards on the north-west side to incorporate the earlier barrow. At that point the distance between ramparts 1 and 2 widens to a maximum of 11m.

Entrances

Not much more than half of the site perimeter survives and there is no clear evidence for entrances from the excavations. Several gaps are apparent in the banks, however, at least from the pre-excavation survey (Fig. 1.4). In the absence of excavation it is not possible to show that any of them are original, or indeed ancient, but one of them (possible entrance gap 4, rampart 3, Fig. 1.4) appears superficially to provide oblique entry through the banks, while four others (possible entrance gaps 1 and 2, rampart 2, and nos 6 and 7, rampart 3, Fig. 1.4) seem to form funnelled entrances. The oblique angle of entrance 4 may relate to its position immediately north of the barrow, which would have

prevented movement between ramparts 2 and 3 in this area.

There is some indication of a causeway across ditch 3 opposite nos 6 and 7. The most convincing causeway is at gap no. 7, where well-defined terminals are opposite a U-shaped gap in bank 3 which does not, however, appear to penetrate through the entire width of the bank. There is no clear evidence for an entrance through rampart 1 although there is a slight indication of a possible causeway across ditch 1 on the western side (possible entrance gap 8, Fig. 1.4). If any of the gaps represent entrances, and accepting that much of the perimeter of the enclosure does not survive, there is a suggestion that the entrances could have been staggered.

If the entrances were staggered, this would provide an explanation for the berms since access and movement between the ramparts would have been an essential aspect of this defensive arrangement. Newman (1997, 178–80) has recognised a group of just four sites that have four or five ramparts (for the Rath of the Synods this involves the inclusion of the secondary modification represented by the 'subsidiary' ditch F228); these sites, the Rath of the Synods, Tlachtga (Wardstown), Co. Meath (Moore 1987, 93), Raheen, Co. Donegal (Lacy *et al.* 1983, 187, fig. 103a), and Rathra, Co. Roscommon (Herity 1987, 137–8), are also unusual in having berms between the ramparts (Grogan 2005b, 130).

Secondary features

Two secondary enclosing elements were identified. The 'subsidiary' ditch (F227) was inserted between ditch 1 and bank 2. Although the evidence is not entirely conclusive, it appears that the 'subsidiary' ditch was a modification of the primary enclosure. The construction of this feature, which may have had a revetted inner bank, required an alteration in access to the site since it would have reduced the berm between ditch 1 and bank 2 to a narrow strip averaging about 1m in width on either side of it. The 'subsidiary' ditch was identified in all the relevant cuttings on the northern, western and south-western sides of the site but did not occur on the southern side in cutting 8/23.

The 'secondary' ditch (F228) cut into the upper fill of

ditch 1 and was therefore a much later, and very much less substantial, feature. It also appears to be a later feature than the 'subsidiary' ditch. It is not possible to determine whether it represents the final phase of continuous use of the Rath of the Synods or a later reuse of the site.

The habitation phase

Occupation within the enclosure dates from the period between the third and fourth centuries AD (see below). The habitation layer within the central enclosure appears to abut the inner edge of bank 1, which was constructed by the community who occupied the site. The main focus of the habitation was concentrated in the northern, and especially the north-eastern, part of the inner enclosure, although some activity is represented elsewhere within the inner enclosure and at a few locations elsewhere within the overall defences.

The houses (Fig. 4.2)

There is good evidence for at least two structures. The house (F20) appears to be a small rectangular structure (c. 4m by 3.5m) defined by light upright posts; the other structure (F66) is smaller but also appears to be rectangular (c. 3.5m by 2.75m). While the size of the structures suggests that they were not the principal domestic buildings of the occupants, both produced habitation debris and a paved and cobbled area. There seemed to be a small yard immediately outside F66 on the southern side. Further concentrations of post- and stake-holes, as well as fireplaces and pits, on the southern side of the inner enclosure probably represent other, possibly substantial, buildings. A large part of the centre of the inner enclosure had suffered considerable damage during the British-Israelite investigation and it is possible that the main house or houses stood in this area.

A quantity of burnt earth and charcoal came from the immediate vicinity of the house, including charcoal from part of a slot-trench (F27) on the north-west side. The evidence suggests that the house was destroyed by fire.

Material assemblage

The finds fall into three broad categories. The first category consists of objects of probable local manufacture, such as the striated ring and bracelet, the chape fragments and the uncontexted stone cone, which have close parallels in the region but usually from burial contexts. It is possible that burials from the earlier cemetery within the inner enclosure were disturbed during the occupation phase and that these objects represent disturbed grave-goods. Indeed, some of this material could have been associated with the pre-burial ceremonial enclosures. Amongst this material are the penannular brooch fragment (E615:220, Fig. 4.10), part of a striated bracelet (E615:195, Fig. 4.15), a striated ring (E615:193, Fig. 4.10 and Pl. 1) and possibly the binding strip (or chape) fragments (E615:138, Fig. 4.10) from an object or objects similar to the chape from trench F, phase 2. The stone cone should be included in this assemblage (B. Raftery 1983, 230, fig. 185). Most of this material can be paralleled in late Iron Age contexts in Ireland, such as the striated rings and cones from the burials at Knowth, or the striated bracelet from the ring-barrow at Oranbeg (see Chapter 2). It should be noted, however, that the striated bracelet would be just as acceptable in a contemporary Romano-British context.

Another group of objects can be paralleled on both Irish and Roman sites of the early centuries AD. Amongst these are copper-alloy penannular rings (E615:21a, 21b, 21c, Fig. 4.15), a strip ring (E615:172, Fig. 4.16), the pin stem (E615:66, Fig. 4.15), the iron buckle pivot (E615:170a, Fig. 4.11) and the spherical glass pinhead (E615:216, Fig. 4.13; see Appendix A), portions of plain (E615:168, Fig 2.11 and Pl. 1) and decorated glass bracelets (E615:136, Fig. 4.16 and Pl. 1), sheet copper alloy (E615:211, Fig. 4.15), and the copper-alloy mount (★E615:225).

The third group consists of items that are clearly imports from the Roman world, most of them probably from Britain (Table 5.2). This consists of the pottery, mainly southern Gaulish *terra sigillata* but including sherds of flagons of the first or second century AD, the glass vessels (Appendix C), which are of second- to fourth-century AD date, copper-alloy items, including the spring possibly from a bow brooch (E615:187, Fig.

Table 5.2—Material from the Rath of the Synods and Rath na Ríogh imported from the Roman world.

	E no.	Object	Context	Phase	Probable date range
Ceramic	*E615:5	Sherd Roman pottery	Sq. 6, sod layer	?	First to second century AD?
	E615:10	Sherd Roman pottery	Cutting 1, ditch 1	4	First to second century AD?
	E615:17a	Sherd	Sq. 8	?	First to second century AD?
	E615:35	Sherd Roman flagon	Cutting 4, sod over bank 3	?	First to second century AD?
	E615:68	Sherd Roman pottery	Cutting 10, ext. E, ditch 1	4	First to second century AD?
	E615:127	Spindle-whorl/Roman sherd	Sq. 52	4	First to second century AD?
	E615:137	Sherd Roman flagon	Sq. 47	4	First to second century AD?
	E615:146	Twelve sherds *terra sigillata*	Sq. 53 (F16)	4	First to second century AD?
	E615:150	Sherd *terra sigillata*	Sq. 54	?	First to second century AD?
	E615:165d	Sherd *terra sigillata*?	Sq. 52 with E615:165a	4	First to second century AD?
	E615:174	Sherd Roman pottery	Cutting 15	4	First to second century AD?
	E615:183a–b	Two sherds Roman pottery	Sq. 59 ext., ditch 1	4	First to second century AD?
Glass vessels	E615:140	Rim sherd of Roman bowl	Sq. 38	4	First to second century AD?
	E615:145	Three fragments	Sq. 53	4	First to second century AD?
	E615:151	Bowl fragment	Sq. 42	4	First to second century AD?
	E615:154	Nine cone beaker rim/body sherds	Sq. 52	4	First to second century AD?
	E615:198	Fragment	Cutting 21, ditch F228	4	First to second century AD?
	E615:200	Fragment	Sq. 55	4	First to second century AD?
Glass	E615:71	Globular dark blue	Cutting 8, ditch 1	4	First century BC to third century AD?
	E615:130a	Globular dark blue	Sq. 52	4	First century BC to third century AD?
	E615:131	Mid-blue cylindrical	Sq. 55	4	Third to fourth century AD?
	E615:132	Opaque turquoise	Sq. 42	4	Post-first century AD
	E615:136	Part decorated ultramarine bracelet	Sq. 43	4	First century BC to third century AD?
	E615:168	Part ultramarine bracelet	Sq. 43	4	First century BC to third century AD?
	E615:182	Blue spherical	Sqs 36/37	4	First century BC to second century AD?
	E615:204	Green spherical	Sqs 46/54	4	First century BC to second century AD?
	E615:214	Blue glass waste	Sq. 52	4	
	E615:216	Blue pinhead	Sqs 37/43	4	First to fourth century AD?
	*E615:270	Round inset bevelled edges	Unknown	?	Second to third century AD?
Copper alloy	*E615:92	Nail, mushroom head	Sq. 22	?	Very long use period
	E615:187	Fibula spring?	Cutting 21 (F228)	4	Very long use period
	*E615:212	Mirror fragment?	Sqs 38/42	4	First to fourth century AD?
	E615:251	Dividers?	Cutting 21 (F228)	4	
Lead alloy	E615:124	Seal	Sq. 42		
Iron	E615:164	Stud with trefoil head	Sq. 45	4	?
	E615:167	Barrel padlock	Sq. 37	4	Third to fourth century AD?
	*E615:231	Joiner's dog	Rath na Ríogh	?	Very long use period
Nails	E615:128	Nail, pyramid head	Sq. 42	4	Very long use period
	E615:139a–b	Nails	Sq. 55	4	Very long use period
	E615:147a–b	Nail and stem	Sq. 54 (F16)	4	Very long use period
	E615:148	Nail, pyramid head	Sq. 37 (F5)	4	Very long use period
	E615:153	Stem of E615:148	Sq. 37 (F5)	4	Very long use period
	E615:159a–b	Nail and stem	Sq. 36	4	Very long use period
	E615:166a	Nail	Sq. 37	4	Very long use period
	E615:166b	Nail	Sq. 37	4	Very long use period
	E615:166c	Staple	Sq. 37	4	Very long use period
	E615:173	Nail	Sq. 37 (F16)	4	Very long use period
	*E615:181a	Nail	Sqs 37/43 (F5)	4	Very long use period
	*E615:207	Nail	Rath na Ríogh	U	Very long use period
	*E615:226	Nail	Rath na Ríogh	?	Very long use period
	*E615:230	Nail	Sq. 45 (F16)	4	Very long use period
	E615:235	Nail?	Sqs 37/43 (F5)	4	Very long use period

4.15), the dividers (E615:251, Fig. 4.15), a possible mirror fragment (★E615:212), the lead seal (E615:124, Fig. 4.10 and Pl. 1), a glass inset for a ring or brooch (E615:32, Pl. 1), glass beads (E615:130b, 132, 182, 204, Fig. 4.13) and the mushroom-headed bronze stud (★E615:92). The stud occurs mainly in first-century BC to first-century AD contexts in Britain (Appendix A). The iron barrel padlock is definitely imported and dates from between the first and fourth centuries AD (Appendix B). The nails are discussed below.

The excavation yielded 513 finds and samples, of which 66% were contexted; of the 310 finds, 60% were contexted and these 187 finds came from phase 2 (13%), phase 3 (8%), phase 4 habitation and the ramparts (70%), and Rath na Ríogh (9%).

The number of finds that can clearly be identified as Roman imports is 55, although this is a conservative number since much of the iron material, such as the smaller nails and blade fragments, is corroded and difficult to type. Of the contexted finds (186), 46 or 24.7% were clearly Roman imports or manufactured in the Roman fashion, with three from phase 2, two from phase 3, 22 from phase 4 and one from Rath na Ríogh.

Dating

In advance of the results from a scientific dating programme (Appendix J) and taking all of the evidence into account, including the probable currency of the phase 2 enclosures, the nature of the phase 3 burials as well as the assemblage, it seems that the enclosure was constructed not earlier than the late second century AD. Within the date range for the exotic material there is a median period, in the second to third century, when the majority of the finds were current in Britain. Since the bulk of the material comes from a homogeneous occupation phase of the enclosure, occupation did not continue beyond the early part of the fourth century AD.

Another consideration here is the preceding cemetery (phase 3), which, by comparison with other burials from Ireland and accepting the influence of changing burial customs in the Roman world, should span the period from the first into the second century AD. It is probable that some time elapsed before the cemetery area was reused for occupation, but the

enclosure-builders' knowledge of some funerary activity on the site is indicated by the careful avoidance of damage to the barrow, and a knowledge of the unmarked cemetery is not impossible. The damage to some of the burials in the flat cemetery suggests, however, that the occupants were not aware of these burials prior to the construction of the site.

Coins

While there appears to be no satisfactory record of the other material found during the British-Israelite search at the Rath of the Synods (Carew 2003), it is known that coins were discovered (Appendix E). Two possible coins were found during Ó Ríordáin's excavation: one of copper from burial E, phase 1 (★E615:178), and a second, much less probable example of silver (★E615:191) from the top of the habitation layer within the enclosure (see Chapter 3, burial E).

The flint assemblage

A small quantity of flint and chert artefacts and waste came from various parts of the site (Appendix D). Some of this occurred in phase 3 (burials) and phase 4 (habitation, particularly in house F20) contexts, but it appears that all of this material was fortuitously incorporated into later features and it is probable that the material represents a single episode of early prehistoric activity at the Rath of the Synods. None of the material is sufficiently diagnostic to indicate a firm date but it may have been associated with the primary ditched enclosure. A fragment of a polished stone axe (★E615:15) was found in the British-Israelite disturbance at the western part of the central enclosure.

The flint came from a wide scatter across the site but the overall quantity suggests that it does not represent a major phase of activity.

Animal bone

The samples that were retained were frequently preserved in bags containing more than one type of sample, e.g. charcoal mixed with animal bone, but around 70% was contexted. Ó Ríordáin's draft report shows that most of the animal bone was not retained (Appendix F). Some analysis was conducted on these samples prior to discarding them, however. Over 136kg of bone from the site was noted and *c.* 90% came from cutting 1 alone, most of this from ditch 1.

As well as the above draft report, another list (excluding ditch 1) of discarded but identified animal bone was found in the archives. This is reproduced in Appendix F. Some of these bones—large dog or wolf, bird, field mouse and claw of a small rodent—were 'sent to Dublin' but their location is unknown. The list also notes two horse bones, one of which is from cutting 21.

Tools and manufacture

The assemblage contained some 30 tools—awls, blades, chisels, points, staples, rubbing stones, etc.—indicating manufacturing activity on the site. Any tools from this period are extremely rare (see below).

The tool assemblage, although corroded, is remarkable because of the dearth of such objects from this period in Ireland. Barry Raftery notes that '. . . the only tool we have yet recovered from an Iron Age context in Ireland is an iron chisel from Feerwore, Co. Galway' (1994, 149), although, more recently, tools including a socketed iron axe came from excavations at Rath na Ríogh at Tara (Roche 2002). The Rath of the Synods yielded a tool assemblage, some showing that fine craftsmanship was practised on the site. For example, the awls and points from the habitation level, E615:133, E615:135b (Fig. 4.11) in iron and ★E615:29 and ★E615:22 in bone, were used for fine work, and some delicate chisels were recovered, ★E615:190 and E615:189a (Fig. 4.15, phase 4) and ★E615:267 (uncontexted). Seven contexted blades were found—★E615:83 from phase 3, ★E615:11, ★E615:156, E615:160 (Fig. 4.11), ★E615:165b and E615:166d (Fig. 4.12) from phase 4 and ★E615:253 from Rath na Ríogh—and three more were uncontexted (★E615:162, ★E615:194 and E615:196, Fig. 4.16).

The small staple (★E615:61) from phase 2 and the bolt (E615:166a, Fig. 4.12) from the habitation level indicate woodworking, but the joiner's dogs ★E615:231 and ★E615:246 from Rath na Ríogh point to larger construction. As noted above, the staple might indicate one means by which the palisade was jointed. These objects are found on Romano-British sites (W. H. Manning 1985, R52-3), from the Roman period in Scotland (Piggott 1955, 37, fig. 10: C54) and at the fourth-century site at Shakenoak Farm, Oxfordshire (Brodribb *et al.* 1968, 106, fig. 36, 67 and 75).

The nails, as noted above, are unique in Iron Age Ireland. Some, at least, of the nails, particularly the larger examples (e.g. E615:128, E615:139a, E615:148, E615:166b, E615:166c, E615:173 and E615:235, Fig. 4.12) and a few of the smaller ones (e.g. ★E615:181a, ★E615:188a, ★E615:207 and ★E615:226), were either imported or manufactured in the Roman manner. The complete examples range from 30mm to 140mm in length; 54% have round sections, 33% are square or rectangular in section and 13% have oval sections. The larger examples, such as E615:235, E615:128, ★E615:230, E615:159a, E615:139a and E615:166a, were probably used in construction, although they may have been imported for their exotic value, particularly as these were used in the building of Roman forts. The latter fall into two groups: those over 100mm in length (such as E615:235 and E615:128) and those under 60mm. Among the eighteen nails from contexted locations, including the longest example at 140mm, the average length is 53mm. The small, wide-headed nails or tacks (★E615:226, ★E615:241) could be from shoes.

Industrial activity

Metalworking debris and burnt material were scattered throughout the site, with most, *c.* 70%, in the central habitation area. Two dumps of metalworking waste occurred, one in ditch 1 and the other at the Rath na Ríogh ditch (see below). The phase 2 ditches produced *c.* 10% of this material. While it was unfortunately not possible to obtain expert analyses of the retained animal bone and metalworking material, it is thoroughly archived and would reward future study.

Most of the industrial activity took place close to the habitation area, including some evidence for production within the habitation area itself. Some of the ironworking, however, seems to have been focused away from the habitation, on the south-west side of the site immediately inside bank 3, for example, or outside the enclosure. The ironworking noted (below) at Rath na Ríogh pre-dates the occupation phase of the Rath of the Synods (Roche 2002).

Evidence of metalworking is shown in the contexted iron debris and copper waste and crucible fragments. A small amount (*c.* 10%) of the iron waste came from phase 2, the rest being almost equally divided between ramparts 1 and 3. The copper-working waste and crucible fragments came from ditch 1, phase 4 north, and the 'secondary' ditch, with a concentration of debris in ditch 1. The stone mould (E615:65, Fig. 4.16) was uncontexted, however. Four grinding stones were recovered (★E615:256, ★E615:258, ★E615:169 and ★E615:84) and two were contexted, ★E615:258 from phase 2 and ★E615:84 from phase 4.

Evidence for copper-working came from the base of ditch 1 on the south-west side of the site in cutting 2. The material consisted of light glassy slag, some with a red powdery coating, copper residue, charcoal and burnt clay. This deposit also produced three copper-alloy rings (E615:21a–c, Fig. 4.15), which either may have been cast in the area or were being melted for reuse. A copper waster (S201) came from cutting 21 beside it, and a very considerable area of intense burning, possibly associated, came from an area *c.* 5m to the south-east in cutting 8. It is possible that a kiln may have been located in the sheltered base of the ditch close to the habitation area.

Glass-working or melting for reuse is shown by the waste fragment (★E615:214) with its fine tool mark. Allason-Jones (Appendix A) thought that one of the beads (E615:204, Fig. 4.13) from the habitation level might be recycled Roman window or bottle glass. Both objects came from the habitation layer.

Antler-working is shown by the partially worked antlers (★E615:278 and ★E615:279) from the subsidiary ditch on the north-east side and from ditch 2 on the north-west side beside the barrow. No finished items have been recovered, however. The bone objects are missing from the assemblage but could well have been manufactured on the site.

The spindle-whorl (E615:127, Pl. 2) from the habitation phase may indicate textile-working, but its manufacture from Roman pottery could make it an exotic import.

The Rath of the Synods and Roman material in Ireland

The imported Roman finds from the rest of Ireland have been characterised as falling into two chronological frames, an earlier (first to second century AD) and a later (fourth to fifth century AD) (Bateson 1976; B. Raftery 1994, 214). The earlier material is not unusual in light of Ireland's proximity to Britain, where the Roman invasion and expansion (with some resistance) occurred at that time. This would have engendered enough disruption to create refugees and mercenaries. Trade and tribute cannot be discounted at this time, however, since Roman Britain was well aware of Ireland. 'An Irish prince, expelled from his home by a rebellion, was welcomed by Agricola, who detained him, nominally as a friend, in the hope of being able to make use of him', and 'Ireland could be reduced and held by a single legion with a fair-sized force of auxiliaries' (Tacitus, *Agricola*, 24) (translation by H. Mattingly, who examined the Tara coins). Even taking into account the conqueror's bias and the panegyric nature of Tacitus's words, some contact with Ireland was inevitable at this time.

Thus the earlier Roman material in Ireland is concentrated along the east coast, and in particular in the areas around the mouths of the Boyne and Liffey rivers (Fig. 5.1). The material from Lambay Island, Co. Dublin (Macalister 1929; Rynne 1976), and from Stoneyford, Co. Kilkenny (Bourke 1989; 1994), suggests the burial of British immigrants. Imports of the first to second century AD at Drumanagh, Co. Dublin, on the coast opposite Lambay (B. Raftery 1994, 207–8), burials with coins of Trajan (AD 97–117) and Hadrian (AD 117–138) at Bray, Co. Wicklow, and domestic material amongst the very large assemblage of mainly votive material at Newgrange (Carson and O'Kelly 1977) indicate that Lambay was not the only site with a significant Romano-British element. Other sites in this region with imports of this period are Freestone Hill, Co. Kilkenny (B. Raftery 1969a), Uisneach, Co. Westmeath (Macalister and Praeger 1928–9; Donaghy and Grogan 1997), and Millockstown, Co. Louth (C. Manning 1986). Other finds include the fibula from near St Anne's Well, Randalstown, Co. Meath, a strap-tag from Rathgall, Co. Wicklow (B. Raftery 1969b), fibulae from Dún Ailinne, Co. Kildare (Wailes 1990), *terra sigillata* from Knowth (Eogan 1968) and, further north, metalwork and *terra sigillata* from Clogher, Co. Tyrone (Richard Warner, pers. comm.).

By comparison there is a slightly more dispersed distribution of the fourth- to fifth-century AD Roman finds in Ireland (B. Raftery 1994, 214). This may relate to the breakup of the empire and the resulting raids. The turmoil is shown in a panegyric by the poet Claudian of Stilicho's consulship: 'After an introduction depicting Britannia with the trappings of a Caledonian savage, she is made to declare: "When I too was about to succumb to the attack of neighbouring peoples—for the Scots had raised all Ireland against me and the sea foamed under hostile oars—you Stilicho fortified me"' (Salway 1981, 420). Stilicho's success must have been uncertain or short-lived, however: 'Yet only a month after the detailed eulogy of January 400 the trumpeted claims of major success disappear, and they do not reappear. In mid 402 Claudian gives us news of troop withdrawals from Britain' (*ibid.*).

Within the Rath of the Synods material, at least 24% of the contexted finds were clearly of Roman origin, the only such domestic assemblage yet found in Ireland. In combination, the date range of these individual objects spans a considerable period from the first century BC to the early fourth century AD or even later. As discussed above, some items, such as the striated ring and bracelet (E615:193, Fig. 4.10 and Pl. 1; E615:195, Fig. 4.15) and the stone cone, have good Irish parallels from first- to second-century contexts such as Knowth and Oranbeg. Amongst the imported material, a few items, such as four of the glass beads (E615:71, E615:130a, E615:182, E615:204, Figs 4.13 and 4.15), could be as early as the first century (see Appendix A), while the *terra sigillata*, another bead (E615:132, Fig. 4.13), the fragment of a possible bow brooch (E615:220, Fig. 4.10), the mirror (★E615:212), the dividers (E615:251, Fig. 4.15) and possibly the seal (E615:124, Fig. 4.10 and Pl. 1) are of more general first- to second-century date. The only items that might be significantly later are the glass bead (E615:131, Fig. 4.13) and the zoomorphic brooch, which would generally be considered to belong to the third to fourth century (Fowler 1960).

The overall range of finds—pottery, glass vessels, ornaments, high-status personal items such as the padlock and seal, as well as tools—from the Rath of the Synods points to a community with a familiar relationship with the Roman world. In fact, the inhabitants of the site could have been of British origin, whether traders, mercenaries, refugees or settlers. The implication of the burial evidence from Lambay Island and Bray Head, and perhaps from Stoneyford, is that some settlements were established in the first to second century by people from, or on the fringes of, the newly Romanised parts of Britain. What is missing for the purposes of comparison with the Rath of the Synods is the settlements associated with these funerary sites.

There are two principal considerations in the determination of the cultural origin of the enclosure's occupants. First, the assemblage contains no material, other than the striated bronze ornaments and the stone cone, that might have a background in Ireland. Second, the presence not only of the ornaments and personal effects but perhaps more significantly of the more mundane items, such as the nails, joiner's dogs, staples and tools, with no parallels in Ireland suggests a largely Romano-British origin for the assemblage.

A problem with this interpretation is the relative dearth of pottery that would be expected from an immigrant settlement, but this could be the result of isolation after the settlement was established. This is not remarkable in light of the apparent gap in Roman finds in Ireland in the third century (above).

An element of caution must be observed in dating the domestic assemblage from the site. While the pottery is undoubtedly of first- to second-century AD date, its condition suggests that it could have become abraded during a lengthy period of activity on the site. The date of manufacture is likely to be earlier than the context within which the pottery occurs. In addition, the other artefacts for which British parallels have been cited cannot be firmly affixed to narrow date ranges. Glass beads, for example, can have a lengthy currency of use, even when their date of manufacture can be established with reasonable accuracy. Other items, such as the seal, dividers, lock, mirror and the tools and nails, are not closely datable and were current in the Roman world from the first to the fourth century AD.

Nevertheless, the presence of the material within a homogeneous occupation context, the probable date range of the objects, both singly and collectively, and the absence of material, other than the zoomorphic penannular brooch fragment, generally dated to the third to fourth century indicates a date in the latter part of the third century AD for the occupation phase at the Rath of the Synods. This is the lacuna between the two Irish Roman assemblages discussed above.

In her assessment of the assemblage Allason-Jones (Appendix A) comments that 'there are obvious and serious gaps' which 'support the conclusion that the finds from the Rath of the Synods represent a settled, limited-income domestic group rather than a high-status group with important political, military, religious or mercantile connections'. This provides an interesting contrast with Barry Raftery's (1994, 212) assessment that 'these imported items, concentrated together at a single site, are indicative of an affluent elite'. The evidence at present certainly confirms that much of the assemblage was exotic and would, despite its relative poverty when compared with high-status sites within the Roman Empire, have conferred considerable prestige on its owners in a late Iron Age Irish context. These assessments tend to confirm the theory of a family or community at the Rath of the Synods with strong Romanised or sub-Roman contacts. Certainly the importance of the Hill of Tara implies that these people were sufficiently powerful and influential to establish and maintain a defended settlement within what appears to have been an otherwise exclusively ritual landscape throughout prehistory. It is also possible that the group derived additional prestige through their foreign contacts or even relatives and their ability to source exotic foreign material. Perhaps this, with the aid of local alliances, and indeed alliances in Romano-Britain, provided the context within which a domestic settlement could be established at Tara.

Comparative sites

The date range for the Rath of the Synods places it early in, if not wholly outside, the conventional chronology of Irish ringforts (e.g. Caulfield 1981; Edwards 1990, 15–19). Indeed, there is little evidence for any ringfort of comparable or earlier date. Nevertheless, the construction of the site is consistent with many of the features of earthen multivallate ringforts. An unusual aspect of this site is the presence of berms between the ramparts, which contrasts with the closely spaced ramparts of most Irish multivallate sites. Perhaps of particular significance in the case of the Rath of the Synods is the possibility of staggered entrances, an arrangement that is only possible if a thoroughfare between the ramparts is provided by the berms.

It may also be that the oblique or angled entrances that have been tentatively identified would have added to the ease of access to the passage between the ramparts. Unfortunately none of the possible entrances were excavated so it is not possible to tell what further elaborations may have existed in the settlement defences.

The element of closely spaced multivallation has frequently been discussed as resulting from external influence, particularly from Britain or, more particularly, the Veneti of north-western France (Raftery 1976). Just such a possibility is raised by Barry Raftery (1994, 208) in relation to the coastal promontory fort at Drumanagh, Co. Dublin, which has produced Romano-British material (first-century AD Gallo-Roman Samian ware; see Mitchell and Ryan 1997), while first- to second-century AD coins have been found close to the site.

The contrasting morphology of the Rath of the Synods indicates that its origins cannot be so narrowly defined. It is evident that enclosed occupation sites began in the Neolithic, and small-scale enclosed habitations defined by stone-revetted rubble banks have been identified as a common form of site during the middle to late Bronze Age (Grogan 2005a; 2005b; Grogan et al. 1996, 38–44). One such site, at Aughinish, Co. Limerick (B. Raftery 1994, 32), appears to span the late Bronze Age–early Iron Age transition. While there do not appear to be any clearly dated domestic enclosures from the latter part of the Iron Age, two aspects of the record appear to be relevant. First, the technique of multivallation is represented on hillforts; most of these sites date from the late Bronze Age (Grogan 2005b; Mallory 1995; B. Raftery 1994) but it is possible that others belong to the Iron Age. The ramparts on these sites are usually widely spaced and it is possible that the Rath of the Synods was influenced by this layout. Second, Edwards (1990, 17–18) has pointed out the nature of pre-enclosure activity at a number of ringfort sites. Amongst these may be Feerwore, Co.

Galway, where habitation material and a cremation burial in a cist might pre-date the rampart of the enclosure, possibly a ringfort. At the multiperiod site of Millockstown a large enclosure, *c.* 66m by 53m in internal diameter, was defined by a ditch (C. Manning 1986). Activity within this enclosure produced a type A1 zoomorphic penannular brooch and pebbles possibly from a gaming set. This phase was dated to cal. AD 230–620 (1595 ± 70 BP, GU-1781). Other objects from disturbed contexts on the site that may be from this period include a stone cone and an iron penannular brooch with expanded terminals. In phase 2 an enclosure characterised by the excavator as a ringfort was constructed within the earlier site. This would have had an internal diameter of *c.* 33m. The pre-ringfort enclosure at Uisneach has already been mentioned in relation to the phase 1 ditch at the Rath of the Synods.

CHAPTER 6

THE RATH OF THE SYNODS: GENERAL DISCUSSION

Introduction

The evidence from Ó Ríordáin's excavations at the Rath of the Synods indicates that this was a significant location within the Tara complex during the final stages of the prehistoric era at least. While there is good stratigraphic evidence for the four major phases presented here, there is also a lack of firm chronological information for all but the final residential stage. Nevertheless, comparative archaeology from the similar complexes at Emain Macha and Dún Ailinne provides some context for the phase 2 palisade enclosures, while some evidence from the recent excavations at Rath na Ríogh may help to clarify the date of the burials from phase 3.

The phase 1 enclosure

While the date of the primary, phase 1, enclosure is unknown, it probably belongs to the early Iron Age or earlier, and the remnants suggest that it may originally have constituted a significant monument possibly similar to Rath Grainne—a ceremonial enclosure defined by a ditch and an external bank (Newman 1997). The evidence from geophysical survey in the immediate vicinity indicates the presence of a larger enclosure measuring 210m north–south by 175m east–west that appears to be centred on the Rath of the Synods, and perhaps specifically on the phase 1 feature (Fenwick and Newman 2002). While the date of this ditch and pit enclosure is unknown, Fenwick and Newman (2002, 11–14), in discussing the range of potential parallels, identified comparable elements amongst a number of ceremonial enclosures, including late Neolithic 'henges' such as Ballynahatty, Co. Antrim (Hartwell 1998), and Newgrange, Co. Meath (Sweetman 1985), and the

predominantly Iron Age complexes at Emain Macha, Dún Ailinne, Rathlin and possibly Rathcroghan, Co. Roscommon (Fenwick et al. 1999). Some elements of the late Bronze Age sites at Lugg, Co. Dublin (Kilbride-Jones 1950; Roche and Eogan 2007), and Haughey's Fort, Co. Armagh, are also analogous, as is the recently identified early Iron Age enclosure complex at Lismullin, Co. Meath, on the western flank of Skreen Hill, c. 2km to the east of Tara (O'Connell 2007; Grogan, O'Connell et al. 2007). Regardless of the specific date of the ditch and pit enclosure, it is further evidence of the importance of this area of the Tara complex.

The phase 2 palisade enclosures

During this phase there is a general sequence represented by a figure-of-eight enclosure (enclosures A/B, the post circle and C) replaced at a later stage by a larger circular enclosure defined by palisades D and E. A small quantity of material from this phase, and possibly some disturbed artefacts redeposited in phase 3 and 4 levels, give a very general indication of a late La Tène context for phase 2. Some striking parallels for these enclosures are provided by the sites at Emain Macha and Dún Ailinne, and the much better dating sequences for these sites suggest that the activity at the Rath of the Synods may date from the century or so before c. 100 BC.

The cemeteries

Two areas of the site, consisting of a barrow on the north-west side and a flat cemetery centred on the southern side, were used for burial in the late prehistoric period. The flat cemetery clearly post-dates the phase 2 activity and is probably also later than the ditch of Rath na Ríogh. While the barrow is certainly earlier than the phase 4 residential enclosure, there is no direct stratigraphic evidence for its relationship to either the phase 2 enclosures or the flat cemetery. Nevertheless, it is probable that the two areas of burial were in broadly contemporary use. Cremations and both crouched and extended inhumations are represented in the burial rite. As none of the burials is securely dated there is only tentative stratigraphic evidence to indicate a broad sequence, but it is possible that this is initially represented by cremations that were, in turn, followed by crouched and then extended inhumations. In view of the presence of Neolithic cremations around the perimeter of the Mound of the Hostages, c. 25m to the south (O'Sullivan 2005, 29–40), there is a possibility that the cremations at the Rath of the Synods are of a much earlier date than the inhumations.

Close parallels with the extended cemetery at Knowth suggest a broad date range for the inhumations at the Rath of the Synods of between the first century BC and the early second century AD. This dating is compatible with the evidence for inhumation burials from the ditch of Rath na Ríogh.

The phase 4 residential enclosure

It is evident that the occupants of the residential enclosure had attempted to establish ownership of this sacred site and its landscape. The site is positioned as close to the Iron Age ritual enclosure of Rath na Ríogh as was possible without encroaching directly onto the heart of the prehistoric complex. Indeed, the position on top of the phase 2 enclosures and both the primary ditched enclosure and the later cemetery is a powerful statement of status and a highly visible assertion of control over the complex and its history. A certain element of timidity in not occupying the inner sanctum of the hilltop may well represent both a reflection of the sacred nature of Tara and a caution regarding the potential wider societal perception of arrogance or presumption. In this regard it is worth noting that the church, immediately to the east but positioned further from the heart of the complex, appears to reflect a

similar degree of caution and contrasts with, for example, the location of the church site on the summit of the hilltop at Skreen on the opposite, eastern, side of the Tara–Skreen Valley.

The status of this residential group, this kinship unit or family, was probably not new-found but it may well have been the subject of powerful new political or social aspirations. The selection of an appropriate suite of material possessions appears to have played a significant role in the pursuit of these ambitions. While there are a small number of artefacts that were otherwise current in Ireland, the majority were imported or were copies of imported pieces. These range from the simplest items, such as nails and possibly the small tools such as chisels, to the more exotic material brought from the fringes of the Roman world in Britain. The selectivity of this assemblage is highlighted by the choice of drinking vessels in pottery and glass, as well as by the absence of more common domestic utensils such as cooking pots. While, as both Allason-Jones and Evans point out (Appendices A and G), this would not constitute a significant or particularly high-status collection in Britain, the material would certainly have been perceived as rare, exotic and prestigious in late Iron Age Ireland. Given the domestic context, some of the items, such as the lead seal and the possible dividers and mirror, may have had remarkable social value as unique curios.

Evans (Appendix G) has noted the absence of ceramic material that would be expected even from sites on the fringes of Roman Britain. These include Black Burnished Ware (Tyers 1996, 182–6), produced on an industrial scale in the Dorset region from the late first to the early fifth century AD, as well as terra sigillata from Colchester and, more especially, related material from southern and central Gaul, which collectively have a wide distribution in England, Wales and southern Scotland. The Tara assemblage contains small quantities of Oxfordshire Slip Ware (ibid., 175–8), found extensively in central and southern England, and a more substantial quantity of Severn Valley Ware, which has a predominantly western distribution in Britain, with several identified kilns (Darlington and Evans 1992). Production of the Oxfordshire material began c. AD 240 but it has a wide currency in the late third and early fourth centuries AD. Severn Valley Ware flourished in the second and early third centuries. The absence of so-called grey wares, including amphorae and cooking utensils, is certainly in contrast to the British evidence, as is the particular selection at Tara of small drinking bowls, including the two fine Déchelette 72 examples.

The date range for the Tara pottery is in the second to fourth centuries, which accords well with the dating of the glass vessels (Bourke, Appendix C). Another interesting correlation between the pottery and the glass is the dominance of drinking vessels in both media, an aspect of the site that appears to contrast with both Irish Iron Age sites and contemporary evidence in Britain. The deliberate selection of these vessels, and the absence of more common domestic wares in pottery, is one apparently strong indicator that the occupants of the Rath of the Synods were indeed Irish.

There is no direct evidence for the mechanism by which this material was acquired. It may represent straightforward trade items, although there is little other evidence for the existence of a significant market for contemporary Romano-British artefacts in Ireland. A more direct relationship with communities or families on the other side of the Irish Sea may have provided the source for the assemblage. It is tentatively suggested here that this may have been a group or network on the fringes of Roman Britain with access to a wider, and often more functional, range of material: the probable origins of the pottery, in particular, may indicate sites in the Severn Valley, or perhaps further north along the coastal areas of Cumbria or Lancashire. Ties with such groups, whether through trade contact or familial bonds, could have provided strategic support for the Tara occupants' aspirations, and alliances with powerful élites in Britain may well have been a significant component in the pursuit of regional political and social ambitions.

Conclusions

While our understanding of the Bronze Age and Iron Age at Tara is still at an early stage of development, it is clear that the Rath of the Synods spans a significant part of the final late prehistoric history of the complex. While many of the finer details of this evidence, and its close chronology, were not resolved through Ó Ríordáin's

excavations, his work has certainly provided an important insight into the intensity and complexity of activity on this part of the hilltop. It is further evidence that Tara maintained a position of more than regional status from the middle Neolithic, at least, until the end of the prehistoric era.

The overall evidence indicates that the settlement dates from a period during the second to fourth centuries AD. It is probable that it was the high-status homestead of a native Irish group with familial ties in the region of Romano-Britain on the fringes of the empire, possibly in the Severn Valley.

Bibliography

Adams, J.-P. 1984 *La construction Romaine: materiaux et techniques*. Paris. Picard.

Alarcão, J., Delgado, M., Mayet, F., Moutinho Alarcão, A. and Ponte, S. 1976 *Fouilles de Conimbriga. Vol. VI. Céramiques diverses et verres*. Paris. M.A.F.P./M.M.C.

Allason-Jones, L. 1989 *Ear-rings in Roman Britain*. British Archaeological Reports, British Series 201. Oxford.

Allason-Jones, L. and Miket, R.F. 1984 *Catalogue of small finds from South Shields Roman fort*. Society of Antiquaries of Newcastle upon Tyne Monograph Series 2. Newcastle upon Tyne. Society of Antiquaries of Newcastle upon Tyne.

Bateson, J.D. 1973 Roman material from Ireland: a reconsideration. *Proceedings of the Royal Irish Academy* **73C**, 21–97.

Bateson, J.D. 1976 Further finds of Roman material from Ireland. *Proceedings of the Royal Irish Academy* **76C**, 171–80.

Beckett, J.K. 1979 *Planting native trees and shrubs*. Norwich. Jarrold and Sons.

Benton, S. 1931 The excavation of the Sculptor's Cave, Covesea, Morayshire. *Proceedings of the Society of Antiquaries of Scotland* **65**, 177–216.

Bhreathnach, E. 1995a *Tara. A select bibliography*. Discovery Programme Monograph 3. Dublin. Royal Irish Academy.

Bhreathnach, E. 1995b The topography of Tara: the documentary evidence. *Discovery Programme Reports* **2**, 68–76.

Boone, G.C. 1967 A penannular brooch from Kings Weston Roman villa. *Transactions of the Bristol and Gloucestershire Archaeological Society* **86**, 195–6.

Bourke, E. 1989 Stoneyford: a first-century Roman burial from Ireland. *Archaeology Ireland* **10**, 56–7.

Bourke, E. 1994 Glass vessels of the first nine centuries AD in Ireland. *Journal of the Royal Society of Antiquaries of Ireland* **124**, 163–209.

Brodribb, A.C.C., Hands, A.R. and Walker, D.R. 1968 *Excavations at Shakenoak Farm, near Wilcote, Oxfordshire*, Part 1. Oxford. Published privately.

Brodribb, A.C.C., Hands, A.R. and Walker, D.R. 1971 *Excavations at Shakenoak Farm, near Wilcote, Oxfordshire*, Part 2. Oxford. Published privately.

Brodribb, A.C.C., Hands, A.R. and Walker, D.R. 2005 *Excavations at Shakenoak Farm, Oxfordshire, 1960–1976*. British Archaeological Reports, British Series 395. Oxford.

Burley, E. 1955–6 A catalogue and survey of the metal-work from Traprain Law. *Proceedings of the Society of Antiquaries of Scotland* **89**, 118–226.

Butler, H. and Foster, R.F. 1990 *The sub-prefect should have held his tongue and other essays*. Harmondsworth. Allen Lane.

Byrne, F.J. 1973 *Irish kings and high kings*. London. Batsford.

Carew, M. 2003 *Tara and the Ark of the Covenant*. Dublin. The Discovery Programme.

Carson, R.A.G. and O'Kelly, M.J. 1977 A catalogue of Roman coins from Newgrange, Co. Meath. *Proceedings of the Royal Irish Academy* **77C**, 35–55.

Casey, P.J., Davies, J.L. and Evans, J. 1993 *Segontium*. CBA Research Report 90. London. Council for British Archaeology.

Caulfield, S. 1981 Some Celtic problems in the Irish Iron Age. In D. Ó Corráin (ed.), *Irish antiquity: essays and studies presented to Professor M. J. O'Kelly*, 205–15. Cork. Tower Books.

Collins, A.E.P. 1955 Excavations at Lough Faughan crannog, Co. Down, 1951–2. *Ulster Journal of Archaeology* **18**, 45–81.

Cooney, G. and Grogan, E. 1994 *Irish prehistory: a social perspective*. Wordwell. Bray.

Cree, J.E. 1923 Account of the excavations on Traprain Law during the summer of 1922. *Proceedings of the*

Society of Antiquaries of Scotland 57, 180–226.

Cross, S. 1991 An intensive survey of the early prehistoric archaeology in the environs of Fourknocks, Co. Meath. Unpublished MA thesis, University College Dublin.

Daniels, M.J. and Williams, B.B. 1977 Excavations at Kiltierney Deerpark, County Fermanagh. *Ulster Journal of Archaeology* 40, 32–41.

Darlington, J. and Evans, J. 1992 Roman Sidbury, Worcester excavations 1959–1989. *Transactions of the Worcestershire Archaeological Society* 13, 5–104.

Déchelette, J. 1927 (1913) *La Collection Millon: Antiquités préhistoriques et Gallo-Romaines.* Paris. Geuthner.

Dolley, M. 1968 Two numismatic notes. *Journal of the Royal Society of Antiquaries of Ireland* 98, 57–65.

Donaghy, C. 1991 Barrel padlocks and their keys in Ireland. Unpublished MA thesis, National University of Ireland.

Donaghy, C. and Grogan, E. 1997 Navel-gazing at Uisneach, Co. Westmeath. *Archaeology Ireland* 42, 24–6.

Dwyer, M. 1988 Tara excavations. *Lough Gur and District Historical Society Journal* 3, 39–47.

Edwards, N. 1990 *The archaeology of early medieval Ireland.* London. Batsford.

Eogan, G. 1963 A Neolithic habitation-site and megalithic tomb in Townleyhall townland, Co. Louth. *Journal of the Royal Society of Antiquaries of Ireland* 93, 37–81.

Eogan, G. 1968 Excavations at Knowth, Co. Meath, 1962–5. *Proceedings of the Royal Irish Academy* 66C, 299–382.

Eogan, G. 1974 Report on the excavations of some passage graves, unprotected inhumation burials and a settlement site at Knowth, Co. Meath. *Proceedings of the Royal Irish Academy* 74C, 11–112.

Evans, J. 2004 The pottery vessels. In H. E. M. Cool, *The Roman cemetery at Brougham, Cumbria*, 333–62. Britannia Monograph Series No. 21. London. Society for the Promotion of Roman Studies.

Evans, J. (forthcoming) The pottery from Cefn Cwmwd, Melin Y Plas and Cefn Du.

Fenwick, J. and Newman, C. 2002 Geomagnetic survey on the Hill of Tara, Co. Meath, 1998–9. *Discovery Programme Reports* 6, 1–17.

Fenwick, J., Brennan, Y., Barton, K. and Waddell, J. 1999 The magnetic presence of Queen Medb: magnetic gradiometry at Rathcroghan, Co. Roscommon. *Archaeology Ireland* 47, 8–11.

Fowler, E. 1960 The origins and development of the penannular brooch in Europe. *Proceedings of the Prehistoric Society* 26, 149–77.

Fowler, E. 1963 Celtic metalwork of the fifth and sixth centuries AD. A reappraisal. *Archaeological Journal* 120, 98–160.

Frere, S.S., Roxan, M. and Tomlin, R.S.O. (eds) 1990 *The Roman inscriptions of Britain, Volume II. Instrumentum domesticum (personal belongings and the like), Fascicule 1: The military diplomata; metal ingots; tesserae; dies; labels; and lead sealings (RIB 2401–2411).* Stroud. Alan Sutton.

Gale, R. 2003 Wood-based industrial fuels and their environmental impact in lowland Britain. In P. Murphy and P. E. J. Wiltshire (eds), *The environmental archaeology of industry*, 30–47. Oxford. Oxbow.

Gale, R. and Cutler, D. 2000 *Plants in archaeology: identification manual of artefacts of plant origin from Europe and the Mediterranean.* London. Westbury Publishing and the Royal Botanic Gardens, Kew.

Grogan, E. 1983–4 Excavation of an Iron Age burial mound at Furness. *Journal of the Kildare Archaeological Society* 16, 298–316.

Grogan, E. 2005a *The North Munster Project, Vol. 1. The later prehistoric landscape of south-east Clare.* Discovery Programme Monograph 6. Bray. Wordwell.

Grogan, E. 2005b *The North Munster Project, Vol. 2. The later prehistoric landscape of North Munster.* Discovery Programme Monograph 6. Bray. Wordwell.

Grogan, E. and Eogan, G. 1987 Lough Gur excavations by Seán P. Ó Ríordáin: further Neolithic and Beaker habitations on Knockadoon. *Proceedings of the Royal Irish Academy* 87C, 299–506.

Grogan, E., Condit, T., O'Carroll, F., O'Sullivan, A. and Daly, A. 1996 Tracing the late prehistoric landscape in North Munster. *Discovery Programme Reports* 4, 26–46.

Grogan, E., O'Connell, A., Kinsella, A. and O'Connor, E. 2007 The archaeological complex at Lismullin. Unpublished report for Archaeological Consultancy Services Ltd.

Grogan, E., O'Donnell, L. and Johnston, P. 2007 *The Bronze Age landscapes of the Pipeline to the West: an integrated archaeological and environmental evaluation.* Bray. Wordwell.

Guido, M. 1978 *The glass beads of the prehistoric and Roman periods in Britain and Ireland.* Reports of the Research Committee of the Society of Antiquaries of London 35. London.

Guinan, B. 1992 Ploughzone archaeology in north Dublin. The evidence from a lithic collection and field walking study. Unpublished MA thesis, University College Dublin.

Harden, D.B. 1947 The glass. In C. F. Hawkes and M. R. Hull (eds), *Camulodunum*, 287–305. Society of Antiquaries Research Report XIV. Oxford.

Hartley, K.F. and Webster, P.V. 1973 The Romano-British pottery kilns near Wilderspool. *Archaeological Journal* **130**, 77–103.

Hartnett, P.J. and Eogan, G. 1964 Feltrim Hill, Co. Dublin: a Neolithic and Early Christian site. *Journal of the Royal Society of Antiquaries of Ireland* **94**, 1–37.

Hartwell, B. 1998 The Ballynahatty Complex. In A. Gibson and D. Simpson (eds), *Prehistoric ritual and religion*, 32–44. Stroud. Sutton Publishing.

Hather, J.G. 2000 *The identification of the northern European woods. A guide for archaeologists and conservators.* London. Archetype Publications.

Haverfield, F. 1913 Ancient Rome and Ireland. *English Historical Review* **28**, 1–12.

Healy, J. 1900 Tara. *Journal of the Royal Society of Antiquaries of Ireland* **30**, 176.

Hencken, H. O'Neill 1938 *Cahercommaun, a stone fort in County Clare.* Royal Society of Antiquaries of Ireland, special volume.

Hencken, H. O'Neill 1950 Lagore crannog: an Irish royal residence of the seventh to tenth centuries AD. *Proceedings of the Royal Irish Academy* **53**C, 1–248.

Henig, M. 1978 *A corpus of Roman engraved gemstones from British sites.* British Archaeological Reports, British Series 8. Oxford.

Herity, M. 1987 A survey of the royal site of Cruachain in Connacht III. Ringforts and ecclesiastical sites. *Journal of the Royal Society of Antiquaries of Ireland* **117**, 125–41.

Isings, C. 1957 Roman glass from dated finds. *Archaeologica Traiectina* **2**, 1–185.

Jacobi, G. 1974 *Werkzeug und Gerät aus dem Oppidum von Manching.* Wiesbaden. Steiner.

Jessup, R.F. 1932 Bigberry Camp, Harbledown, Kent. *Archaeological Journal* **89**, 87–115.

Jessup, R.F. 1938 Objects from Bigberry Camp, Harbledown, Kent. *Antiquaries Journal* **18**, 174–6.

Kilbride-Jones, H. 1950 The excavation of a composite Early Iron Age monument with 'henge' features at Lugg, Co. Dublin. *Proceedings of the Royal Irish Academy* **53**C, 311–32.

Lacy, B. *et al.* 1983 *Archaeological Inventory of County Donegal.* Lifford. Donegal County Council.

Lawson, A.J. 1976 Shale and jet objects from Silchester. *Archaeologia* **105**, 241–76.

Lloyd-Morgan, G. 1981 *Description of the collections in the Rijksmuseum G.M.Kam at Nijmegen. IX. The mirrors.* Nijmegen.

Longley, D., Johnstone, N. and Evans, J. 1998 Excavations on two farms of the Romano-British period at Bryn Eryr and Bush Farm, Gwynedd. *Britannia* **29**, 185–246.

Lynn, C. 1986 Navan Fort: a draft summary of D. M. Waterman's excavations. *Emania* **1**, 11–19.

Lynn, C. 1991 Knockaulin (Dún Ailinne) and Navan: some architectural comparisons. *Emania* **8**, 51–6.

Macalister, R.A.S. 1917–19 Temair Beag: a study of the remains and traditions of Tara. *Proceedings of the Royal Irish Academy* **24**C, 231–399.

Macalister, R.A.S. 1929 On some antiquities discovered upon Lambay. *Proceedings of the Royal Irish Academy* **38**C, 240–6.

Macalister, R.A.S. 1931 *Tara: a pagan sanctuary of ancient Ireland.* London.

Macalister, R.A.S. and Praeger, R.L. 1928–9 Report on the excavation of Uisneach. *Proceedings of the Royal Irish Academy* **33**C, 69–247.

McCabe, A.M. 1973 The glacial stratigraphy of eastern counties Meath and Louth. *Proceedings of the Royal Irish Academy* **73**B, 355–82.

McCracken, E. 1971 *The Irish woods since Tudor times: distribution and exploitation.* Newton Abbot. David and Charles.

Mahr, A. 1932 *Christian art in ancient Ireland, Vol. 1.* Dublin. Stationery Office.

Mallory, J. 1995 Haughey's Fort and the Navan Complex in the Late Bronze Age. In J. Waddell and E. Shee Twohig (eds), *Ireland in the Bronze Age*, 73–89. Dublin. Stationery Office.

Manning, C. 1986 Archaeological excavation of a succession of enclosures at Millockstown, Co. Louth. *Proceedings of the Royal Irish Academy* 86C, 135–81.

Manning, W.H. 1985 *Catalogue of the Romano-British iron tools, fittings and weapons in the British Museum.* London. British Museum.

Marguerie, D. and Hunot, J. 2007 Charcoal analysis and dendrology: data from archaeological sites in north–western France. *Journal of Archaeological Science* 34 (9), 1417–33.

Meduna, J. 1961 *Staré Hradisko.* Katalog der Funde im Museum der Stadt. Boskovice. Brno. Fontes Archaeologicae Moravicae.

Mitchell, G.F. 1965 Littleton Bog, Tipperary; an Irish agricultural record. *Journal of the Royal Society of Antiquaries of Ireland* 95, 121–32.

Mitchell, [G.]F. and Ryan, M. 1997 *Reading the Irish landscape.* Dublin. Town House.

Moloney, A., Jennings, D., Keane, M. and McDermott, C. 1993 *Excavations at Clonfinlough, Co. Offaly.* Irish Archaeological Wetland Unit Transactions 2. Dublin. Crannóg Publications.

Moore, M. 1987 *Archaeological Inventory of County Meath.* Dublin. Stationery Office.

Neal, D.S. 1974 *The excavation of the Roman villa in Gadebridge Park, Hemel Hempstead, 1963–8.* Reports of the Research Committee of the Society of Antiquaries of London 31. London. Thames and Hudson.

Nelson, E.C. 1993 *Trees of Ireland.* Dublin. The Lilliput Press.

Neville, R.C. 1856 Description of a remarkable deposit of Roman antiquities of iron, discovered at Great Chesterford, Essex, in 1854. *Archaeological Journal* 13, 1–13.

Newman, C. 1993a Sleeping in Elysium. *Archaeology Ireland* 25, 20–3.

Newman, C. 1993b The show's not over until the Fat Lady sings. *Archaeology Ireland* 26, 8–9.

Newman, C. 1997 *Tara: an archaeological survey.* Discovery Programme Monographs 2. Dublin. Royal Irish Academy.

Newman, C., O'Connell, M. and Dillon, M. 2007 Interpretation of charcoal and pollen data relating to a late Iron Age ritual site in eastern Ireland: a holistic approach. *Vegetation History and Archaeobotany* 16, 349–65.

O'Brien, E. 1990 Iron Age burial practices in Leinster: continuity and change. *Emania* 7, 37–42.

O'Brien, E. 1992 Pagan and Christian burial in Ireland during the first millennium AD: continuity and change. In N. Edwards and A. Lane (eds), *The early church in Wales and the west*, 130–7. Oxbow Monograph 16. Oxford.

O'Carroll, E. 2004 Species identifications of charcoal from Kilgobbin townland, Co. Dublin (03E0306). Unpublished report for Margaret Gowen and Co. Ltd.

O'Connell, A. 2007 Iron Age enclosure at Lismullin, Co. Meath. *Archaeology Ireland* 82, 10–13.

Ó Donnabháin, B. 2002 Appendix 4. Human remains from Tara, Co. Meath. In H. Roche, 'Excavations at Ráith na Ríg, Tara, Co. Meath, 1997'. *Discovery Programme Reports* 6, 123–5.

Ogden, J. 1982 *Jewellery of the ancient world.* London. Trefoil.

O'Kelly, M.J. 1982 *Newgrange: archaeology, art and legend.* London. Thames and Hudson.

Ó Ríordáin, S.P. 1940 Excavations at Cush, Co. Limerick. *Proceedings of the Royal Irish Academy* 45C, 83–181.

Ó Ríordáin, S.P. 1947 Roman material in Ireland. *Proceedings of the Royal Irish Academy* 51C, 35–82.

Ó Ríordáin, S.P. 1951 Lough Gur excavations: the Great Stone Circle (B) in Grange townland. *Proceedings of the Royal Irish Academy* 54C, 37–74.

Ó Ríordáin, S.P. 1954a *Tara, the monuments on the hill.* Dundalk. Dundalgan Press.

Ó Ríordáin, S.P. 1954b Lough Gur excavations: Neolithic and Bronze Age houses on Knockadoon. *Proceedings of the Royal Irish Academy* 56C, 297–459.

Ó Ríordáin, S.P. and Ó h-Iceadha, G. 1955 Lough Gur excavations: the megalithic tomb. *Journal of the Royal Society of Antiquaries of Ireland* 85, 34–50.

Orme, B.J. and Coles, J.M. 1985 Prehistoric woodworking from the Somerset Levels: 2. Species selection and prehistoric woodlands. *Somerset Levels Papers* **11**, 7–24.

O'Sullivan, M. 2005 Duma na nGiall. *The Mound of the Hostages, Tara*. Bray. Wordwell.

Oswald, F. and Pryce, T.D. 1920 *An introduction to the study of* terra sigillata. London. Longmans.

Peterson, J.D. 1990 From foraging to food production in south-east Ireland: some lithic evidence. *Proceedings of the Prehistoric Society* **56**, 89–99.

Piggott, S. 1955 Three metal-work hoards of the Roman period from southern Scotland. *Proceedings of the Society of Antiquaries of Scotland* **87**, 1–52.

Pitt-Rivers, A.H.L. 1887 *Excavations in Cranbourne Chase*. London. Privately published.

Price, J. 1976 Glass. In D. Strong and D. Brown (eds), *Roman crafts*, 111–27. London. Duckworth.

Rademacher, F. 1942 Fränkische Gläser aus dem Rheinland. *Bonner Jahrbücher* **147**, 285–344.

Raftery, B. 1969a Freestone Hill, Co. Kilkenny: an Iron Age hillfort and Bronze Age cairn. *Proceedings of the Royal Irish Academy* **68C**, 1–108.

Raftery, B. 1969b A decorated strap-end from Rathgall, County Wicklow. *Journal of the Royal Society of Antiquaries of Ireland* **100**, 200–11.

Raftery, B. 1976 Rathgall and Irish hillfort problems. In D. W. Harding (ed.), *Hillforts: later prehistoric earthworks in Britain and Ireland,* 339–57. London. Academic Press.

Raftery, B. 1981 Iron Age burials in Ireland. In D. Ó Corráin (ed.), *Irish antiquity: essays and studies presented to Professor M. J. O'Kelly,* 173–204. Cork. Tower Books.

Raftery, B. 1983 *A catalogue of Irish Iron Age antiquities*. Veröffentlichung des Vorgeschichtlichen Seminars Marburg, Sonderband 1. Marburg.

Raftery, B. 1984 *La Tène in Ireland*. Veröffentlichung des Vorgeschichtlichen Seminars Marburg, Sonderband 2. Marburg.

Raftery, B. 1994 *Pagan Celtic Ireland: the enigma of the Irish Iron Age*. London. Thames and Hudson.

Raftery, J. 1938–9 The tumulus cemetery at Carrowjames, Co. Mayo, Part I. *Journal of the Galway Archaeological and Historical Society* **18**, 157–67.

Raftery, J. 1940–1 The tumulus cemetery of Carrowjames, Co. Mayo; Part II, Carrowjames II.

Journal of the Galway Archaeological and Historical Society **19**, 16–85.

Raftery, J. 1944 The Turoe Stone and the Rath of Feerwore. *Journal of the Royal Society of Antiquaries of Ireland* **74**, 23–52.

Roche, H. 2002 Excavations at Ráith na Ríg, Tara, Co. Meath, 1997. *Discovery Programme Reports* **6**, 19–82.

Roche, H. and Eogan, G. 2007 A re-assessment of the enclosure at Lugg, County Dublin, Ireland. In C. Gosden, H. Hamerow, P. de Jersey and G. Lock (eds), *Communities and connections: essays in honour of Barry Cunliffe*, 154–68. Oxford University Press.

Rynne, E. 1976 The La Tène and Roman finds from Lambay, County Dublin: a reassessment. *Proceedings of the Royal Irish Academy* **76C**, 231–44.

Salway, P. 1981 *Roman Britain*. The Oxford History of England. Oxford University Press.

Schweingruber, F.H. 1978 *Microscopic wood anatomy*. Birmensdorf. Swiss Federal Institute for Forest, Snow and Landscape Research.

Scott, B.G. 1990 *Early Irish ironworking*. Belfast. Ulster Museum.

Stead, I.M. and Rigby, V. 1986 *Baldock: the excavation of a Roman and pre-Roman settlement, 1968–72*. Britannia Monograph Series No. 7. London. Society for the Promotion of Roman Studies.

Stevenson, R.B.K. 1955 Pins and the chronology of brochs. *Proceedings of the Prehistoric Society* **21**, 282–94.

Stuijts, I. 2005 Wood and charcoal identification. In M. Gowen, J. Ó Néill and M. Philips (eds), *The Lisheen Mine Archaeological Project 1996–8,* 137–86. Bray. Wordwell.

Sweetman, P.D. 1976 An earthen enclosure at Monknewtown, Slane, Co. Meath. *Proceedings of the Royal Irish Academy* **76C**, 25–73.

Sweetman, P.D. 1985 A Late Neolithic/Early Bronze Age pit circle at Newgrange, Co. Meath. *Proceedings of the Royal Irish Academy* **85C**, 195–221.

Tyers, P. 1996 *Roman pottery in Britain*. London. Batsford.

Wailes, B. 1970 Excavations at Dún Ailinne, Co. Kildare, 1968–9: interim report. *Journal of the Royal Society of Antiquaries of Ireland* **100***,* 79–90.

Wailes, B. 1976 Dún Ailinne: an interim report. In D. W. Harding (ed.), *Hillforts—later prehistoric earthworks in Britain and Ireland*, 319–38. London. Academic Press.

Wailes, B. 1990 Dún Ailinne: a summary excavation report. *Emania* **7**, 10–21.

Wainwright, G.J. 1979 *Gussage All Saints, an Iron Age settlement in Dorset*. Department of the Environment Archaeological Reports 10. London. HMSO.

Wainwright, G. 1989 *The henge monuments: ceremony and society in prehistoric Britain*. London. Thames and Hudson.

Ward-Perkins, J. and Claridge, A. 1976 *Pompeii AD 79*. London. Royal Academy.

Waterman, D.M. 1997 *Excavations at Navan Fort 1961–71* (ed. C. J. Lynn). Belfast. HMSO.

Wheeler, E.A., Bass, P. and Gasson, P.E. 1989 IAWA list of microscopic features for hardwood identification. *IAWA Bulletin* **10** (3), 219–332. Leiden. Rijksherbarium.

Wheeler, R.E.M. and Wheeler, T.V. 1932 *Report on the excavation of the prehistoric, Roman and post-Roman site in Lydney Park, Gloucestershire*. Oxford University Press.

Wheeler, R.E.M. and Wheeler, T.V. 1936 *Verulamium: a Belgic and two Roman cities*. Report of the Research Committee of the Society of Antiquaries of London 11. Oxford.

Willmot, G.F. 1938 Three burial sites at Carbury, Co. Kildare. *Journal of the Royal Society of Antiquaries of Ireland* **68**, 130–42.

Woodman, P.C. 1992 Excavations at Mad Man's Window, Glenarm, Co. Antrim: problems of flint exploitation in East Antrim. *Proceedings of the Prehistoric Society* **58**, 77–105.

Young, C.J. 1977 *Oxfordshire Roman pottery*. British Archaeological Reports, British Series 43. Oxford.

Ancient sources

Pliny the Elder, *Natural History* (ed. John F. Healy) (New York, 1991).

Tacitus, *The Agricola and The Germania* (ed. Betty Radice) (Harmondsworth, 1948).

APPENDICES

THE SMALL FINDS

Lindsay Allason-Jones

The small finds from the Rath of the Synods form an interesting group with some significance for the debate about Roman activities in Ireland. The objects that can be positively identified are mostly of a domestic nature. None of the items can be categorised as booty or status gifts as none would have been of great monetary value at the time and none are of particularly fine workmanship. They are merely items that people would have used about their homes. The lead seal, although of a type that was used by Roman military or judicial authorities, could equally have been used by an individual to seal a bale, crate or document. The chape, bindings and knife fragments are also likely to have been used by civilians. Nothing was found that was indisputably military in origin. The picture is therefore of a small group of people living at Tara who were either from one of the peripheral Roman provinces, possibly Britain, or who were in contact with such an area to the extent of being familiar with its basic domestic equipment.

The ironwork forms the largest group of the finds but is mostly in poor condition; little is identifiable or datable. The nails indicate that they deteriorated *in situ* and were not from a dismantled building. The other datable finds range from the first century BC to the late fourth century AD.

Comparing the assemblage with the Roman material found in the rest of Ireland catalogued by Bateson (1973; 1976), there are obvious and significant gaps. There are, for example, no bow brooches, although the brooch spring is likely to have come from a bow brooch. This may suggest that the type of Roman costume that required pinning with brooches was not commonly worn at Tara. Nor are there any of the metal vessels or toilet implements that have been found in some numbers in the rest of Ireland. The lack of gold artefacts, silver ingots and religious material is also of some

importance. These gaps support the conclusion that the finds from the Rath of the Synods represent a settled, limited-income domestic group rather than a high-status group with important political, military, religious or mercantile connections.

Copper-alloy objects

E615:21a. Ditch 1, fill (Fig. 4.15). Penannular ring of circular section with overlapping terminals, one of which is tapered. Int. D 11mm, T 2mm.

E615:21b. Ditch 1 fill (Fig. 4.15). Incomplete circular-sectioned ring. Int. D 12mm, T of shank 2mm.

E615:21c. Ditch 1 fill (Fig. 4.15). Several fragments of a thin, circular-sectioned ring. Int. D 15mm, T 2mm.

E615:66. Bank 1 (Fig. 4.15). Two fragments of a circular-sectioned tapering pin or needle shank. L 66mm, max. T 3.5mm.

E615:125. Phase 4 habitation (Fig. 4.10). Incomplete penannular brooch of D-shaped section with a flat filed back. The convex face has a series of closely spaced transverse grooves up to the neck of the elongated zoomorphic terminal. The head is stylised with incised nostrils and is little wider than the shank of the brooch. The pin is missing.

The size and terminal motif of this brooch put it into Fowler's type E or E1, two other examples of which have been found in Ireland at Cahercommaun, Co. Clare, and Ballinderry 2, Co. Westmeath (Fowler 1960; 1963, 137). Examples that have been found in well-dated contexts indicate a date range from the late third to the late fourth century AD; although the majority were lost in the mid- to late fourth century, many are worn or broken and seem to have enjoyed a long period of use. Int. D 28mm, W 2mm, T 1.5mm.

E615:126a. Phase 4 habitation. Pin of circular section tapering to a point. The head is broken off but the scar suggests that the head projected forward from the neck in the manner of a ring-headed pin. Cast pins of this type occur from the second century BC and were particularly popular in Scotland up to the fourth century AD. Undated examples come from Castletown, Co. Meath, and elsewhere in Ireland (Mahr 1932, pl. 1, nos 3, 6, 7; see also pl. 19, 1–3).

E615:134. Phase 4 habitation (Fig. 4.10). Penannular ring of circular section with one blunt and one rounded terminal. This cannot have been worn as a finger-ring or ear-ring: the internal diameter is too small and the scar down the inner face, made when the wire was drawn, is still rough and unpolished. Int. D 11mm x 8mm, W 1.5mm, T 1.5mm.

E615:138. Phase 4 habitation (Fig. 4.10). Fragment of U-sectioned binding similar to E615:161. L 35mm, W 4mm.

While pieces of U-sectioned binding of the type listed above were used in military contexts for edging shields and scabbards, they were also used by civilians on scabbards for hunting knives and daggers. The width of the chape (E615:161) is more suggestive of a narrow-bladed hunting knife than an army *pugio*.

E615:149. Phase 2, trench C (F4) (Fig. 2.11). Penannular ear-ring of oval section with one surviving rounded terminal. An indented area of wear near the broken end suggests that the ear-ring was decorated with a pendant bead. This type (type 1) is common to many cultures and impossible to date (Allason-Jones 1989, 2–3). Int. D 11mm, W 2mm, T 2mm.

E615:161. Phase 2, trench F (F137) (Fig. 2.11). Dagger chape of U-section that splays at the pierced rounded terminals. L 61mm, W across arms 30mm, W of channel 4–5mm.

E615:172. Uncontexted, British-Israelite disturbance (Fig. 4.16). Two fragments of a strip ring with overlapping terminals. The outer face is decorated with two longitudinal grooves. The ends are tapered. Int. D 16mm x 10mm (distorted), W 1.25mm, T 5mm.

E615:177. Phase 3, burial E (F97) (Fig. 2.11). Undecorated oval knife guard with an oval hole to take the tang of the handle. L 20mm, W 14mm, T 0.5mm.

E615:187. Ditch 1, fill (Fig. 4.15). Brooch spring of oval-sectioned wire, wound eight times. L 9mm, int. D 2mm.

E615:193. Phase 4 habitation (Fig. 4.10; Pl. 1).

Penannular ring of circular section with blunt ends. The hoop is entirely covered with encircling transverse lines. Int. D 12mm, W 1.5mm, T 1.5mm.

E615:195. Phase 4, ditch 1 (Fig. 4.15). Curved fragment of circular section with a band of transverse grooving on the outer face of the curve only. Part of a bracelet that has had bands of decoration interspersed with plain areas (see Wheeler and Wheeler 1932, fig. 17.S). L 15mm, T 3mm.

E615:211. Bank 2. Slightly curved sheet with parallel edges. There are roughly tooled oblique grooves across the face. L 39mm, W 18mm, T 0.25mm.

★*E615:212*. Phase 4 habitation. Fragment of a copper-alloy sheet with two surviving parallel straight edges. One face is pitted, the other polished smooth, which may suggest that this was part of a mirror. Rectangular metal mirrors were popular from the first century AD, sometimes with decorated edges but often in plain wooden frames (see Lloyd-Morgan 1981). W 34mm, surviving L 32mm, T 1mm.

E615:213. Phase 4 habitation (Fig. 4.13). D-sectioned strip with traces of lead/tin alloy on the back. L 44mm, W 3mm, T 2.5mm.

E615:217. Phase 4 habitation (Fig. 4.10). Small fragment of U-sectioned binding similar to E615:161. L 30mm, W 5mm.

E615:220. Phase 4 habitation (Fig. 4.10). Undulating brooch of oval section. The point is tapered and decorated on its upper face with a series of transverse lines; the other end has broken as it splays and curls into a hinge. From a penannular brooch. L 32mm, W 1.25mm, T 1mm.

★*E615:225*. Rath na Ríogh. Two strips with parallel sides, flat backs and shallow convex faces that show traces of white metalling. One piece is pierced by a circular rivet, the end of which has been polished flush with the curve of the face before the application of the white metalling. The end is split along a casting flaw. L 29mm, 17mm, W 6mm, T 1mm, D of rivet 2mm.

E615:251. Secondary ditch (Fig. 4.15). Pair of dividers. The arms have flat backs and faceted faces and are hinged by a circular rivet at the pointed head. This is an unusual example as the majority of the compasses or dividers found in the Roman period have plain rectangular-sectioned arms that expand to flat circular heads (Adams 1984, pl. 84; see also pl. 78 for depictions on stone). It is closer in appearance to an example from Pompeii (Ward-Perkins and Claridge 1976, no. 281). L 87mm, W of arms 5mm, D of rivet 2mm, T of each arm 2mm.

Lead objects

E615:124. Phase 4 habitation (Fig. 4.10, Pl. 1). Lead sealing with an oval impression showing the raised figure of a bird standing facing right and holding a rolled document(?) in its beak. The bird is not set square within the oval; the feet finish in the bottom left corner, and as a result it looks as if it is toppling forward. The face of the device or intaglio which made the impression was flat. A cord was passed through the lead when still molten in order to secure it for use and this has left a small circular hole through the back.

The identification of the bird is open to speculation. The closest parallels on intaglios are to Indian parrots, for example London (Henig 1978, no. 686) and Colchester (*ibid.*, nos 685 and 687), but note also a raven from Fishbourne, Sussex (*ibid.*, no. 674). Although eagles are the most commonly depicted birds on intaglios, because of their association with Jupiter and the Roman army, they are usually shown standing erect with just the head turned rather than in full profile. It is very tempting to see the bird's somewhat unbalanced stance as confirming its identification as a parrot as there was a popular belief that because parrots had weak legs they tended to topple onto their beaks (Pliny, *Natural History,* X. 58).

Lead seals were used by the Roman military or judicial authorities as well as by individuals for sealing bales, boxes or documents, and many were impressed with a device in order to identify the sender or to provide additional security against interference in transit. The style of this example suggests that the device used belonged to an individual rather than a military unit and may have had a personal significance for that individual (see Frere *et al.* 1990, 87–124, for a general discussion and parallels in Britain). L 28mm, W 19mm, impression 10mm x 13mm.

Iron objects

★*E615:6*. Phase 2, trench D1 (F143). Oval penannular band with a small ring projecting away from one terminal. Scabbard mount? (Cf. Lambay, Co. Dublin: B. Raftery 1984, fig. 47 (bronze).) L 53mm, H 11mm.

★*E615:113*. Phase 1, trench D (F142). Tapered rod of circular section with a rounded end. L 50mm, T 4mm.

E615:126b. Phase 4 habitation (F174) (Fig. 4.10). Circular-sectioned rod. L 13mm, T 2.5mm.

E615:128. Phase 4 habitation (Fig. 4.12). Large nail with a square-sectioned shank bent to an angle. The head is square and domed. L 110mm, head 19mm x 20mm.

★*E615:129*. Phase 4 habitation. Fragment of a circular-sectioned ring. Int. D 14mm, W 3mm, T 5mm.

E615:133. Phase 4 habitation (Fig. 4.11). Tapered circular-sectioned rod with a rounded head. Needle? L 61mm, W 5mm.

E615:135a. Phase 4 habitation (Fig. 4.11). Fragment of a ring of oval section. Int. D 25mm, W 5mm, T 9mm.

★*E615:135b*. Phase 4 habitation. Fine rod of circular section that tapers to both ends. L 49mm, T 3mm.

E615:139a. Phase 4 habitation (Fig. 4.12). Nail with incomplete bar head and a rectangular-sectioned shank. L 41mm, W of head 15mm.

★*E615:139b*. Phase 4 habitation. Fragment of a circular-sectioned rod. L 13mm, T 3mm.

★*E615:144*. Phase 2, trench B (F100). Fragment of a ring of oval section. D *c.* 22mm.

E615:147a. Phase 4 habitation (Fig. 4.12). Incomplete oval-sectioned rod. L 37mm, W 7mm, T 5mm.

E615:148. Phase 4 habitation (F5) (Fig. 4.12). Top portion of nail with flattish pyramid head and square-sectioned stem, similar to E615:128. L 50mm, head 21mm x 20mm.

★*E615:152a*. Phase 4 habitation. Fragment of a circular socket with copper core and part of a straight-sided blade. Insufficient survives to state whether this was a weapon or a tool. L 20mm.

E615:153. Phase 4 habitation (F5) (Fig. 4.12). Rectangular-sectioned stem of nail. L 63mm, W 5mm, T 5.5mm.

★*E615:158*. Phase 4 habitation. Oval-sectioned rod with one pointed end. Pin or needle? L 41mm, T 3mm.

E615:159a. Phase 4 habitation (Fig. 4.12). Nail with square-sectioned stem and bulbous head. L 64mm, T 3mm.

E615:159b. Phase 4 habitation (Fig. 4.12). Circular-sectioned rod with a tapered end. L 41mm, T 4mm.

E615:160. Phase 4 habitation (F8) (Fig. 4.11). Plate with parallel sides. L 32mm, W 19mm.

★*E615:163.* Uncontexted, phase 4 area. Doubly spiked loop with a strip curve and lozenge-sectioned arms (see W. H. Manning 1985, 130–1). W across loop 35mm, H 53mm, max. T 9mm.

E615:164. Phase 4 habitation (Fig. 4.11). Small stud with a circular-sectioned shank and an incomplete trefoil head. L 14mm, W of head 12mm.

★*E615:165b.* Phase 4 habitation. Flat plate with a rounded tip. Knife blade? L 35mm, W 20mm.

E615:166a. Phase 4 habitation (Fig. 4.12). Circular-sectioned rod with a small globular head and a slightly expanded rounded end. L 43mm, D of head 8mm, T of shank 4mm.

★*E615:166b.* Phase 4 habitation. Incomplete nail with a square-sectioned shank and a disc head. L 48mm.

★*E615:166c.* Phase 4 habitation. Nail with a bent square-sectioned shank. Most of head is missing. L 36mm, T 4mm.

★*E615:166d.* Phase 4 habitation. Fragment of a triangular-sectioned blade. L 25mm, depth of blade 13mm.

E615:170a. Phase 4 habitation (Fig. 4.11). Circular-sectioned rod with bulbous ends: pivot bar from a large buckle (see B. Raftery 1983, no. 870: Loughy, Co. Down (bronze)). L 34mm, D of head 8mm, T of shank 5mm.

E615:173. Phase 4 habitation (Fig. 4.12). Large nail with bulging rectangular-sectioned shank that has faceted edges. The head is a solid dome. L 140mm, D of head 32mm, shank 15mm x 12mm.

E615:176. Burial E (F97) (Fig. 2.11). Fragment of a ring of tapering circular section. Int. D 11mm, T 3–4mm.

★*E615:180.* Phase 4 habitation. Several fragments of a strip collar with out-turned edges. W 26mm.

E615:181a. Phase 4 habitation. Small nail with a bent rectangular-sectioned shank and a disc head. L 29mm, D of head 18mm.

★*E615:188a.* Phase 4 habitation. Small nail with a circular-sectioned shank and a globular head. L 14mm, D of head 11mm.

E615:189a. Bank 2 (Fig. 4.15). Tapering square-sectioned shank with a wide fanned head that has a circular-sectioned rivet through it. Part of a hinge? L 49mm, W of head 29mm.

★*E615:194.* Uncontexted phase 4 area. Rectangular-sectioned strip with one blunt end and one narrowed end. L 42mm, W 9mm, T 5mm.

E615:190. Phase 4 habitation. Tapering rectangular-sectioned rod with rounded end. L 71mm, W 7mm, T 5mm.

★*E615:207.* Uncontexted Rath na Ríogh area. Small nail with a short oval-sectioned shank and a disc head. L 23mm, D of head 12mm.

★*E615:223b.* Phase 4. Fragment of a circular-sectioned rod. L 22mm, T 5mm.

E615:226. Rath na Ríogh (Fig. 2.11). Small nail with a square-sectioned shank and a disc head. L 21mm, D of head 12mm.

★*E615:230.* Phase 4 habitation. Incomplete circular-sectioned rod. L 51mm, T 4mm.

★*E615:231.* Rath na Ríogh. Bar of rectangular section with angled tapered ends. Joiner's dog for joining timbers (cf. W. H. Manning 1985, R52–3). L 96mm, W of shank 7mm, T of shank 5mm, L of arms 25mm.

★*E615:232.* Rath na Ríogh. Rod of rectangular section with an oval-sectioned rounded end. L 46mm, W 10mm, T 6.5mm.

E615:235. Phase 4 habitation (F5) (Fig. 4.12). Large nail with a rectangular-sectioned shank and an incomplete disc head. Total L 124mm, T 8mm x 7mm.

★*E615:240a.* Phase 4 habitation. Plate with no original edges surviving. L 67mm.

★*E615:240b.* Phase 4 habitation. Very corroded sheet with no original edges surviving. L 57mm.

★*E615:246.* Rath na Ríogh. Bar of rectangular section with down-turned ends. A third strip seems to protrude from the shank. L 10mm, T 7mm.

★*E615:253.* Rath na Ríogh. Strip with parallel edges ending in a tang. Too corroded to be certain if one edge is sharpened. L 66mm, W of blade 20mm, W of tang 7mm.

★*E615:267.* Uncontexted. Rectangular-sectioned shank that bulges in the centre and terminates in a wedged head. Possibly a modelling tool (cf. W. H. Manning 1985, C12). L 46mm, W of head 10mm.

★*E615:155, 156 and 224.* Unidentifiable fragments of iron.

Glass objects

E615:71. Ditch 1 (Fig. 4.15). Globular bead of dark blue translucent glass. Guido group 7iv. D 6mm, H 4mm, D of hole 3mm.

E615:116. Phase 2, trench C (F4) (Fig. 2.11). Cylinder bead of very bright cobalt blue glass with both ends cut obliquely. D 4mm, H 4mm, D of hole 2mm.

E615:130a. Phase 4 habitation (Fig. 4.13). Small globular bead of dark blue translucent glass. Traces of iron inside the hole suggest that the bead was strung on iron wire. D 7.5mm, H 6mm, D of hole 3mm.

These two beads fall within Guido's group 7iv but are not itemised in her catalogue (Guido 1978, 171). The type was popular from the first century BC and continued to be manufactured for several centuries. A necklace that included such beads was found in a first-century BC–first-century AD context at Loughey, Donaghadee, Co. Down, and others are known from Lagore crannog, Co. Meath (Guido 1978).

E615:130b. Phase 4 habitation (Fig. 4.13). Annular bead of translucent cobalt blue glass (Guido 1978, 160: Guido 6ivb). This is a common type with a long history from the sixth century BC. Guido has suggested that their importation throughout the British Iron Age may have been up the Bristol Channel and north into the Irish Sea. In Ireland many examples appear on sites as late as the seventh–tenth centuries AD, but a single example from Dunshaughlin crannog, Lagore, Co. Meath, may have come from an earlier context and a number have been found on undated sites (*ibid.*, 67, 160). D 5mm, H 2mm, D of hole 2.5mm.

E615:131. Phase 4 habitation (Fig. 4.13). Mid-blue opaque cylinder bead of tapering rectangular section (Guido 1978, 214). Guido has suggested that beads of this form were 'mostly rather late in the Roman period . . . for the most part they date from the 3rd to 4th centuries' (*ibid.*, 96). W 3–3.5mm, H 3.5mm, D of hole 1.5mm.

E615:132. Phase 4 habitation (Fig. 4.13). Small annular bead of opaque turquoise glass See Guido 1978, 163: group 6vii: 'these are not a common form and none of them appears to be pre 1st century AD'. D 4mm, L 3mm, D of hole 1.5mm.

E615:182. Phase 4 habitation (Fig. 4.13). Globular bead of blue glass. D 4mm, H 3.5mm, D of hole 1mm.

Both this and E615:204 are listed in Guido's catalogue (1978, 169) and form part of her group 7iii. The date of this group is confined to the first century BC to the first century AD and examples are rarely found in Britain north of Chester. An outlying example from Covesea, Moray, however, was found with second-century AD imported glass (Benton 1931).

E615:204. Phase 4 habitation (F20) (Fig. 4.13). Globular bead of 'natural' green glass, possibly recycled Roman window or bottle glass. D 9mm, H 8mm, D of hole 2mm.

E615:214. Phase 4 habitation (Fig. 4.13). Fragment of cobalt blue glass that may have come from bead-making waste. L 5.5mm.

E615:216. Phase 4 habitation (Fig. 4.13). Tiny glass sphere of cobalt blue glass with opaque white marvered vertical stripes. A small hole in the base is surrounded by traces of iron corrosion and wear damage. Two identical objects were found at Knowth (K78.GL3) (G. Eogan, pers. comm.) and it is possible that all three were pinheads. There is nothing about the glass that argues against a Roman date or source, but glass beads from metal pins of this period tend to be larger and of plain glass rather than patterned: cf. South Shields (Allason-Jones and Miket 1984, nos 5.94 and 3.505; see also B. Raftery 1983, fig. 140, no. 448, for a small pin with a minute iron rivet that may have held a similar head). D 4mm, hole less than 0.5mm.

E615:270. Uncontexted (Fig. 4.16; Pl. 1). Incomplete disc with a chamfered edge and a rounded base, made from two layers of glass. The lower stratum is transparent glass of very dark red or brown colour; the upper stratum is of opaque pale blue glass with a lighter blue swirl that appears to be the result of inefficient mixing rather than a deliberate attempt at decoration. Inset for a ring or brooch. D 13mm, H 4mm, upper stratum 1.5mm.

Layered glass insets were popular in the Roman provinces, particularly Britain, in the second and third centuries AD as imitations of 'nicolos': this term refers to a method of cutting semiprecious stones in order to take advantage of different coloured strata but is mostly used when referring to blue/white onyx (see Ogden 1982, 109, pl. 18).

Stone objects

E615:26b. Phase 2, trench D1 (F143) (Fig. 2.11). Rounded rim of a narrow-necked sandstone vessel with straight outer wall and sloping inner wall. Incomplete profile. H 37mm, ext. D 120mm, int. D 80mm.

E615:27. Phase 4, uncontexted (Fig. 4.16; Pl. 1). Section of an undecorated oval-sectioned ring. Possibly part of a hair-ring (cf. Silchester: Lawson 1976, no. 59). Int. D 16mm, W 16mm, T 14mm.

E615:65. Uncontexted, bank 1 area (Fig. 4.16). One half of a two-piece mould of micaceous sandstone. The shape is roughly oval and has two opposed tie grooves plus a third groove that shows signs of burning. The channel is narrow and oval in shape. It would appear that this is the upper half of the mould; the channel is not deep enough to make an object worth casting and it is more likely that it was intended merely to take the surplus metal, the main channel being on the lower, missing, stone. W of groove 2mm, depth of groove 1mm, ext. D of groove 62mm x 38mm.

★E615:84. Barrow, phase 3. Disc that has broken from a circular-sectioned rod of fine sandstone. Whetstone? L 25mm, D 57–60mm.

★E615:255. Phase 2, trench A (F101). Roughly circular, flat sandstone pebble with one well-polished face. The rounded edge has been smoothed to shape and the polishing on the face stops 5mm short of this edge. There are traces of iron-staining around this line, suggesting that this was a palette that was held in an iron frame. Rectangular and oval stone palettes were used for mixing ointments and pigments and were often held in metal frames (cf. Allason-Jones and Miket 1984, no. 12.68). D 63mm x 67mm, T 13mm.

★E615:258. Phase 2, trench A (F101). Bun-shaped pebble of coarse micaceous sandstone. The flat face is well worn. Gaming piece? D 46mm, T 26mm.

★E615:259. Phase 2, trench D (F142). Water-worn ovoid pebble. Gaming piece? D 26mm x 21mm, T 9mm.

APPENDIX B

THE RATH OF THE SYNODS BARREL PADLOCK

Caroline Velzian Donaghy

The barrel padlock and bolt (E615:167) from the Rath of the Synods are now in poor condition. A drawing was, however, made by Paddy Healy at the time of excavation (Fig. 4.11). Both objects are of type 1a (Donaghy 1991), a type found on Romano-British sites from the late second century AD (Wheeler and Wheeler 1936, 219) to the late Roman period (W. H. Manning 1985, 96, pl. 43, O.67).

The technology of all barrel padlocks is simple. The security comes from the expansion of barbs on a spine within the padlock case, rendering it incapable of release until the barbs are compressed.

This padlock has an oval case with an asymmetrical U-shaped arm-hasp attached by a short arm to the top of the case opposite the bolt hole and extending past the case. The bolt has a round aperture to engage the hasp at one end and a barb-spring at the other to secure it inside the case. Case: L 95mm, D 30–40mm. Hasp: L 235mm, D 6mm, round-sectioned. Bolt: L 160mm, W 4mm, depth 10mm, rectangular-sectioned. Although the Tara padlock case is oval, other examples of cases of similar size may be square, like the late Roman examples from the hoards at Lakenheath (*ibid.*) and Great Chesterford (Neville 1856, 7–8, pl. 2, 24 and 26), and an example with a round case was recovered from Verulanium (Wheeler and Wheeler 1936, 220, pl. lxv, 15).

The single barb-spring bolt has a loop at the terminal to engage the arm-hasp and a stop-ridge for the bolt hole. A similar bolt, undated, which also tapers from the terminal to the stop-ridge, comes from Wylye in Wiltshire (W. H. Manning 1985, 96, pl. 43, O.68) and an example dated to the second or early third century was found at Shakenoak Farm (Brodribb *et al.* 1971, 120, fig. 51.93). Manning notes that this type of bolt is usually for a smaller padlock, and indeed there is evidence that the Tara bolt is not the original bolt for the padlock. The padlock has a loop corroded on to the arm-hasp which

does not belong to the bolt. The original bolt would have had a double loop and, in addition to the loop on the arm-hasp, a second loop was found with the padlock fragments. Examples of double-loop bolts came from the Great Chesterford hoard (Neville 1856, 7–8, pl. 2, 24 and 26). The loop fragment from Tara would have been the terminal loop, and the loop corroded on to the arm-hasp would have been the inner loop. A double-looped bolt dated to the late third or early fourth century was recovered from Shakenoak Farm (Brodribb *et al.* 1968, 102, fig. 34.1). The bolt and padlock from Tara, however, could have been used together but the locking area for the hasp would have been reduced. It is still a large area, however, and could have held shackles (although no restraining chains were recovered from the excavation) or a door, window or large box hasp. Notwithstanding the dichotomy between the padlock and the bolt, both of these objects are from the same type, 1a, and both have good parallels in habitation, military and hoard sites in Romano-Britain.

The concept of the barbed bolt has its origins in Iron Age Europe, and sprung bolts were found on the Continent at Staré Hradisko (Meduna 1961, 39:6) and Manching (Jacobi 1974, 163:41). In England sprung bolts were found at the late Iron Age/Roman sites of Gussage All Saints (Wainwright 1979, 107–8, fig. 82:1131) and Woodcuts (Pitt-Rivers 1887, 73, pl.:xxiv). The sprung bolt continued into the late Roman period in England, however, as at Shakenoak (Brodribb *et al.* 1968, 104, fig. 35:37, 38) and Baldock (Stead and Rigby 1986, 68–71, fig. 31:27), where it was found with a box in a burial.

The earliest actual barrel (or barb-spring) padlocks appear to have been used to restrain humans, and an example was found with a slave-chain in a hoard at Chalon-sur-Saône in France, along with iron objects including a La Tène II sword and an axe described as

'Gallic' (Déchelette 1927, 184–7, figs 30–31 and pl. xxxviii). Another apparently early example comes from gravel pits at Bigberry Camp in Kent, England, where a fragment of a barrel padlock was attached to a neck collar (Jessup 1938, 174, pl. xlix). The gravel pits at Bigberry contained Iron Age objects, including pottery probably of the first century BC (Jessup 1932, 87–115, figs 4–5 and pl. III). The Romans were not averse to shackling humans either, as demonstrated by the shackles found in the Great Chesterford hoard in Essex, England (Neville 1856, 9, pl. 2:21, 22). Barrel padlocks, in diverse forms, have continued in use until the present time and can still be seen in the bazaars of the Middle and Far East today.

One Romano-British key of the type that would have unlocked the Tara padlock is known from Ireland. This comes from Uisneach, Co. Westmeath (Macalister and Praeger 1928–9, 121, pl. xix:8), significantly another important site which, like Tara, has interesting mythical and early Irish importance. The key was found during an excavation in the 1920s of an early medieval annexed ringfort, which revealed, again like Tara, a penannular ditch beneath the earthwork, of Iron Age significance. Recent survey of this site shows that the larger element of the ringfort is in fact a hilltop enclosure of Iron Age date, *c.* 100 BC–AD 200 (Donaghy and Grogan 1997).

Padlocks basically represent ownership, control and exclusion, of property and sometimes lives, and the Tara padlock must have been a powerful symbol of prestige and control in Ireland at the time of its currency.

APPENDIX C

THE GLASS VESSELS FROM THE RATH OF THE SYNODS

Edward Bourke

Introduction

During the first nine centuries AD there is no evidence to suggest that glass vessels were manufactured in Ireland. The vessels present are all of soda glass and represent the products of the Roman glass industry. Iron present in all sands causes soda glass to be blue-green in colour; this colour can be removed by using decolourants such as manganese or antimony (Price 1976, 116). Other colours can be produced by the addition of various oxides and by varying the time spent in the kiln and oxidising conditions. The ability to choose colour and to produce vessels with a high-quality metal was fully utilised by the Romans, and E615:151, E615:200 and E615:198 are of decolorised transparent metal.

Glass of the second–fourth centuries

Mould-blown bowl (E615:140)

The example from the Rath of the Synods (Fig. 4.14) is of an unusual form, with a thickened everted rim and a horizontal rib running below the rim. It has parallels from Conimbriga, an urban site in Portugal, and Dura Europus, Syria (Alarcão *et al.* 1976, 186, fig. XL, no. 166). These examples date from the second half of the second century to the first half of the third century AD. The Tara sherd is of a clear, transparent, decolorised metal typical of the highest-quality Roman table glass. These vessels are probably drinking glasses.

The sherd was retrieved from a pit containing animal bone, teeth, a deer horn and lumps of charcoal; there were no further associated artefacts. On typological grounds the sherd suggests settlement at the Rath of the Synods during the second or third century AD.

Unclassified bowls

*E615:151 is clear glass with no diagnostic features and few bubbles (Fig. 4.14). It was found in the upper of the two phase 4 habitation layers in square 42. It is associated with a fragment of an unidentified seal from a wax-covered writing tablet.

*E615:198 is clear, colourless, translucent metal, has no diagnostic features and is probably from a bowl (Fig. 4.14). This sherd was found in the secondary ditch (F228). There were no associated artefacts.

E615:200 was of clear glass and had weathering/strain marks, few bubbles and no diagnostic features (Fig. 4.14). Its context points to a third-century date. It was found in the baulk between squares 55 and 56 in the phase 4 habitation layer and was associated with a penannular brooch with zoomorphic terminals. A close parallel for this brooch was found in a wall at the Roman villa dating from AD 268–70 at Kings Weston (Boone 1967). Another example from Lydney is dated to AD 275–378 by coins. Thus the most likely date for this vessel is in the late third to the early fourth century AD.

Cone beaker (E615:154)

These joining rim and body sherds, with faint horizontal wheel-incised lines on the interior below the rim, are from a cone beaker of Isings form 106a, b2 or d (Fig. 4.14). All these types are found in fourth-century contexts throughout western Europe and all have examples with wheel-engraved decoration (Isings 1957, 126–31).

The simple thickened rim on the vessel from the Rath of the Synods is most closely paralleled in form 106d; all the other forms have knocked-off and ground-down rims. These vessels with solid or thickened bases are the ancestors of the Frankish cone beakers of the fifth and sixth centuries (Rademacher 1942, 296). The clear transparent metal, however, places this vessel in the tradition of Roman high-quality table ware, as does the wheel-engraved decoration, neither of which are found in Frankish cones. Most of these vessels in the west were probably drinking vessels, although some may also have functioned as lamps (Harden 1947).

This vessel, which was retrieved from the upper of two habitation layers in square 52, was found in association with glass beads (E615:130a–b), glass waste (E615:214) and possible *terra sigillata* (E615:165d, Pl. 2) pottery. On typological grounds the vessel is datable to the fourth century and indicates the presence of high-quality imports at Tara at this time.

Discussion

The vessels of the second–fourth centuries from the Rath of the Synods are part of a usage of imported glass drinking vessels on high-status sites that continues beyond this period. The Tara material, which is all decolorised, high-quality glass, points to trading contacts with Roman Britain in the second–fourth centuries. There is ample historical and archaeological evidence for contact and trade between Ireland and the later Roman Empire, and these vessels are indicative of a small part of this trade.

Catalogue

E615:140 (Fig. 4.14)
Rim sherd of a small mould-blown or mould-pressed bowl, of soda glass with one tiny pinprick bubble. Clear, colourless, transparent metal. Thick everted rim, sides almost vertical. One horizontal rib 4mm below rim. Dulled and few strain cracks, no iridescence.

Square 38, from the upper levels of a pit with dark soil mixed with bone, teeth, lumps of charcoal and a deer horn. No associated finds.

Height 17mm; width 43mm; thickness 1.5–4mm; original rim diameter *c.* 90mm.

E615:151 (Fig. 4.14)
Body sherd of bowl, of soda glass with some bubbles. Clear, colourless, translucent metal with some black impurities. Surface slightly scratched and pitted. No diagnostic features.

Sq. 42 in upper habitation layer, consisting of humus, bones, charcoal and black clay. Associated with a portion of a seal (E615:124, Fig. 4.7).

Height 19mm; width 16mm; thickness 1.1mm; original body diameter *c.* 80mm.

E615:154 (Fig. 4.14)
Body and rim sherds (joining) of a cone beaker of soda glass with few tiny bubbles. Clear, colourless, transparent metal. Rim slightly inturned and thickened. Sides taper inwards and downwards. Two faint horizontal wheel-engraved lines on the interior, below rim. Slight dulling, no iridescence. Isings form 106b.

Sq. 52, in upper habitation layer. Associated with glass beads, pottery and flint.

Height 33.5mm; width 40mm; thickness 1.1mm; original rim diameter *c.* 78mm.

E615:198 (Fig. 4.14)
Body sherd of a vessel of soda glass with some bubbles. Clear, colourless, translucent metal. Probably from a bowl. No diagnostic features.

Cutting 21, in dark fill of the secondary ditch (F228) with charcoal and bone. This, and the earlier ditch 1 into which it is cut, are the only ditches with substantial habitation debris; the outer ditches silted up and are only lightly flecked with charcoal. No associated finds.

Height 19mm; width 16mm; thickness 0.8mm.

E615:200 (Fig. 4.14)
Body sherd of bowl or squat jar of soda glass with few bubbles. Clear, colourless, translucent metal. Surface striations caused by either weathering or strain. No diagnostic features.

Baulk between sq. 55 and sq. 56. From the phase 4 habitation layer. From the description this appears to underlie a stony layer containing a penannular brooch with zoomorphic terminals (E615:125) dating probably from the third century.

Height 15mm; width 22mm; thickness 0.5mm; original body diameter *c.* 80mm.

THE LITHIC ASSEMBLAGE

Fiona Dillon

Introduction

There are 42 lithics in the assemblage: 28 pieces of flint, twelve of chert and two of quartz. These were recovered from cuttings 1, 5, 6, 7, 9, 15 and 21. In approaching the analysis of this assemblage two aspects need consideration. First, the lithics were disturbed either in antiquity or in modern times, resulting in a virtually uncontexted assemblage. Second, it is likely that there was a selective collection of the lithics, as was usual during the period when the site was excavated (see Grogan and Eogan 1987). In the analysis a simple model was adopted from field-walking collections (Peterson 1990) and was used to establish the nature of the assemblage.

The raw material

Flint, chert and quartz were present. Flint is the predominant raw material, and includes Antrim and glacially deposited flint. The Antrim flint is caramel (E615:118) and grey (E615:25) in colour with a slightly abraded cortex, indicating that it was derived from nodules in Antrim coastal deposits. Different local sources of pebble flint were exploited, as there are small pebbles with a smooth brown cortex and grey flint with a thick white cortex. Seven patinated and two burnt flints were identified. Nineteen flints bear patination, which in all cases had formed after knapping. Both chert and quartz were exploited, forming 15% and 3% of the assemblage respectively.

Pebble flint, chert and quartz are present in small quantities in the glacial drift to the north of the Hill of Tara (McCabe 1973, 357–9). More extensive deposits of pebble flint are present on the Dublin, Meath and Louth coasts (Cross 1991; Guinan 1992). As a result the raw material was available locally.

Technology

The analysis of the assemblage shows that production of tools took place within the site. Although two cores are present, E615:18i was discarded after testing and E615:63, a chert core, is badly damaged and examination of the flake scars shows that the flakes were small and inefficient. The presence of core rejuvenation flakes shows that some other flint-knapping took place. E615:118 is of Antrim flint, indicating that it was knapped on site rather than imported as a blank (Woodman 1992, 87–90). The low incidence of cortical flakes confirms the lack of knapping evidence. An analysis of the flake platforms shows the predominance of prepared platforms especially for retouched pieces. This shows a favouring of percussive rather than bipolar reduction, indicating that reasonably sized pebbles were available for knapping.

Comment

Pebble flint is the predominant raw material. This was supplemented by imported Antrim flint and to a lesser extent by locally available chert and quartz. There are no diagnostic pieces in the assemblage. Of the seven modified tools, three can be paralleled: the tanged flakes from a Beaker context at Monknewtown, Co. Meath (Sweetman 1976, fig. 18: 539, 526a), and the end and concave scrapers found in early Neolithic to Beaker contexts (Hartnett and Eogan 1964, fig. 5: 73, 90, 100; Sweetman 1976, fig. 18: 522–4).

Catalogue

Cores (complete: E615:18i, 63 (chert))
There are two cores. E615:18i is an irregularly shaped water-rolled pebble with a thick brown patina. It is a uniplane core with a conical platform. E615:63 is a core of poor-quality chert, dual-platformed and knapped on two faces, with damaged edges.

Core rejuvenation flakes (complete: E615:25, 51, 59ii)
E615:25 and 51 are tertiary flakes that rejuvenate the flaking surface of the core. E615:25 is Antrim flint and E615:59ii is pebble flint. E615:51 is a small pebble split by bipolar reduction.

Unutilised flakes (complete: E615:18iii, 100b, 184i; incomplete: E615:7, 12, 14 (burnt), 24, 28, 87)
There are ten unutilised flakes. Cortical analysis shows that there are six tertiary flakes, three secondary flakes and one primary flake. All are made of pebble flint.

Utilised flakes (complete: E615:18ii, 18a, 25a, 250; incomplete: E615:186, 18vi (Fig. 4.15) (chert))
There are six flakes with edge damage.

Concave scraper (incomplete: E615:59i)
This has a shallow concavity on the lateral edge of a proximal fragment of a blade. The retouch is abrupt, forming a steep working edge with severe use wear. Parallels for this type are Eogan's (1963, fig. 3: 21–8, 44–5) group C hollow scrapers from the pre-tomb habitation level at Townleyhall 2, Co. Louth.

End scraper (complete: E615:118)
This is an end scraper with invasive retouch forming a steep working edge at the distal end of a secondary flake of pebble flint. It is partly patinated, which formed post-deposition, and is caramel in colour with an abraded gritty cortex derived from nodules of Antrim flint. Parallels for this piece may be found from the Neolithic to the Beaker period (Hartnett and Eogan 1964, fig. 5: 5, 73, 90; Sweetman 1976, fig. 18: 522–4).

Tanged flake (complete: E615:120)
This has a semicircular notch at the distal end of a tertiary flake. A parallel for this occurs at Monknewtown (Sweetman 1976, fig. 18: 539, 526a), although there is lateral retouch on the Tara example.

Retouched flakes (complete: E615:69; incomplete: E615:184ii, 24c)
E615:69 is a tertiary flake with abrupt retouch on the bulbar face of the lateral edge. E615:184ii and 24c have intermittent abrupt retouch on the lateral and distal edges.

Flake fragments (E615:31 (chert), E615:121 (burnt), E615:37)
There are three flake fragments which do not have intact edges and cannot be assigned to a particular flake type.

Chip (E615:39)
There is one chert chip.

APPENDIX E

THE ROMAN COIN HOARD FROM THE RATH OF THE SYNODS

Eoin Grogan

A hoard of fifteen copper coins of Constantine the Great (306–37) was reputedly found during the British-Israelite diggings at the Rath of the Synods in 1899 and was described in a letter to the *Daily Express* (21 August 1899) by the Reverend John Healy (see also Healy 1900). Although the information is very imprecise, the location of the coins appears to have been at a depth of *c.* 45cm (18in.) beneath the sod over, or close to, a 'trench', either the primary ditched enclosure or the inner ditch of the ringfort. Regrettably, the present location of the coins is unknown, but Carew (2003, 113–17), in an extensive account of the issue, suggests that they were later sent to Bellinter House, the residence of the landlord at Tara, Mr Gustavus Villiers Briscoe (see below).

The circumstances of discovery of the coins have been commented on by several writers, most of whom accepted the discovery as genuine (e.g. Healy 1900; Haverfield 1913; Macalister 1917–19; Ó Ríordáin 1947). The most significant accounts, however, are the dismissal of the hoard as a hoax by Dolley (1968, 62–4) and the acceptance of this claim by Bateson (1973, 59–60). Dolley's view was based on three factors: that the coins were of a common type, that they were found close to the surface and, most significantly, that a statement was made in 1967 asserting that the coins had been deliberately deposited on the site by local landowners out of sympathy for the diggers, who were finding very little. This account was by Wing-Commander Frank Fowler, who had been brought up in Meath and was told it by his mother, who heard it from 'the survivor' of those responsible for 'salting' the site (quoted in full in Dolley 1968, 63–4). Several elements in the statement, such as the suggestion that the British-Israelites' work was headed by 'an American' or that the digging was stopped in 1899 through the intervention of local landowners, are erroneous. The coins are known to have been found in that year (Healy 1900) while the activity continued into 1901. A significant apocryphal element in this story is that two of the three individuals (all unnamed) reputedly died in quick succession soon after the 'salting' incident, while the third 'came to the conclusion that there might be some truth in a legend that he had heard that whoever dug for the ark would surely die, withdrew his permission to dig, and sent the diggers packing' (Fowler, reported in Dolley 1968, 64).

It is also significant that the story is one of a number of 'revised memories' of the events surrounding the work of the British-Israelites, such as the invented story quoted (in good faith) by Hubert Butler (Butler and Foster 1990, 68–70). This indicated that the British-Israelites did not dig at Tara but that some small-scale work was carried out by a misguided young man, Mr Groome (this is Charles Groom), from London. This account, related to Butler by his cousin Mrs Synolda French (née Butler) in 1969, suggests that it was believed that other material was also placed on the site by locals:

'So this Mr. Groome took a side-car out to Bellinter and told Gussie (Briscoe, one of the landowners at Tara) he wanted to dig for the Ark of the Covenant. Gussie was fascinated and said "Of course!" and told two of his men to dig for him and paid their wages, for the young man hadn't a penny. And they dug three big holes near the wall of the Protestant church at Tara a long way from the mounds. We were all highly delighted and amused. There were all kinds of jokes. We were very hard up at the time and were saying that we would turn Staffordstown into a hotel for all the Jews who would come to see the Ark and we would make a lot of money. Shirley and Cecil (Ball) hid all kinds of things for the young man to find, teapot lids and so on, and Shirley hid Lady Dillon's napkin-ring. But the young man was very good humoured and just laughed' (Butler and Foster 1990, 69).

Whether or not the site was being 'salted' during the British–Israelite campaign, the story of the hoax is not necessarily supported by Dolley's three main pieces of evidence. The common availability of small-denomination Roman copper coins is of little relevance, particularly in view of the discovery of fourth-century AD Roman, or Romano-British, material during Ó Ríordáin's excavation. This fact is not alluded to by either Dolley (1968) or Bateson (1973). The depth at which the coins were allegedly found presents no difficulties either. Healy's (1900) description suggests that they were found over an 'outer' trench c. 5.5m wide, which from his account may be the inner ditch (ditch 1) of the ringfort. If this interpretation of the information is correct, then the coins were in a position high up in the fill of the ditch at a level coinciding with the digging of the secondary ditch (F228) into the upper fill of ditch 1. This appears to have occurred towards the end of the occupation phase. If Healy's location is less reliable and the coins were found near, rather than over, the ditch, then a depth of c. 0.45m could place the coins at a low level in the primary occupation phase of the ringfort. In either case, it is reasonable to suggest that the coins come from the habitation phase (phase 4) of the ringfort.

The story related by Fowler cannot, unlike that of Mrs French, for example, be simply dismissed as a fabrication. Nevertheless, in view of the nature of some accounts of the British–Israelites' presence at Tara, and in particular what appears to be a memory of the period revised to play down local acquiescence in their digging, it is unreasonable to accept the assertion that the coins were deliberately placed on the site during this period. The date and apparent location of the coins are entirely in keeping with the other evidence from Ó Ríordáin's excavation, and a genuine fourth-century context at the Rath of the Synods appears to be a far more probable explanation.

LIST OF IDENTIFIED BUT DISCARDED ANIMAL BONE

Transcript of manuscript by Seán P. Ó Ríordáin

Overall assessment

Identification

The total weight of animal bone was 300lbs [136kg]. Of this *c.* 200lbs [90.7kg] were ox. Apart from ox, pig bones were more numerous than others. Other types found: horse, red deer (a few fragments of antler and one large bone), two fragments of dog, a few fragments of bird (type unidentified). A notable feature was the almost complete lack of sheep (three fragments found). In a few cases there were bones of very large pig and very large ox.

Distribution

By far the greater number of bones came from the fill of the inner ditch [ditch 1]. Proportion by weight between inner, middle and outer was 20:1:1?. This proportion is based on the bones found in cutting 1.

Bones occurred all down through fill of inner ditch. A remarkable feature was a concentration of ox jaw bones in the upper fill of the ditch. In cutting 1 these occurred in grey sticky soil just under the 'pebbly' shale line (? 17.4m W, depth: 0.62m). In cutting 8 they lay in the black fill on stones at a depth of 0.70–0.80m.

A large number of bones occurred in the ditch of the mound (barrow) and to a lesser degree scattered through the mound. The dog fragments occurred only in the mound and below the old turf line.

List of animal bones, other than those from cutting 1, from the Rath of the Synods

Sq. 35: Ox and pig fragments, some burnt, charcoal.
   Fill of black pit, under bridge in central area, young pig, calf, many fragments, young sheep (not lamb) (what seemed to be a burial).
Sq. 36: Ox, pig and sheep.
Sq. 36: Deep pit NW corner, one sheep, two pig and one ox.
Sq. 36: E baulk, pits and post-holes, ox and field mouse (sent to Dublin).
Sq. 37: Two pigs, fragments ox, one bird (sent to Dublin).
Sqs 37/43: Baulk, ox, pig.
Sq. 38: Pit in W sector, depth: 0.88m, pig, ox, deer (worked tine).
Sq. 38: Trench, ox and pebble.
Sqs 38/37/42/43: Baulk, fragments of several pigs, several ox, one horse.
Sqs 38/42, 41/43, 37/43: Baulks, fragments of several pigs and ox.
Sq. 41: Several pigs, one ox.
Sq. 41: Dark stratum in fill of fosse, two pig, one ox, horse.
Sq. 41: Two pigs, large and small, one horse, one ox (horse, metacarpal, teeth).
Sq. 41: Rock-cut trench, several pigs, large, two ox, fragment horse.
Sq. 41: Top of ditch fill, many fragments pig, some of ox, one canine tooth.
Sq. 42: Many fragments pig, ox, some sheep, one horse.
Sq. 42: Charcoal area, many fragments ox, pig.
Sq. 42: Charcoal area, one horse, pig and ox fragments. House trench (red trench?) central area with charcoal, fragments pig, one fragment ox.
Sq. 42, ext.: Two fragments pig, two fragments ox.
Sq. 42: Upper levels, small quantity ox, horse, pig.
Sq. 43: Pit in SE corner, under flags, fragments pig and ox.
Sq. 43: S side, fragments ox, pig.
Sq. 43: Upper levels, fragments ox, pig.
Sq. 43: Dark habitation layer, a few bones (pig, ox).
Sq. 43: Habitation, one pig, one ox.
Sqs 43/42/37: Baulk, around burial I, one good-sized dog (or wolf), fragment of shed antler of red deer, several pigs, one horse tooth, several ox of various age. Some bone burnt.

Sq. 45: British-Israelite dump down to habitation layer, large dog or wolf (sent to Dublin), pig and one ox.

Sq. 46: Fragment horse.

Sq. 52: E baulk, pig and ox.

Sqs 55/56: Baulk, near bottom of pit in red-filled trench, fragments ox.

Pit/trench, *c.* 9.70E *c.* 2.90N, depth: 0.36m, small fragments sheep, pig, claw of small rodent (sent to Dublin).

Sq. 59, ext.: Dark layer, depth 0.80m, one pig and one ox, many fragments, one horse tooth.

Sq. 59, ext.: From palisade, one horse, one ox, one pig (infant).

Sq. 63, ext. E: One ox, pig, sheep, deer, horse.

Sq. 63, ext. E: One pig, one ox, one horse (fragmentary).

W from fill of subsidiary ditch, depth: 0.90m, two pigs, one ox, (fragmentary) red deer tine.

Sq. 63: Fill of subsidiary ditch, pig and ox.

Cutting 13: Upper layers, ox and pig fragments.

Cutting 15, ext.: Two fragments pig, one horse, ox.

Cutting 15, ext.: One pig, one ox, fragments.

Cutting 15, ext.: Fragments ox, pig.

Cutting 15, ext. E, near S face: Remains of two pigs and two oxen.

Cutting 19: Fill of ditch, ox and one fragment pig.

Cutting 19: Inner bank of ditch 3, small fragments ox.

Cutting 21: Ditch fill, two pigs, many fragments ox, deer antler, distal end of tibia of horse.

Cutting 22: Top sod, fill of ditch 3, a few bones ox and pig.

Bottom of Rath na Ríogh ditch, depth: 2.55m, under large stone in west face, horse.

THE ROMAN POTTERY FROM THE RATH OF THE SYNODS

Jeremy Evans[1]

Introduction

The first thing that must be stated is that the collection of pottery from the site is very small—24 surviving sherds and a minimum of eight surviving vessels, with fragments of a further one or two (in Nash-Williams's 1952 report, see below) no longer available for study—so that any conclusions must be of a tentative nature. By the standards of collections of Roman sherds from Ireland, however, this is a large assemblage.

Discussion

Despite the size of the group, an assemblage in which (with the exception of the single missing mortarium sherd) all the sherds are oxidised, colour-coated or Samian ware is not typical of Roman pottery. It would be possible to argue that this was a recovery bias, but on a site with very few ceramics of any sort it is highly improbable that greyware or blackware sherds were simply overlooked, especially as some of the colour-coated sherds have black surfaces. Rather this is an assemblage apparently totally lacking in the usual Romano-British greywares and Black Burnished ware. This is significant, since it makes very clear that this collection is just that: a series of selected vessels, not a representative sample of Romano-British pottery from anywhere in Britain.

The Tara collection is very different from assemblages found on rural sites in North Wales, Mid Wales and Anglesey (Evans, forthcoming, table 5), where assemblages are dominated by BB1 jars (Black Burnished ware) and Samian ware. On the Welsh sites, assemblages with a status-display aspect, such as those from Cefn Cwmwd and Bryn Eryr (Evans, forthcoming; Longley *et al.* 1998), contain a high proportion of decorated Samian ware, in the form of Dr 37 bowls. Interestingly there is no evidence from Tara of any Dr 37 having reached there.

The pottery from the Welsh rural sites is also a selection in part, in that, compared with their source at the Segontium *vicus*, on most only Black Burnished ware and Samian ware have been acquired, leaving out the greywares and oxidised wares found in quantity at Segontium. Essentially those upland sites wanted Black Burnished ware for cooking pots, and sometimes Samian for status display, and left everything else (Evans, forthcoming).

Six of the nine Tara vessels would be classed as finewares, but five of them are drinking vessels. In this context it is worth noting that the common Samian ware cups, Dr 27 and Dr 33, are absent. The much less common Déchelette 72 is, however, present, apparently in two examples. It may be significant that this form would appear to have a rather larger capacity, like the beakers, than the more dainty Dr 27 and Dr 33 cups, which were presumably designed for wine-drinking.

Functionally, therefore, the Tara pottery would seem to be largely associated with drinking, using relatively high-status vessels. Pleasingly, this evidence seems to correlate neatly with that of the vessel glass. Bourke (Appendix C) shows that the Tara glass is dominated by bowls and beakers, both being drinking vessels.

To turn to how the pottery was deposited, it is clear from the generally fragmentary nature of the material that it was broken and discarded and not ritually deposited in the ground (in which case complete or largely complete vessels would have been recovered). The lack of ritual deposition at Tara is reinforced by the small finds (Allason-Jones, Appendix A), which completely lack any votive-type objects.

Whilst the Tara pottery was not ritually deposited in the ground, it is of note that several vessels seem to be represented by more than single sherds, particularly both the Déchelette 72 beakers. The functional composition of

[1] 67 Dovey Road, Moseley, Birmingham.

the group, and the glassware, and the use of the site as a cemetery may explain this. It seems to this author that the assemblage may largely represent the remains of funerary meals/toasts, with the vessels discarded on the surface. There are well-evidenced cemeteries in Italy where drifting sand has preserved the old ground surface that illustrate this. In Britain the unstratified collection from the Brougham cemetery (Evans 2004) also exhibits characteristics that can only be explained in this manner.

In seeking a locus in Britain for the material at Tara, the presence of Severn Valley ware (or sherds in that tradition at least) and colour-coated ware likely to be of Wilderspool origin (Hartley and Webster 1973) as well as the presence of Oxfordshire ware all point to the Cheshire–southern Lancashire area as the point of contact (although this material could conceivably have been assembled from the *vicus* at Segontium, for example (Casey *et al.* 1993)).

In terms of the dating of the material, the colour-coated oxidised ware sherds are probably Wilderspool products of second-century date. The Severn Valley ware sherds and the spindle-whorl are undatable, except to say that they are Roman. The Oxfordshire C20 body sherd is given a date range of AD 270–400+ by Young (1977). Amongst the Samian, the Déchelette 72 vessels are mid–late second-century, leaving the Dr 18/31 body sherd (E615:150, Fig 4.16 and Pl. 2) and the indeterminate fragment (E615:165, Pl. 2). Both could benefit from a Samian specialist's opinion as to whether they might be south Gaulish. The lost mortarium was dated by Nash-Williams (*in litt.* 1952) and Richmond to the third–fourth centuries. Currently material can be positively dated to the second century and the fourth century. This seems to correlate well with the second–fourth-century date range given to the glass (Bourke, Appendix C).

Bateson (1973) pointed to a theory of Collins (1955) that the Roman pottery in Ireland was not a contemporary importation but was brought in during the post-Roman period. Whilst this view is not one shared by this author, this explanation is not so easily ruled out for the Tara group, because most of it is fineware and oxidised. Collections of Roman pottery in Britain from *grubenhuser* and medieval sites tend to be disproportionately of red-slipped finewares, and it is possible that these sherds were being reused, perhaps for cosmetic purposes.

Were the collection made from a site in Britain in the early post-Roman period by field-walking, selecting chiefly oxidised pieces, its composition would be surprising, however. The vast majority of Samian wares on British sites are table wares (dishes and bowls) but these are not reflected in the Tara material. Similarly there are large parts of two of the Samian vessels that would not be expected either. Thus the composition of this assemblage, and its correlation with the nature of the glassware vessels assemblage, tends to argue against this. Bateson (1973) also pointed out that the find-spots of Samian in Ireland produce 'not one piece which can be said to have come from a context that is incontrovertibly post-Roman in date and there is no reason to believe that they were not imported during the normal period of currency of samian ware'.

Catalogue

E615:1, 17, and 123 (Pl. 4). Three sherds forming the base and lower wall of Samian form Déch. 72, a type in use in the second half of the second century. Central Gaulish. Burnt brown. See Oswald and Pryce 1920, pls LXXVII and LXXIX. Weight 82g. BE 100%.

E615:10. Phase 4, ditch 1 (Pl. 2). Fragment of fine oxidised, finely micaceous sherd from a closed form. Probably Severn Valley ware. Weight 7g.

E615:35. Uncontexted bank 3 (phase 4) area (Pl. 2). An oxidised body sherd from a closed form with a blue-grey core and orange margins and surfaces, soapy with moderate organic temper voids. Severn Valley ware or an allied fabric. Weight 7g.

E615:68. Phase 4, ditch 1 (Pl. 2). A closed-form body sherd in a fine fabric with a grey inner margin and orange outer margin, with a black colour-coat on the exterior. Possibly Wilderspool. Weight 2g. Perhaps from same vessel as E615:137 and E615:183a–b.

E615:70a. Phase 3, barrow. Small ball of yellow ironstone/haematite. Weight 0.8g, D 8.5mm.

E615:127 (Pl. 2). A spindle-whorl made from an oxidised sherd with a soapy texture and some fine organic temper voids, with a pale grey core and orange margins and surfaces. From a closed form, perhaps a jar. Severn Valley ware or an allied fabric. This author suspects that this object was imported as a spindle-whorl rather than as a vessel from which the spindle-whorl was subsequently made. Weight 10g, diam. *c.* 45mm, diam. of hole 6mm.

E615:137. Phase 4 habitation (Pl. 2). An oxidised sherd with a brown colour-coat with a barbotine tendril under the slip. Inner margins grey and exterior orange. Fabric fine with some very fine sand. Fragment of a similar beaker 68 above. Weight 2g. Perhaps from same vessel as E615:68 and E615:183a–b.

E615:146, 1 of 12. Phase 4 habitation (Pl. 3). A thin-walled Samian closed-form body sherd, exterior largely excoriated, interior apparently unslipped. Around 2mm thick. Weight 0.2g.

E615:146, 2 of 12. Phase 4 habitation (Pl. 3). A thin Samian closed-form body sherd, interior unslipped, as 146: 3 of 12. Central Gaulish. Weight 1g.

E615:146, 3 of 12. Phase 4 habitation (Pl. 3). A thin Samian body sherd, interior excoriated or unslipped, exterior partly excoriated. Possibly once decorated. From a closed-form, Déch 72 etc. Central Gaulish. Weight 2g.

E615:146, 4 of 12. Phase 4 habitation (Pl. 3). A thin Samian closed-form body sherd, exterior slipped, interior unslipped, as 146: 3 of 12. Weight 1g.

E615:146, 5 of 12. Phase 4 habitation (Pl. 3). An oxidised micaceous body sherd with blue-grey core and orange margins, exterior red colour-coated. The sherd is from an indented beaker. Oxfordshire colour-coated ware (Young 1977) type C20, AD 270–400+. Weight 3g.

E615:146, 6 of 12. Phase 4 habitation (Pl. 3). A thin Samian sherd, exterior largely excoriated, interior unslipped, a closed form, as 146: 3 of 12. Weight 2g.

E615:146, 7 of 12. Phase 4 habitation (Pl. 3). A totally excoriated Samian ware flake, central Gaulish, as 146: 3 of 12. Weight 0.3g.

E615:146, 8 of 12. Phase 4 habitation (Pl. 3). A thin Samian closed-form body sherd, probably decorated, central Gaulish, as E615:146: 3 of 12. Weight 1g.

E615:146, 9 of 12. Phase 4 habitation (Pl. 3). A Samian fragment, perhaps from a foot-ring, a thin-walled vessel, as 146: 3 of 12. Central Gaulish. Weight 1g.

E615:146, 10 of 12. Phase 4 habitation (Pl. 3). Fragment of a globular jar/beaker of central Gaulish *terra sigillata*, Déchelette type 72, mid–late second century, as 146: 3 of 12. No inner surface survives. Weight 3g.

E615:146, 11 of 12. Phase 4 habitation (Pl. 3). A thin Samian closed-form body sherd, exterior partly excoriated, interior unslipped, exterior perhaps decorated, as 146: 3 of 12. Weight 0.2g.

E615:146, 12 of 12. Phase 4 habitation (Pl. 3). A thin flake, completely excoriated, as E615:150 (below).

E615:150. Uncontexted beneath British-Israelite upcast (Fig 4.16; Pl. 2). A Samian, possibly south Gaulish, body sherd with a single incised line across the face. Dr. 18/31 wall sherd, late first century AD (or second century if not south Gaulish). Weight 2g.

E615:165d. Phase 4 habitation (Pl. 2). Abraded Samian fragment with no surfaces surviving. Possibly from a foot-ring, source uncertain. Weight 1g.

E615:174. Phase 4, ditch 1 (Fig. 4.15; Pl. 2). A beaker body sherd in a fine orange fabric with some fairly fine sand temper, exterior and interior having a brown colour-coat, exterior rouletted. Probably Wilderspool. Weight 0.5g.

E615:183a. Phase 4, ditch 1 (Fig. 4.15; Pl. 2). A closed-form, probably a beaker, body sherd with a grey inner margin and orange exterior margin and a black colour-coat. A fine fabric very similar to E615:137. Weight 4g. Perhaps same vessel as E615:68, E615:137 and E615:183b.

E615:183b. Phase 4, ditch 1 (Fig. 4.15; Pl. 2). A black colour-coated body sherd with barbotine decoration from a closed form, probably a beaker. Interior margin grey and exterior one orange, with some very fine sand temper. Weight 1g. Perhaps same vessel as E615:68, E615:137 and E615:183a.

Missing material

At the time of excavation, the Roman pottery sherds with their excavation cards were sent to specialists in Britain. The first batch went to V. E. Nash-Williams at the National Museum of Wales. He in turn sent them to John P. Gillam, Kings College, Newcastle, who forwarded them to R. E. M. Wheeler.

Nash-Williams (below) reported on a mortarium sherd (no. 5 in his report), which is definitely no longer present in the collection and cannot be located. Other notes from the archive (from Mortimer Wheeler and possibly Ian Richmond) are also reproduced here.

POTTERY-FRAGMENTS FROM TARA (IRELAND)

E615:5. Fragment of <u>mortarium</u>. Fairly fine whitish-buff ware. The interior was originally thinly sprinkled with medium-sized grains of grit or spar, which have since worn or weathered away. A characteristic Romano-British type. In the absence of a rim the piece cannot be narrowly dated, but the fabric suggests a hammer-headed or flanged vessel of the type which was in vogue in Britain in the later Roman period (3rd–4th century AD).

E615:6. Similar fabric to no. 10, but showing traces of chocolate-red glaze on the exterior surface. At first glance the fragment gives the impression of a badly weathered Gaulish Samian sherd, but the fabric is hardly of Samian type and quality. Possibly an imitation-Samian vessel. Shape indeterminate. Date: ?2nd–3rd century AD.

E615:7. Fragment of jug (?), with crinkled foot-ring. Coarse mica(?)-speckled pinkish-red ware, with grey core. The form and the harsh sandy texture of the fabric are both consistent with a medieval date. 13th–14th century AD.

E615:1, 17, 123. Base of pedestalled jar or small flagon. Fine soft dull pink ware (showing traces of burning), coated externally with a smooth matt chocolate glaze (changing to black in places due to burning). The internal surface is speckled with mica (?) particles. The fabric is akin to that of E615:17. The form of the vessel recalls that of certain Samian jars, e.g. Déchelette 72 and Dragendorff 54[(1)]. Date: ?2nd–3rd century A.D.

Apart from the medieval fragment (E615:67), all the above sherds give the impression of belonging to, or deriving from, the Roman period, but, except for the last (no. 1–17–123), they suggest a Romano-<u>native</u> rather than a Roman context. No. 1–17–123 would not be usual for a Romano-British site, and I should suspect Gallo-Roman rather than Romano-British affinities.

V. E. Nash-Williams
National Museum of Wales,
CARDIFF.
5th December, 1952

Tara sherds

Nos 1, 17, and 123. These represent a good copy of Samian form Déch. 72, a type in use in the 2nd half of the 2nd century and in the early years of the 3rd. It is good work and is probably an importation from Gaul. Its slip was doubtless red but has been burnt brown. See Oswald and Price (1920), pls LXXVII and LXXIX.
Sherd 5. This is a piece of mortarium, not datable.
Sherd 67. Fragment of a waster, probably late Roman but not closely datable.
REMW
[R. E. M. Wheeler]

Pottery from Tara

127. Spindle whorl made from a sherd of hard, reddish buff ware of Roman date, possibly from a jug.
REMW
[R. E. M. Wheeler]

There is also a note, dated May 1954, in the archive (possibly by Ó Ríordáin) on remarks by Ian Richmond (Department of Greek and Roman, UCD) concerning two of the missing sherds.

> *5—Mortarium—not likely to be before 3rd and might be early 4th (probably hammer-headed rim type). (See E615:5 above)*
> *67—Waster—one of latest pieces in collection—almost might be 4th century.*

Nash-Williams's description of the sherd numbered no. 6 in his report suggests that while it may be missing it could in fact be E615:68 (Pl. 2) and the related colour-coated sherds (although it could also be another sherd of Oxfordshire ware). Nash-Williams also describes (his no. 7) part of a jug no longer present in the collection, as well as another sherd (his no. 67) which is probably from a medieval vessel: to this author this sherd also seems likely to account for Wheeler's sherd no. 67.

APPENDIX H

UNCONTEXTED FINDS AND SAMPLES BY AREA

Caroline Velzian Donaghy and Eoin Grogan

This list includes material with conflicting or clearly inaccurate coordinates, as well as material from the sod layer and from disturbed areas (Fig. 1.5).

In the finds descriptions the following conventions are used: ★not illustrated; underlining indicates that the object cannot be located. The location of the finds (where available) is given from the centre point ©.

L= length; W = width; T = thickness; D = diameter; H = height; BI = British-Israelite.

Phase 2

S19: Slag, 200g. Sq. 6, trench D. No location/context card with sample but bottom of box says sq. 6. The notebook states that iron fragments, slag and nails came from the 'charcoally' (*sic*) fill of F142 (trench D): it is possible that this sample represents part of that deposit.

Phase 3—barrow

Silver
★E615:88a: Modern silver plate cutlery terminal. Cutting 6, barrow, centre of mound, towards 9mW, 0.75mN?, depth 0.72m.

Copper alloy
★E615:79: Corroded semicircular object, possibly a button, D 13mm. Cutting 13, disturbed area.
★E615:80: Coin, Victorian penny with modern objects. Cutting 7, extension west, barrow, sod of mound.
★E615:227: Button with loop for fastening, D 19mm. Cutting 14, depth 0.4m.

Iron
★E615:38a: Fifteen fragments of corroded stems and staples. Cutting 5, rising slope of barrow, inside bank.
★E615:49: Rectangular-sectioned nail, corroded head, L 37mm. Cutting 7, west end of cutting, soft fill, depth 0.35m.

★E615:89a: Corroded rectangular-sectioned stem with expanded head, L 157mm, W 4–9mm, T 5–7mm. Cutting 12, under sod.

Glass
★E615:88c: Rim of glass vessel. Cutting 6, barrow, centre of mound, towards 9mW, 0.75mN?, depth 0.72m.
★E615:99: Body sherd of blue glass vessel, 30mm x 24mm. Cutting 6, centre of barrow.

Ceramic
E615:1 (Pl. 4): Roman base sherd, central Gaulish. Sq. 8, north of square along east face, in layer under sod, depth 0.25m.
E615:17a and b (Pl. 4): Roman base sherd, central Gaulish. Sq. 8, north of square along east face, in layer under sod, depth 0.25m.
★E615:38b: Body sherd of cream stoneware. Cutting 5, barrow, rising slope of mound inside bank.
★E615:58: Body sherd of modern pottery. Cutting 5, barrow, top of mound, depth 1m.
★E615:85: Stoneware body sherd. Cutting 5, barrow, disturbed area among large stones at top of mound.
★E615:88b: Modern pottery sherd. Cutting 6, barrow, centre of mound, towards 9mW, 0.75mN?, depth 0.72m.
E615:123 (Pl. 4): Roman base sherd, central Gaulish. Sq. 8, north of square along east face, in layer under sod, depth 0.25m.

Clay pipe
★E615:89b: Clay pipe stem.
★E615:103: Clay pipe stem, with six fragments of animal bone.

127

Stone

★E615:59b: Flint flake. Cutting 7, barrow, sod in disturbed area in centre of mound.

★E615:74: Flint flake. Cutting 6, barrow, top of mound in small stones, 9mW, 0.6mN, depth 1.1m (Appendix D).

★E615:120: Tanged flint flake. Cutting 7, under sod.

Samples

S33: Clay, seven pieces of vitrified organic material. Cutting 5, top of barrow, amongst stones, depth 0.3m.

S48: A few wood fragments. Cutting 11 under sod, depth 0.7m.

S91: Clay, lightly burnt with charcoal, two fragments of cremated bone. Cutting 12, clay at edge of cairn.

S140: Six fragments of animal bone. Cutting 9, under sod.

S151: Bone and tooth. Cutting 10, inner edge, mainly ditch.

S167: Two fragments of animal bone. Cutting 10, east part of cut, under sod.

Phase 4

Silver

E615:115 (Fig. 4.16): Ringed pin with round head, L 55mm, T 1–2mm. Decoration extends for 24mm from head of pin; five incised lines laterally below head then lattice cross-hatching for 17mm, ending in six lateral incised lines. Ring, about one half survives, D 1.5mm, corroded into the head. Possibly Roman but could be of later date. Sqs 3 and 4, bottom of humus, above hard layer, depth 0.4m.

Copper alloy

★E615:92: Copper-alloy nail with solid mushroom head, L 36mm, square section 3mm, D head 4mm, Roman(?). Sq. 22, north face, depth 0.5m.

E615:172 (Fig. 4.16): Strip ring with overlapping tapered terminals, now in two parts, rectangular section, 5.5mm x 1.5mm, outer face decorated with two linear grooves set along the edges. Original internal D *c.* 16mm x 10mm. Sq. 35, north-east corner in disturbed soil at the base of the British-Israelite cut, depth 0.35m.

★E615:262: Fragments, convex, largest 5mm x 3.6mm x 0.5mm. Sq. 53/52, baulk.

Iron

★E615:56: Iron chisel or gouge. Sq. 1, *c.* 0.6mW, 1mN, depth 0.6m, BI disturbance.

★E615:76: Spatulate object, L 126mm x 6mm x 4mm, terminus 28mm x 7–11mm x 5mm. Sqs 5 and 8, baulk, bottom of humus.

★E615:97: Iron nail. Sq. 4, BI rubble, *c.* 10mW, 1mN, depth 0.45m.

★E615:100b: Three stems: (a) L 39mm x 10mm x 5mm; (b) L 36mm x 4mm; (c) nail L 20mm x 3mm, head 4.5mm. Cutting 1, extension south, *c.* 13mW, above clay floor at post-hole.

★E615:157: Rectangular-sectioned strip staple, L 77mm, arm 15mm, 5mm x 3mm plus fragment, L 32mm. Sq. 38, immediately above habitation level.

★E615:162: Blade fragment, 48mm x 7mm; two stems, 28mm x 3mm and 18mm x 4mm. Sq. 52, humus layer below BI dump.

★E615:163: Loop with double spike, strip curve and lozenge-sectioned arms, ext. *c.* 47mm x 42mm, int. *c.* 37mm x 35mm; bar 9mm. Sq. 53, humus layer, possibly Roman (W. H. Manning 1985, 130–1) (Appendix A).

★E615:179: Flat-headed nail or tack, L 21mm, square stem 3mm, flat head D 10mm. Sq. 43/44.

★E615:194: Rectangular-sectioned strip with one blunt and one narrowed end, tanged blade, 43mm x 5–9mm x 4mm. Sq. 45, north baulk.

E615:196 (Fig. 4.16): Tanged blade or strip, corroded, 69mm x 11–22mm x 7mm. Sq. 54, sod layer, on top of dark stratum in north baulk, *c.* 1.8mW, 9.5mN, depth 0.38m.

★E615:197: Disc, coin or button. Sq. 44/52 baulk, BI disturbed upcast, *c.* 3.6mE, *c.* 6.4mN, depth 0.96m.

★E615:210: Stem fragments. Sq. 43/44 baulk, top of humus, over habitation level.

★E615:241: Two nails or tacks, L 23.5mm and 18mm. Sq. 44, humus layer under BI turf line, under west baulk.

Glass

★E615:3b: Vessel sherd. Sq. 1, *c.* 5mW at edge of cutting, depth 1m.

E615:136 (Fig. 4.16; Pl. 1): Fragment (one quarter to one fifth) of D-sectioned, 6.5–7.5mm, ultramarine bracelet, decorated with lines of white glass fused to surface running at a slight angle on outer face; original ext. D *c.* 72.5mm, int. *c.* 61mm, inner surface rough. From spoil on northern side of ringfort interior.

★E615:151: Clear, colourless body sherd of bowl. Sq. 42, upper level of humus (bones, charcoal, black clay layer), 5.15mN, 11mE, depth 0.25m.

★E615:209: Seven pane fragments. Sq. 44/52, *c.* 6mE, 7.2mN, depth 0.72m, in humus under BI upcast, 0.13m from top of humus, 0.5m from habitation layer.

Ceramic

E615:150 (Fig. 4.16; Pl. 2): A Samian, possible south Gaulish, body sherd with single incised line across the face. Late first century AD (Appendix G). Sq. 54, humus layer, beneath BI upcast.

Clay pipe

★E615:3c: Pipe stem. Sq. 1, *c.* 5mW at edge of cutting, depth 1m.

Stone

★E615:25b: Flint core. Sq. 4, BI rubble, *c.* 10.5mW.

E615:27 (Fig. 4.16; Pl. 1): Section of shale, undecorated, oval-sectioned ring, *c.* one half, polished, elliptical section, D 13–14mm x 16mm. Sq. 7, sod, stony soil, 2.2mW, 5.2mS, depth 0.25m.

★E615:46: Sixty-five water-rolled pebbles. From 9m north-west of sq. 9, sod.

★E615:55: Iron Age artefact, finely smoothed siltstone cone, gaming piece, H 37.5mm, base 17mm x 16mm. Sq. 1, disturbed, at edge of cutting, *c.* 5mW, depth 0.35m (see Raftery 1983, 230, fig. 185).

★E615:100b: Unutilised flint flake. Cutting 1, extension south, *c.* 13mW, above clay floor at post-hole.

★E615:169: Elliptical quartz or sandstone rubber, tracked stone, both faces flat, 69mm x 66mm x 47mm. Sq. 52, sod line, depth 0.6m.

★E615:171: Spherical stone, calcareous sandstone, possible working on one side, 64mm. Sq. 43, sod.

★E615:257: Pebble. Sq. 41, BI disturbed.

Samples

S39: Animal bone fragments. Sq. 38, upper levels, immediately above habitation level.

S52: Charcoal, bone. Sq. 55/56 baulk.

S57: Charcoal fragments from baulk. Sq. 37/38/42/43.

S58: Charcoal fragments from baulk. Sq. 37/38/42/43.

S81: Charcoal and clay, bone, tooth. Central area, *c.* 6.2mN, post-hole east of north/south baulk.

S86: Charcoal fragments. Sq. 5, *c.* 0.46mW, 7mS.

S92: Fragment of charcoal. Sq. 45.

S93: Five fragments of charcoal, tiny fragment of quartz. Sq. 55, west baulk.

S122: Charcoal and bone. Sq. 36.

S127: Charcoal and bone. Sq. 43, southern sector.

S130: Shell. Sq. 54.

S138 (E615:97a): Cremated bone. Sq. 4, BI rubble, *c.* 10mW, 1m?, depth 0.45m.

S203 (E615:25): Bone and cremated bone fragments. Sq. 4, BI rubble, *c.* 10.5mW.

Bank 1

Stone

E615:65 (Fig. 4.16): Incomplete stone mould, 84mm x 68mm x 33mm; for description see Appendix A. Cutting 8, sod in inner part of bank 1.

Ditch 1

Iron

★E615:72a: Hooked rod, square section, hooked end 17mm. Cutting 10, fill of ditch 1, depth 0.68m.

★E615:96: Stem of nail. Sq. 2, upper fill of ditch 1, depth 0.44m.

Glass

★E615:8: Two sherds. Cutting 1, ditch 1 edge, layer 1, over shale layer, *c.* 18.28mW, 1.56m?, depth 0.2m.

★E615:72b: Two sherds of blue/green vessel. Cutting 10, fill of ditch 1, depth 0.68m.

★E615:105: Six vessel sherds, one rim sherd. Cutting 1, ditch 1 edge, above shale layer 1, *c.* 18.28mW, 1.56m?, depth 0.2m.

Ceramic

★E615:67: Base of Roman waster, 52mm x 36mm x 3–12mm. Ditch 1, probably upper fill of ditch.

Samples

S177: *Circa* 60 fragments of animal bone and teeth, tusk. Cutting 11, ditch 1 fill.

Bank 2

Iron

★E615:53: Rectangular-sectioned stem fragment. Cutting 2, bank 2, inside bank, depth 0.24m.

Glass

★E615:101: Sherd, 34mm x 24mm. Cutting 2, bank 2, under sod.

Stone

E615:39b (Fig. 4.16): Roof slate with aperture, non-local slate. Cutting 1, sod, *c.* 33.10mW, 2.17mN?, in vicinity of bank 2, 'from the adjacent church?'.

Bank 3

★E615:93: Eighteenth-century coin. Cutting 1, sod, *c.* 27mW, 1mN?, depth 0.15m. Over bank 3.

Iron

★E615:32b: Iron nail. Cutting 5, inside bank 3 sod.

Ceramic

E615:35 (Pl. 2): Body sherd of Severn Valley ware, *c.* first–second centuries AD, 25mm x 32mm x 6–7mm. Cutting 4, under sod on bank 3. See Appendix G.

Clay

★E615:91: Four clay pipe stems. Cutting 5, bank 3 spill.

Samples

S141: Cremated bone fragments. Cutting 4, under sod on bank 3.

S143: Bone, epiphysis. Cutting 4, under sod on bank 3.

S166: *Circa* twenty fragments of animal bone, one tooth. Cutting 5, outside outer ditch, from 'soil profile' cutting, depth 0.6m.

Rath na Ríogh

Copper alloy

★E615:203: Halfpenny *Gratia* coin. Cutting 23, Rath na Ríogh, sod over bank.

Iron

★E615:207: Nail, now in four pieces, L 26mm; stem 4mm x 3mm, tapering to 3mm x 2mm; flat head, D *c.* 14mm. Upper levels under sod.

★E615:264: Nail, L 13.7mm, stem 3mm x 2.4mm, head 11mm x 10mm x *c.* 6mm. Cutting 23, upper fill of Rath na Ríogh ditch, depth 0.3m.

★E615:266: Stem. Rath na Ríogh.

Samples

S13: Slag, 10g. Cutting 23, Rath na Ríogh, fill of ditch, depth 1.45m.

S42: Six shells and fragments. Cutting 23, fill, Rath na Ríogh ditch.

Uncontexted site

Copper alloy

★E615:73: William and Mary halfpenny, 1698. Sq. 16, sod (Dwyer 1988, 43).

Iron

★E615:4: Fragment with hollow stem. Sq. 6, sod.

★E615:31b: Iron fragments. Sq. 10, depth 0.24m.

★E615:45: Corroded stem, tool?, L 49mm. Sq. 6.

★E615:94b: Stem, tool, rectangular-sectioned, tapering to round terminal, L 29mm x 3–6mm. Sq. 15, sod.

★E615:100a: Iron punch, binding strip, nail, three iron stems. Cutting 1, extension south, above clay floor at post-hole, *c.* 13mW.

★E615:102: Nail, corroded. Sq. 16, sod.

★E615:119: Nail. Sq. 7, sod.

★E615:122: Object with two arms, 43mm and 24mm rectangular section. Cutting 10, disturbed, depth 0.3m.

★E615:143: Nail embedded in wood. Cutting 15, ext. BI disturbed?, depth 1.3m, part of modern fence.

★E615:233: Nail, clay pipe stem, daub *c.* 25mm. Cutting 16, sod.

★E615:263: Flat, rectangular, corroded stem, with rivet in it. Sq. 6, sod.

★E615:267: Tool, tanged firmer chisel for fine work, probably Roman, L 46mm x 5–10mm (W. H. Manning 1985, C12). Context unknown.

Glass
★E615:9: Three glass sherds. Cutting 1, near edge of ditch, *c.* 16.6mW, 0.94mN?, depth 0.53m, BI rubble.
★E615:33: Vessel sherd, clear, 21mm x 11mm. Cutting 2, sod.
★E615:52: Oval setting, green bubbly glass, bevelled edge, 36mm x 33mm x 4mm. Sq. 6, sod, depth 0.25m.
★E615:106: Vessel sherd. Cutting 10, sod.
E615:107 (Pl. 1): Setting, white insets, round base, D 35mm. Sq. 18, BI fill, depth 0.88m.
★E615:206: Vessel sherd, 27mm x 12mm x 1.45mm. Sq. 59, extension BI cutting.
★E615:261: Bubbly green opaque vessel sherd, 67mm x 48mm x 7–14mm. Sq. 63, extension east; the museum card also states 'Ráth na Ríogh'.
★E615:270: Inset, half of round inset, bevelled edge, fused dark/light blue, D 13mm. Roman, second–third centuries AD (Appendix A).

Ceramic
★E615:5: Roman vessel sherd, lost. Sq. 6, sod, depth 0.25m.
★E615:95: Three sherds of post-medieval stoneware. Cutting 12.
★E615:202: Four sherds of pottery, grey with yellow glaze, one rim buff-glazed. Cutting 21 sod, top of humus layer, depth 0.3m.

Clay
★E615:3a: Two pipe stems. Cutting 16, top of stone layer under humus, depth 0.43m.
★E615:7: Clay pipe bowl fragment. Sq. 4, depth 0.36m.
★E615:31a: Four clay pipe stems. Sq. 10, depth 0.24m.
E615:221 (Fig. 4.15): Clay Parnell Pipe bowl with stem fragment, stamped 'The Parnell MP Pipe'. Sq. 63, extension west, depth 0.3m.
★E615:245: Clay pipe stems. Cutting 19, sod.

Stone
★E615:15: Polished stone axe fragment. Sq. 3, western

part, BI tip layer.
★E615:25: Flint flake. Cutting 15, extension.
E615:33b (Fig. 4.16): Roof slate, 49mm x 63mm with aperture, D 4mm. Cutting 2 sod.
★E615:51: Flint flake. Sq. 9, sod, depth 0.2m.
★E615:63: Chert flake. Sq. 11, BI disturbed, depth 0.6m.
★E615:94a: Two pebbles worn from rubbing, game or burnishers. Sq. 15, sod, found with pointed iron implement.
★E615:100b: Flint flake. Cutting 1, extension south, above clay floor at post-hole, *c.* 13mW.
★E615:254: Roof slate with aperture, micaceous sandstone, L 205mm x 75–100mm x 10–20mm. Cutting 11, sod, from the adjacent church?
★E615:256: Sandstone object, almost circular in plan, elliptical section, 89mm x 86mm x 58mm. Context unknown.
★E615:257: Spherical pebble, 37mm x 35mm x 3mm. Sq. 41, BI disturbance.
★E615:268: Quartz fragment. Sq. 59 extension.

Miscellaneous
★E615:42: Whiskey pot sherds, iron rods. Cutting 5 sod.
★E615:250a–c: (a) Flint flake, (b) lead shot, (c) seven pipe bowl fragments. Cutting 21 sod.

Samples
S25: Ten bones and fragments of cremated bone, two teeth, twenty fragments of charcoal. Cutting 21, under humus layer, depth 0.46m.
S30: Two pieces of daub.
S31: Eight pieces of daub. 'Synods', trench.
S32: Fifteen fragments of wood; *c.* 21mW, 1m?, depth 0.1m, under east baulk face.
S34: Cremated bone and charcoal. 'Synods', trench in centre area east of post-hole.
S44: Charcoal and bone. Sq. 8.
S49: Fifteen pieces of charcoal. Sq. 10.
S51: *Circa* 60 fragments of charcoal mixed with soil, fragments of bone and cremated bone, seven fragments of slag. Under bank.
S68: Charcoal, ten fragments, cremated bone, four fragments of burnt clay. Sq. 15.
S89: Charcoal fragment. Sq. 14, trench?
S96: Charcoal and bone fragments. 'Synods'.

S101: Charcoal fragments. Sq. 12, under sod.

S104: Ten pieces of charcoal and two fragments of bone.

S117: *Circa* 40 fragments of charcoal mixed with clay, *c.* 20 fragments of cremated bone, slag. Sq. 59 extension.

S124: Charcoal, burnt clay and cremated bone.

S126: Charcoal. 'Synods', sod.

S129: Slag. Sq. 6, under turf, depth 0.25–0.33m.

S139: Fragments of cremated bone. Sq. 10, depth 0.24m.

S178: Animal bone. Cutting 7, trench in central area.

S182: Animal bone. Sq. 30, east of sq. 25, at wall of churchyard, fill of deep ditch.

S198: Slag. 'Synods', extension east, 0–1mE, depth 1m.

S204: Wood fragments. Cutting 9, north area, depth 0.49m.

S205: Animal bone fragment. Sq. 4, BI rubble, *c.* 10mW, 1m?, depth 0.49m.

S207: Animal bone. Cutting 15, extension.

APPENDIX I

CHARCOAL ANALYSIS

Lorna O'Donnell[1]

Introduction

The analysis of charcoal from archaeological sites relies on the premise that it is unlikely that people would forage too far for firewood if it was to be found in the local environment. We know that during the Iron Age woodlands were managed in Ireland (Stuijts 2005), but it is generally presumed that people did not plant trees and therefore the trees should have germinated in suitable soil or locations. An examination of the conditions in which these trees prefer to grow should therefore provide an insight into the local environment of the Rath of the Synods during the Iron Age. Charcoal identifications can also provide information about the selection of different species for building and fuel.

Methodology

Charcoal was examined from 30 samples from the Rath of the Synods. The samples were processed by the client, and charcoal was extracted by hand from the flots. Each piece of charcoal was examined and orientated first under low magnification (10x–40x).

The pieces were then broken to reveal their transverse, tangential and longitudinal surfaces. Pieces were mounted in plasticine and examined under a binocular microscope with dark ground light and magnifications generally of 200x and 400x. Each taxon or species has its own particular anatomical characteristics and can be identified by comparison with keys (Schweingruber 1978; Hather 2000; E. A. Wheeler *et al.* 1989) and a reference collection supplied by the National Botanical Gardens of Ireland, Glasnevin. It was aimed to identify 50 fragments per sample, or at least as many as possible. The general age group of each taxon per sample was recorded, and the growth rates were classified as slow, medium, fast or mixed. Insect infestation is usually recognised by round holes and is considered to be caused by burrowing insects. Their presence normally suggests the use of decayed degraded wood, which may have been gathered from the woodland floor or may have been stockpiled. Ring curvature, along with other factors, can denote whether the charcoal is derived from smaller or larger branches (Fig. I.1).

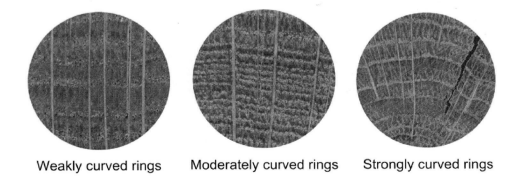

Weakly curved rings   Moderately curved rings   Strongly curved rings

Fig. I.1—Test card for curvature of rings (after Marguerie and Hunot 2007, 1421).

[1] Margaret Gowen and Co. Ltd, 27 Merrion Square, Dublin 2.

Tyloses in vessels in species such as oak can denote the presence of heartwood. These occur when adjacent parenchyma cells penetrate the vessel walls (via the pitting), effectively blocking the vessels (Gale 2003, 37). In all cases it is assumed that the wood identified represents the native Irish species.

Results

Eleven wood taxa were identified from the Rath of the Synods material. The results were dominated by ash (*Fraxinus excelsior*), oak (*Quercus* sp.) and hazel (*Corylus avellana*) (Fig. I.2). Smaller amounts of alder (*Alnus glutinosa*), blackthorn (*Prunus spinosa*), cherry (*Prunus avium*), elm (*Ulmus glabra*), holly (*Ilex aquifolium*), pomaceous fruitwood (Pomoideae), spindle (*Euonymus europaeus*) and willow (*Salix* spp) were also identified. Ash was present in 23 of the samples, hazel in fifteen, oak in thirteen and elm in

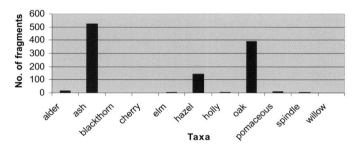

Fig. I.2—Total charcoal identifications from the Rath of the Synods.

seven. Figure I.3 shows that ash dominated twelve of the samples while oak dominated eight. Hazel was the main wood identified in six of the samples. The results will be discussed by phase.

Phase 1
Sample 90—This came from somewhere within the primary ditch (F260). Carbonised ash branches only were identified from this sample, up to 15mm in radius. An ash sample produced a date of AD 24–255 (UBA-8529; see Appendix J), suggesting that this material is from a disturbed context as it dates from the late middle Iron Age.

Phase 2
Sample 36—Hazel, ash, oak and willow were identified from palisade trench D2 (F144). All of the pieces had strongly curved rings, probably representing branches, and were of medium to fast growth. An oak sample produced a date of AD 86–249 (UBA-8527; see Appendix J) during the late middle Iron Age, suggesting that this may be a disturbed context.

Sample 47—Ash and hazel were identified in this sample from palisade trench D (F142). Oak was the main wood present; it was derived from heartwood with tyloses and weakly curved annual rings, with up to twenty annual rings remaining (Pl. 5). The ash fragments were also slow-grown.

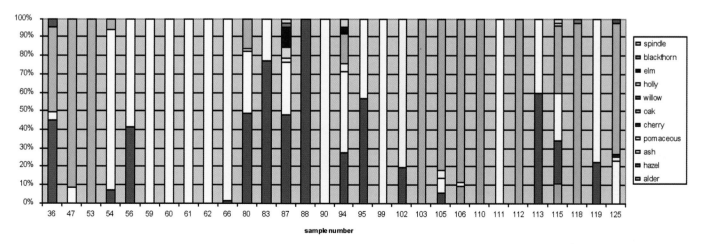

Fig. I.3—Charcoal identifications per sample.

Pl. 5—Slow-grown oak heartwood. Sample 47 (x8).

Sample 60—Small (less than 10mm) fragments of oak only were identified from a palisade trench inside the inner bank, indicating that the palisade may have been constructed from oak. The pieces were too small to determine whether they represented heartwood or branches.

Sample 61—This was from a large bed of charcoal representing one post in palisade trench E (F145). Ash fragments up to 30mm in radius with strongly curved annual rings were present in this sample. The pieces were of slow to medium regular growth and up to fifteen years old at least. A sample produced a date of AD 21–210 (UBA-8528; see Appendix J), suggesting that this feature belongs to a later period.

Sample 80—This sample was derived from a black spread inside the inner bank in palisade trench D (F142). Ash, oak, hazel and pomaceous fruitwood were present. The ash branches were slow- to medium-grown and had up to fifteen annual rings remaining. The hazel branches contained insect holes, suggesting that they were quite degraded when burnt.

Sample 83—Ash and hazel were identified from this sample, which was taken from palisade trench D2 (F144). Both species were derived from medium-grown branches; the hazel pieces had insect holes.

Sample 94—Ash, hazel, oak, pomaceous fruitwood,

elm and spindle tree were identified from palisade trench D2 (F144). The identifications were dominated by ash and hazel branches, both of medium growth. The elm fragments were fast-grown.

Sample 110—A small amount of alder charcoal was identified from the inner bank of palisade trench C (F4). The three fragments probably represent the same piece, as they were all fast-grown. The presence of insect holes suggests that the wood was decayed and degraded when burnt.

Sample 112—This charcoal sample was taken from a post-hole in the burnt area between trenches A and B, possibly a continuation of palisade trench D (F142). Oak only was identified, suggesting that it represents an oak post burnt *in situ.* The rectangular pieces were of medium growth; the weakly curved rings and the lack of tyloses suggest the use of branches rather than oak heartwood.

Sample 113—Ash roundwoods and pieces from larger hazel branches were identified from the fill of palisade trench D2 (F144). The hazel pieces were quite degraded, with many insect holes. The ash fragments were medium- to slow-grown. Both taxa had up to eight annual rings remaining.

Sample 115—Six wood taxa, dominated by oak, hazel and ash, were identified from palisade trench D1 (F143). Alder, holly and spindle were also noted in small quantities. The medium-grown hazel fragments represented both smaller and larger branches, while the ash pieces were fast-grown and contained insect holes. In one case a worm was still intact in the ash fragment (Pl. 6). An alder sample produced an early Iron Age date of 765–416 BC (UBA-8530; see Appendix J), indicating that this feature contained material incorporated from an earlier phase of activity.

Phase 3

Sample 88—This sample of burnt clay taken from the centre of a barrow in cutting 5 had a very low charcoal content. One fragment of hazel only was identified. This produced a date of 3366–3104 BC (UBA-8532), suggesting residual late Neolithic material from beneath the barrow.

Pl. 6—Worm still intact in ash fragment. Sample 115 (x8).

Pl. 7—Strongly curved annual rings in ash. Sample 62 (x8).

Sample 103—Oak only was identified from this sample, taken from a pit (F163). The pieces were slow-grown, with up to fifteen annual rings. The presence of tyloses and weakly curved annual rings indicates that it was derived from heartwood. An oak sample produced a middle Iron Age date of 359–176 BC (UBA-8538; see Appendix J).

Sample 106—The soil for this sample came from a post-hole (F103) under the eastern baulk. Slow-grown oak heartwood and fast-grown alder branches with insect holes were identified. One fragment of ash was also present. An oak sample produced a date of 372–197 BC (UBA-8539; see Appendix J).

Phase 4

Sample 53—This sample was taken from a pit (F157) to the north of burial I with possible metalworking debris. Large fragments (32mm x 40mm x 5mm) of slow-grown oak heartwood with up to twenty annual rings were identified. An oak sample produced a determination of 169 BC–AD 1 (UBA-8534; see Appendix J), indicating a late middle Iron Age date for this feature.

Sample 54—Medium-grown branches of oak, hazel and ash were identified from ash-pit F5 near burial I.

Sample 56—Hazel and ash branches, both of medium to fast growth, were noted from another sample from F5. An ash sample produced a final Iron Age date of AD 259–412 (UBA-8535; see Appendix J).

Sample 59—Ash wood only was identified from the final sample from ash-pit F5. The strongly curved annual rings suggest that this is what remains of an ash branch. Some of the fragments had up to 45 annual rings remaining, which were of medium growth. An ash sample produced a date of AD 257–400 (UBA-8536; see Appendix J).

Sample 62—Large, strongly curved ash fragments only were identified from the charcoal-rich fill of the inner ditch (F31). The pieces were up to 40mm in radius, and were of medium growth (Pl. 7).

Sample 66—Ash roundwoods of mixed growth, with up to twenty annual rings remaining, dominated this sample from the fosse. One hazel fragment, of 10mm radius, was also identified.

Sample 87—Soil from a 2m cutting into rampart 1 contained the largest variety of wood taxa from the site, including hazel, holly, elm, ash, blackthorn, spindle and the pomaceous fruitwood type. Slow-grown, insect-degraded hazel branches dominated the sample. The holly fragments were also slow-grown. In contrast, the ash branches were fast-grown.

Sample 95—Hazel and ash were present in this burnt

pit fill (F5). The remaining hazel fragments were large, up to 20mm in radius, with up to fifteen annual rings remaining. Insect holes were also present, suggesting that the wood was left exposed for a period before being burnt. The ash fragments were also relatively large, up to 20mm in radius. The hazel pieces showed medium growth, while the ash fragments were fast-grown.

Sample 99—Ash only was identified from this post-hole (F62) in the central area of structure F20. The sample represents probably one ash branch, which had strongly curved annual rings and grew at a medium rate. An ash sample produced a final Iron Age date of AD 259–412 (UBA-8537; see Appendix J).

Sample 102—Five fragments of hazel and pomaceous fruitwood only were identifiable from this hard, stony layer within structure F20.

Sample 105—This was derived from post-hole and pit fills from structure F20. The sample contained mainly oak, with some pomaceous fruitwood, ash and hazel. The oak fragments most likely represent heartwood. Insect holes remained on both the ash and hazel fragments.

Sample 111—Fifteen fragments of ash branches were identified from the fill of the inner ditch (F31) of the residential enclosure. An ash sample produced a date of AD 77–216 (UBA-8540; see Appendix J).

Sample 118—Oak, with one fragment of blackthorn, was present in this sample. It may represent structural material as it is from the slot-trench of structure F20. The slow-grown oak heartwood would have been suitable for building owing to its strength and durability. An oak sample produced a date of 359–179 BC (UBA-8541; see Appendix J).

Sample 119—Ash and hazel fragments were identified from this pit (F5), which also contained remnants of bone. The ash and hazel fragments were slow-grown and both were probably derived from branches. Insect holes remained on the hazel fragments.

Sample 125—This sample from a pit (F158) contained oak, ash, pomaceous fruitwood, willow and wild/bird cherry. The sample was dominated by oak fragments, up to 20mm in size and slow-grown. Weakly curved rings and the presence of tyloses in the vessels indicate oak heartwood. In contrast, the strongly curving rings in the hazel fragments indicate that branches were burnt. An oak sample from this pit produced a date of AD 414–540 (UBA-8533; see Appendix J), suggesting at least some disturbance after phase 4.

Discussion

The charcoal identifications provide insight into the timbers selected for construction at the Rath of the Synods. Oak and ash appear to have been the two main structural materials used. A post from phase 2, sample 61, was made probably from one ash piece. The use of ash seems to have continued on into phase 4, as sample 99 also consisted of ash. It seems that the palisade inside the inner bank (phase 2) may also have been constructed from this tree, as ash only was identified from sample 60. Oak was also favoured, however. From phase 2, charcoal from a post-hole in a spread of burnt material in palisade trench D (F142) was identified as oak (sample 112), while oak alone was also identified from the central area of the 'house' slot-trench (sample 118, phase 4). One sample (103) from phase 3 contained oak only; it is described as being from a pit (F163) but may represent an oak post. Ash and oak were frequently chosen for building in both the prehistoric and historic periods. At the late Bronze Age site of Clonfinlough, Co. Offaly, ash was the only species used for the palisade (Moloney et al. 1993). Oak was used during the Neolithic period for structures at Kilgobbin, Co. Dublin, and was then supplemented by ash during the Bronze Age (O'Carroll 2004).

Multiple samples (54, 56, 59) were taken from the ash-pit, F5 (phase 4). Ash only was identified in one (S59), hazel and ash in another (S56), and ash, hazel and oak in the final one (S54). This shows the usefulness of multiple sampling from the different fills of one feature, as a sample from one fill alone may not be representative of all the possible taxa in a feature.

Sample 53 came from the fill of pit F157, which included possible metalworking debris and burnt clay (phase 4). This contained slow-grown oak heartwood only. It is likely that the oak heartwood was used in the smelting process. Generally, oak was the preferred fuel for smelting. Bowl furnaces from early medieval sites excavated at Kiltenan South (02E0574) and at Aghamore (02E0869), Co. Limerick, were probably used for smelting iron slag and the charcoal was dominated by oak. A possible furnace of similar date at Dollas Lower (02E0631), Co. Limerick, also contained mainly oak. At Doohylemore (02E0634), Co. Limerick, a possible metal-making furnace contained mainly oak (Grogan *et al.* 2007). Gale's (2003, 37) results from 24 sites associated with iron-smelting indicate that oak was consistently the dominant fuel from the early Iron Age to the mid-medieval period in England. McCracken (1971, 92) writes that ideally the best charcoal for smelting comes from 25-year-old coppice oak, and that in England the ironmasters practised coppicing to ensure a continuous supply. An acre of coppice gave enough fuel to make a ton of iron every 25 years.

It was not within the scope of this project to measure all the ring widths on the charcoal with a graticule, but some measurements were taken in order to make the scale of slow, medium and fast growth less subjective. Slow growth from this site was considered to be approximately 0.4mm per annum, medium approximately 1mm per annum and fast approximately 2.2mm per annum. In almost all cases the oak pieces were slow-grown, suggesting that optimum conditions for oak growth did not occur around the site. In contrast, ash was almost consistently fast-grown. This indicates that the soil in the area was quite nutrient-rich, a pre-requisite of fast-grown ash, which probably made it suitable for arable agriculture. Growth in the hazel pieces was generally medium. Many of the hazel pieces and some ash contained insect holes, which suggests the gathering of rotten wood from the woodland floor or possibly the stockpiling of fuel.

The Rath of the Synods landscape during the Iron Age

One sample was examined from phase 1 and this contained ash. The eleven samples examined from phase 2 yielded nine of the eleven wood taxa identified from the site. Ash, hazel and oak were the main trees represented overall. Only three samples were analysed from phase 3; hazel, alder, oak and ash were present. Oak and ash were the most important trees, although it is difficult to generalise from only three samples. The greatest number of samples (fifteen) were analysed from phase 4. Ten wood taxa were identified, and neither alder nor birch was present.

The environmental results from the Rath of the Synods present a picture of a mixed woodland dynamic through the centuries. Ash, oak and hazel dominated the charcoal results overall and within phase 2 and phase 4, the source of most of the identifications. There was also a good representation of smaller scrub and shrub trees, such as holly, the pomaceous fruitwood type, cherry and blackthorn/sloe. This suggests that this particular area in Meath was not populated by closed-canopy woodland during the Iron Age.

Oak, ash and hazel are often found together in Irish charcoal assemblages. It is likely that the charcoal from the Rath of the Synods represents an oak, ash and elm woodland, with an understorey of hazel or associated hazel scrub. Ireland has two native oaks, pedunculate (*Quercus robur*) and sessile (*Quercus petraea*). The pedunculate oak will grow in heavy, relatively wet lowland soils, where it will tolerate flooding. In contrast, the sessile oak prefers less fertile, acidic soils (Beckett 1979). Oak and hazel are often found in association with each other. In oak woods hazel will grow as an understorey to oak, providing that there is sufficient light. It can also grow as scrub. Values for hazel have been consistently high in Ireland during the prehistoric period; indeed, McCracken (1971, 19) remarks that 'it was once widespread to a degree that is hard to imagine today'. While ash can grow in wet areas, it will not tolerate permanently waterlogged situations, unlike alder. It requires light to flourish, and only became common in Ireland once the great tracts of oak began to be cleared during the Neolithic. Elm trees will grow on rich, alluvial soils, particularly riverine habitats (Gale and Cutler 2000, 164). The evergreen holly tolerates heavy shade, and so can sometimes be found growing in the understorey of oak woodlands (*ibid.*, 139).

There is evidence for various smaller shrubs and

trees, many of which need light to grow, indicating that the Meath landscape in the vicinity of the site did not consist only of larger-canopy trees. Blackthorn or sloe can be seen in woodland where the canopy is opened, on woodland margins, in scrub and along streams, where it may be found with alder (Orme and Coles 1985, 11). While cherry will tolerate some shade, it also prefers light (Stuijts 2005, 141). The spindle tree can be found growing in marginal woodland and scrub (Gale and Cutler 2000, 107).

The pomaceous fruitwood type includes pear (*Pyrus*), hawthorn (*Crataegus*), rowan (*Sorbus*) and apple (*Malus*). It is unlikely that the pomaceous fruitwood represents pear, as it is not native (Nelson 1993). Hawthorn is shade-tolerant and can frequently be found in Irish hedgerows (Gale and Cutler 2000). Mountain ash is also a common Irish tree, growing well in rocky and mountainous places (Nelson 1993). Both hawthorn and apple-type (*Malus* sp.) produce edible fruits that could have been gathered as foodstuff. These wood types burn slowly and steadily, and provide excellent heat with minimal smoke (Gale and Cutler 2000).

There is also evidence that the site was located near to a water source. Alder was identified in four of the samples. Ireland's native alder is black or grey alder, *Alnus glutinosa*. It commonly grows in wet, waterlogged areas, and will frequently be seen beside rivers or streams. Willow (present in two samples) also prefers to grow in wet areas (Orme and Coles 1985). The main Irish native willows are grey willow (*Salix cinerea*), goat willow (*Salix caprea*) and eared willow (*Salix aurita*).

Pollen analysis conducted at Emlagh bog near Kells, Co. Meath (Newman *et al.* 2007, 358), showed evidence for phases of woodland regeneration and clearance from the end of the third century BC, along with sustained and substantial farming activity. During the period represented by the Rath of the Synods (stretching from the first century AD to approximately the third century AD) there is an expansion of woodland, particularly hazel, ash, elm and yew, on the pollen diagram. Oak is also present (zone C, AD 20–500). The authors interpret this part of the diagram as regeneration of woody vegetation in response to a substantial reduction in farming, followed by initiation of woodland clearance as farming activity increased substantially (*ibid.*). There is a wide diversity of woody plants in the pollen records. The authors note that the 'Late Iron Age Lull' was first described by Mitchell (1965) from the Little Bog complex, indicating that there was a substantial reduction (but not a complete abandonment) of farming during this period. The sequence from Emlagh bog agrees with this (Newman *et al.* 2007, 358). Charcoal from burial-pit fills dates from approximately the third to the fifth century AD. Like the Rath of the Synods charcoal, these were dominated by hazel, oak and ash. While both yew and pine are noted in the pollen record, there are no conifers in the charcoal assemblage (*ibid.*, 359), nor in the Rath of the Synods assemblage. Birch charcoal was also absent from the Emlagh bog charcoal assemblage, which was also the case with the Rath of the Synods identifications.

Charcoal from three Iron Age samples from sites excavated along the Gas Pipeline to the West, extending from Dublin to Limerick, indicated that ash and hazel were important fuels. At the Iron Age levels at Lemanaghan, Co. Offaly, ash and hazel were again dominant (Ellen O'Carroll, pers. comm.; Grogan *et al.* 2007, 51).

Summary

Charcoal was examined from 30 samples from four phases at the Rath of the Synods; 1,101 fragments were identified in total. The results were dominated by ash, hazel and oak. No particular differences were noted between phase 2 and phase 4, which provided most of the samples. The charcoal analysis suggests that the site lay within a mosaic of woodland environments. It was probably located in a relatively open area during the Iron Age, with larger-canopy trees such as oak, elm and ash, and smaller scrubs such as the pomaceous fruitwood, blackthorn and cherry. It is likely that a river or a stream flowed nearby, close to which wetland trees such as alder and willow could grow. The results compare very well to charcoal and pollen analysis from Emlagh bog, near Kells, from the same period. Ash and oak were the preferred trees used for building at the Rath of the Synods. A pit with probable metalworking debris was filled with oak, which compares well with other archaeological sites; oak is frequently found associated with metalworking because of its high calorific value and the fact that it can achieve high temperatures while burning. In some instances the species were chosen carefully, such as oak for building, as it is strong and durable, and for smelting; in other cases a variety of probably randomly gathered fuel was burnt, such as holly, pomaceous fruitwood, alder and spindle.

APPENDIX J

RADIOCARBON DATES FROM THE RATH OF THE SYNODS[1]

Eoin Grogan and Muiris O'Sullivan

Introduction

As indicated above, the assessment of the Rath of the Synods proceeded, from Seán P. Ó Ríordáin's initial analysis of the excavation archive until 2008, without any radiocarbon determinations. This reflected two major concerns.

(1) The site had been excavated in a pre-radiocarbon-dating period, and the treatment, recording and storage of samples, retained mainly for simple palaeoenvironmental analysis, could not be considered secure. As none of those involved with the publication process had participated in the excavation, the extraction of clearly identified samples with specific contexts was an uncertain process.

(2) The site was very complex, and the virtual absence of horizontal stratigraphy required the grouping of some features on the basis of their probable rather than their certain association. On this basis it was considered that dating might reflect small-scale or even very short-term actions on site rather than accurate dates for major activities.

That position continued until the rediscovery (thanks to Lorraine Buckley) of some of the inhumation burials. It is unfortunate that it has not been possible to recover any of the cremations. Nevertheless, it was decided to proceed with dating some of the apparently more secure samples on the basis that they might provide a broad chronological framework for some of the major components of the Rath of the Synods complex. The results, as was anticipated, are fraught with difficulty. Nevertheless, the dates provide some important insights into the site and, in some cases, significant evidence to reassess part of the major phasing—for example, the discovery that the inhumation burials, previously thought to represent a short, homogeneous phase, actually represent a lengthy period of burial extending into the medieval period.

The general stratigraphic evidence

Notwithstanding the radiocarbon dates, three broad statements are borne out by the archaeological record.

(1) The primary ditch (F260) underlies activity represented by the main palisade trenches and the phase 3 enclosure.

(2) The main complex of palisade trenches underlies the phase 3 enclosure.

(3) All of the stages of the barrow construction and remodelling pre-date the phase 3 enclosure.

These general aspects of the site appear to be irrefutable, but that does not mean that all of the features ascribed to them in the report are securely associated: for example, the date of AD 24–255 (UBA-8529, 1898 ± 41 BP) from an unspecified fill in the primary ditch (F260). It is clear that this represents disturbance related to phase 3 activity rather than providing a date for the ditch itself.

---

[1] All dates cited here refer to calibrated results from radiocarbon determinations.

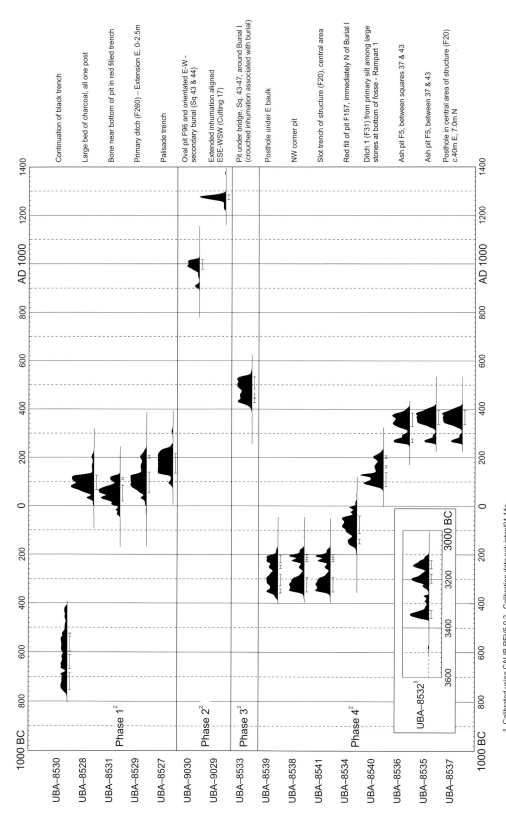

Continuation of black trench

Large bed of charcoal, all one post

Bone near bottom of pit in red filled trench

Primary ditch (F260) – Extension E, 0-2.5m

Palisade trench

Oval pit F96 and orientated E-W - secondary burial (Sq 43 & 44)

Extended inhumation aligned ESE-WSW (Cutting 17)

Pit under bridge, Sq. 43-47, around Burial I (crouched inhumation associated with burial)

Posthole under E baulk

NW corner pit

Slot trench of structure (F20), central area

Red fill of pit F157, immediately N of Burial I

Ditch 1 (F31) from primary silt among large stones at bottom of fosse - Rampart 1

Ash pit F5, between squares 37 & 43

Ash pit F5, between 37 & 43

Posthole in central area of structure (F20) c.40m E, 7.0m N

1. Calibrated using CALIB REV5.0.2. Calibration data set: intcal04.14c.
2. See text for discussion of phasing and radiocarbon dating results.
3. UBA–8532 Centre/core of barrow, in what seems to be undisturbed area under large stones.

Fig. J.1—Rath of the Synods calibrated date probability distributions.

142

Table J.1—Radiocarbon series from the Rath of the Synods.

¹⁴Chrono Centre QUB ref. no.	E615 sample no.	Material	Location as per sample label	Location clarification as per '07 report	C14 determination	E.G. phase	Calibrated C14 date	Comment
UBA-8527	36	Quercus charcoal	From palisade trench (trench D2)	One of slot-trench arcs	1833±30 BP	2	AD 86–249	Broadly contemporary with 61, 90 and 111, but not all these dates are likely to reflect the primary phase of features in question.
UBA-8528	61	Fraxinus charcoal	Large bed of charcoal, all one post (trench E)	One of slot-trench arcs	1910±30 BP	2	AD 21–210	Broadly contemporary with 36, 90 and 111, but not all these dates are likely to reflect the primary phase of features in question.
UBA-8529	90	Fraxinus charcoal	Primary ditch (F260)—extension E, 0–2.5m	Undated central ditch cut by slot-trenches	1898±41 BP	1	AD 24–255	Broadly contemporary with 36, 61 and 111, but not all these dates are likely to reflect the primary phase of features in question, notably F260.
UBA-8530	115	Alnus charcoal	Continuation of black trench (trench D1)	One of slot-trench arcs	2474±33 BP	2	765–416 BC	Seems improbably early for one of the enclosure palisades but similar dates came from Lismullin.
UBA-8531	123	Corylus charcoal	Near bottom of pit in red-filled trench (trench B)	One of slot-trench arcs	1944±33 BP	2	36 BC–AD 128	Close spatial relationship with trench B.
UBA-8532	88	Corylus charcoal	Centre/core of barrow, in what seems to be undisturbed area under large stones	Difficult to unravel	4545±30 BP	3	3366–3104 BC	May date primary phase of barrow, but may also reflect earlier activity on OGL beneath barrow.
UBA-8533	125	Quercus charcoal	Pit under bridge, sqs 43–47, around bur. 1 (crouched inhumation associated with burial)	Charcoal from the pit in which a crouched inhumation (burial 1) occurred	1691±20 BP	3	AD 414–540	Problem re precise context of this sample, as squares 43 and 47 are not adjacent. Squares 43 and 37 are adjacent, but this is some distance from bur. 1, although plausibly near burial B.
UBA-8534	53	Quercus charcoal	Red fill of pit F157, immediately N of bur. 1		2062±30 BP	4	169 BC–AD 1	Close spatial relationship with trench B and reflects the expected date for this phase.
UBA-8535	56	Fraxinus charcoal	Ash pit (F5), between squares 37 and 43		1692±20 BP	4	AD 259–412	Activity in the third and fourth centuries AD.
UBA-8536	59	Fraxinus charcoal	Ash pit (F5), between squares 37 and 43		1707±20 BP	4	AD 257–400	Activity in the third and fourth centuries AD.
UBA-8537	99	Fraxinus charcoal	Post-hole in central area of structure (F20) c. 0.4mE, 7mN	'Houses'—see sample 118 above	1691±20 BP	4	AD 259–412	Activity in the third and fourth centuries AD.
UBA-8538	103	Quercus charcoal	NW corner pit		2184±23 BP	4	359–176 BC	Very tight-knit group with 106 and 118. Show activity near S edge of post circle, possibly including features previously ascribed to phase 4.
UBA-8539	106	Quercus charcoal	Post-hole under E baulk		2202±28 BP	4	372–197 BC	Very tight-knit group with 103 and 118. Show activity near S edge of post circle, possibly including features previously ascribed to phase 4.
UBA-8540	111	Fraxinus charcoal	Ditch 1 (F31) from primary silt amongst large stones at base of fosse—rampart 1	Inner ditch of multivallate enclosure	1872±22 BP	4	AD 77–216	Broadly contemporary with 35, 61 and 90, but not all these dates are likely to reflect the primary phase of features in question.
UBA-8541	118	Quercus charcoal	Slot-trench of structure (F20), central area	Structure F20 interpreted as a post-built house (Fig. 4.2)	2186±22 BP	4	359–179 BC	Very tight-knit group with 103 and 106. Show activity near S edge of post circle, possibly including features previously ascribed to phase 4.
UBA-9030	Bur. H	Human bone from extended inhumation	Burial H	In cluster of burials—central area	1055±26 BP	3	AD 899–919, AD 949–1023	
UBA-9029	Bur. D	Human bone from extended inhumation	Burial D	Isolated, north of main cluster of burials	732±28 BP	3	AD 1227–1294	

Likewise, UBA-8539 (372–197 cal. BC, 2202 ± 28 BP) is recorded as being from a 'post-hole under E baulk' of sq. 36: this feature does not, however, appear on any ground-plans.

Pre-phase 1

There are two dates that indicate activity at the Rath of the Synods apparently pre-dating the available archaeological evidence. A sample from what appears in the record to be beneath the primary stone core of the barrow produced a date of 3366–3104 BC (UBA-8532, 4545 ± 30 BP). While it is not impossible that this dates from the primary construction of the barrow itself, such a monument would be difficult to parallel in the Irish record at this period. It is more probably reflective of activity associated with the middle Neolithic construction and use of the nearby Mound of the Hostages (O'Sullivan 2005).

A date of 765–416 BC (UBA-8530, 2474 ± 33 BP) came from trench D1 (F143): this is stratigraphically earlier than the main phase of enclosure D and appeared to be cut by trench D (F142) (Fig. 2.9). This area produced what appears to be a complex series of intercutting trenches, not all of which were clearly elucidated in either the excavation record or the report. It does not appear probable, given the wider dating of palisade enclosures such as those at Navan Fort and Dún Ailinne, that the tight-knit complex of enclosures at the Rath of the Synods dates from this early phase of the Iron Age. In addition, trench D1 cuts the edge of the primary ditch (F260) at this point and the date may reflect this disturbance of earlier deposits in the ditch. What makes the date interesting, however, is the possibility of activity on the site at this stage, given the dating of the recently excavated post enclosure at Lismullin to c. 520–380/490–370 BC (O'Connell 2007).

Phase 1: the primary ditch

Other than the possibility that the date from trench D1 (discussed above) might be derived from the fill of the primary ditch (F260), there are no dates for this phase.

Phase 1: the palisade enclosures

There are no dates from specific features assigned in the report to this phase. There are, however, five dates from contexts within the phase 1 complex that may be relevant. Three of these, UBA-8538, UBA-8539 and UBA-8541, form a very tight-knit group, notwithstanding that they are all oak dates. They are from the slot (F21) on the western side of structure C20 (ascribed to phase 3) close to the southern edge of the post circle, a pit (F162) that cuts palisade trench F102 (which crosses the presumed entrance to enclosure B), and a 'post-hole under the east baulk' of sq. 36. Regrettably, it is not possible to identify this post-hole. The range of these dates suggests activity dating from c. 350–200 BC, although the oak source requires that these results be treated with caution.

UBA-8538 E615:103 (*Quercus*) 359–176 cal. BC (2184 ± 23 BP)
From north-west corner pit (F162), sq. 36.
UBA-8539 E615:106 (*Quercus*) 372–197 cal. BC (2202 ± 28 BP)
From post-hole under east baulk, sq. 36.
UBA-8541 E615:118 (*Quercus*) 359–179 cal. BC (2186 ± 22 BP)
From slot-trench F21, structure C20.

While it is tempting to associate these dates with the phase 1 enclosures, particularly in view of the general chronology proposed in Chapter 3, there is no direct link between these features and those of the palisade trenches or the post circle. It is possible that UBA-8538 is derived from material disturbed from trench F102, while UBA-8541 could be from material disturbed from post-hole F116 of the post circle, which is cut by trench F21.

What is worth noting here is the presence of broadly contemporary activity at Rath na Ríogh (*Ráith na Ríg*), in particular the ironworking and other industrial activity, and possibly the construction of the great, so-called 'royal', enclosure (Roche 2002, 56–77, table 1).

Two further dates may refer to activity in phase 1. The sample (S123) that produced UBA-8531 is recorded as 'fragments of charcoal near pit bottom in the red filled trench' (palisade trench B). It has not been possible to further identify this feature: only two pits (F98 and F103), forming the termini on either side of the entrance, are shown in the site records as being associated

Table J.2—Summary analysis of the chronology in the main report, informed by the results from the radiocarbon programme.

Main report phase	Main report: suggested date	Features	C14 perspective	Comment
4	Late second–early fourth centuries AD	Residential enclosure and associated 'houses' etc.	Ash sample from primary silt at the bottom of the inner ditch of the enclosure yielded a C14 date calibrating to the first–second century AD. Slot-trench from house gave date of fourth–second centuries BC, but other C14 samples from within the house and a nearby ash pit date from the third–fourth century AD.	Possibly more complex than envisioned, but broadly consistent with relative chronology.
3	First century BC–first/second century AD on basis of dearth of artefacts and mixture of inhumation/cremation burials	Barrow and flat cemetery	Two samples from extended inhumations (H and D) gave dates in the tenth and thirteenth centuries AD respectively. Crouched inhumations, cremations and barrow might date from other periods (see sample 125).	The chronology here is probably more complex than envisioned and the various features are unlikely to date from a single phase.
2	*c.* 100 BC	Slot-trench enclosures	Three dates spanning the late first century BC to the early third century AD, with one very early (LBA/EIA) date.	Main group generally a little later than envisioned, but consistent with relative chronology.
1	Pre-dates slot-trench palisaded enclosures	Primary ditched enclosure	Only direct date appears to be from a secondary feature in the fill, but features within the enclosure yielded dates in the range fourth–second centuries BC.	Still unclear, but consistent with envisioned relative chronology.
N/A	N/A	Charcoal, base of barrow	Mid-Neolithic: 3366–3104 BC.	Cf. the Mound of the Hostages.

with the trench. While the sample may be from one of these, there are later pits, such as F17 and F158, that partly cut the trench. UBA-8534 is from the fill of a pit (F157) that is immediately north of, and may cut, trench B.

UBA-8531 E615:123 (*Corylus*)36 cal. BC–cal. AD 128 (1944 ± 33 BP)   Charcoal, pit bottom in trench B.

UBA-8534 E615:53 (*Quercus*) 169 cal. BC–cal. AD 1 (2062 ± 30 BP)   Red fill of pit F157, north of burial I.

Phase 1 summary

While these five dates demonstrate activity on the site in the middle part of the Iron Age, they do not present a coherent group. UBA-8538, UBA-8539 and UBA-8541 form an impressive cluster, but as they are derived from oak heartwood (with up to fifteen rings identified; O'Donnell, Appendix I) the reliability of the actual date is very doubtful. Furthermore, their date ranges do not overlap with either UBA-8531 or UBA-8534. The latter date ranges overlap only slightly, and UBA-8534 is from oak heartwood (with up to twenty rings identified; O'Donnell, Appendix I) and may represent very much later activity.

The late Iron Age/early medieval period: phase 2 burials

There are three dates that refer to this phase: UBA-8533, UBA-9029 and UBA-9030. There is some confusion regarding UBA-8533: squares 43 and 47 are not adjacent to each other, so we take this to be an error and the record should read 43 and <u>37</u>. While this would place the context at some distance from burial I, it seems certain to refer to burial B, which is in this area. In any case, both burials B and I are crouched inhumations. The date, cal. AD 414–540 (1691 ± 20 BP), is improbably, although admittedly not impossibly, late: once again, however, the identification of the oak from this sample (S125) indicates that it is heartwood and therefore extremely unreliable for radiocarbon analysis. Furthermore, the association with the burial is very uncertain, as the sample is identified as coming from the grave fill but is not clearly recorded as being directly associated with the burial itself.

UBA-8533 E615:125 (*Quercus*) cal. AD 414–540 (1691 ± 20 BP) From pit under bridge, sq. 43–47, around burial I (crouched inhumation). Not I, probably B.

UBA-9030 Human bone cal. AD 899–919 (1055 ± 26 BP), cal. AD 949–1023
Burial H, extended inhumation in main cluster of burials.

UBA-9029 Human bone cal. AD 1227–1294 (732 ± 28 BP)
Burial D: isolated extended inhumation 30m north of main cluster of burials.

UBA-9029 and UBA-9030, from bone samples from the extended inhumations D and H, are amongst the most reliable dates from the site. Burial H is among the main cluster of burials in the centre of the site, and the spatial relationship of the graves suggested a tight-knit and broadly contemporary cemetery. It appears, however, that this location may have been used, perhaps intermittently, for burial over a lengthy period. The undated cremations in this area—V, W and possibly others represented by samples 199/142—appear to represent burial in the prehistoric, and possibly the late Iron Age, period. If the date from burial B (UBA-8533) is accepted as a possible general indication for the inhumations, then it appears that there was a resumption of burial after the abandonment of the phase 3 residential enclosure (see below). The tenth-century date for burial H raises some important issues as by this time it appears that the Church had succeeded in restricting burial to recognised ecclesiastical cemeteries. Is it possible that, despite the absence of any historical records, a church site had been established at Tara, perhaps on the site of the later fifteenth- or sixteenth-century building immediately to the east of the Rath of the Synods (Newman 1997, 38–43)? This possibility might lend greater credence to the holding of synods here by Patrick, Rúadán and Adomnán (in 695; Byrne 1973, 54, 158).

The presence of the other, undated, crouched or flexed inhumation burials (E and I) in the immediate vicinity suggests the possibility that the site was a recognised, if only intermittently utilised, place of burial from an early date in the medieval period. Subsequently, perhaps with the establishment of more formal arrangements, it is possible that the cemetery was located closer to the church site. In this case it might be that burial H is on the western fringes of that putative cemetery. While the thirteenth-century extended inhumation (D) is located 30m to the north-east of the central burial cluster, it is, in fact, slightly closer to the modern churchyard and may be well within this cemetery.

Phase 2: summary

At a general level it is apparent that the area around the Rath of the Synods was considered an appropriate place for burial from the prehistoric period onwards. The barrow, with its associated cremations, was remodelled at least once, while the crouched inhumation (U), which may represent its final funerary use, suggests a link with similar burials in the main cluster. Cremations from other parts of the site, including V, W, A, F and G, indicate that an extensive area was used for funerary activity, although to label this a cemetery might be to over-emphasise what may have been the occasional funerary element in a much wider and more complex ritual arena.

What the radiocarbon dates for the inhumations at the Rath of the Synods do indicate is that there was probably not a discrete, compact phase of burial, nor is it now appropriate to consider this as pre-dating the residential enclosure. In short, there is no 'phase 2', and these burials should probably be viewed as representing a lengthy period of burial, possibly beginning as early as the sixth century and continuing, perhaps intermittently, into the medieval period.

Phase 3: the late Iron Age residential enclosure

The group of seven dates that appear to represent this phase form, at a general level, a cluster that reflects the proposed chronology. Within this there are two distinct clusters that indicate activity centred around *c.* AD 21–255: the oak charcoal date range (UB-8527) falls towards the end of this period, while the other three may indicate a more precise period of *c.* AD 50–150 (see Fig. J.1). Indeed, UB-8527 might, because of the potential

old wood effect, be more closely linked with the second group, UB-8535–8537, which are derived from the final occupation phase *c.* AD 257–412. The probability ranges for these may indicate a more exact date in the fourth century (Fig. J.1).

When these dates are related to the construction and occupation sequence of the residential enclosure some interesting, and potentially very important, patterns emerge. There are two clear construction phases represented by the archaeology. The first is the main construction of the trivallate enclosure—ditch 1/bank 1, ditch 2/bank 2, ditch 3/bank 3. UBA-8540 from the primary fill of ditch 1 (F31) suggests, as indicated above, that this occurred in the period *c.* AD 50–150. Contemporary activity within the inner enclosure is reflected by UBA-8528 and UBA-8529, and possibly also UBA-8531 (see above). The stratigraphic evidence demonstrates that the date, UBA-8529, from the primary ditch (F260) must reflect intrusive activity.

The most intriguing dates from the entire series are UBA-8527 and UBA-8528. The latter is 'from large bed of charcoal, all one post', identified as ash by O'Donnell (S61, Appendix I), which stood in palisade trench E (F145) in sq. 29.

Given the overall evidence, including some of the stratigraphic sequences, it is probable that these dates reflect intrusive activity in the phase 1 trenches. There is another possibility, however. The line of trench E follows, somewhat erratically, the curve of ditch 1 along the south-west side of the site (Fig. 2.1). The written records, supported by the evidence from section T–T[1] (Fig. 4.9), indicate that trench E was sealed beneath the (largely destroyed) bank 1 of the inner enclosure. Another section (L[1]–L[2], Fig. 4.5) shows a more ambiguous picture, however, and suggests that trench E may have been cut through at least the lower layers of the bank. Is it possible that this palisade was associated with the bank, possibly as a strengthening feature within the bank rather than a retaining palisade (given its proximity to the inner edge of ditch 1)? This is particularly interesting, as Ó Ríordáin himself considered this possible scenario, articulated most clearly in a reconstruction sketch. This interpretation is worth pursuing a little further in relation to trench D2 (F144) and UBA-8527. As we have seen, this is at face value contemporary with UBA-8528 (trench E); setting aside, for the moment, the possible old wood effect alluded to above, the position of this palisade trench follows, again erratically, the line of ditch 1, but perhaps more importantly it mirrors trench E very closely (Figs 2.1 and 2.9). Its path is 4.5–5.5m inside the edge of ditch 1 and might indicate an inner retaining palisade. A further possibility, given the oak sample for UBA–8527, is that trench D2 is a later replacement for trench E.

UBA-8527 E615:36 (*Quercus*) cal. AD 86–249 (1833 ± 30 BP) From palisade trench D2.

UBA-8528 E615:61 (*Fraxinus*) cal. AD 21–210 (1910 ± 30 BP) From single post, trench E.

UBA-8529 E615:90 (*Fraxinus*) cal. AD 24–255 (1898 ± 41 BP) Primary ditch (F260).

UBA-8540 E615:111 (*Fraxinus*) cal. AD 77–216 (1872 ± 22 BP) Ditch 1 (F31) from primary silt.

UBA-8535 E615:56 (*Fraxinus*) cal. AD 259–412 (1692 ± 20 BP) From ash pit F5, between sqs 37 and 43.

UBA-8536 E615:59 (*Fraxinus*) cal. AD 257–400 (1707 ± 20 BP) From ash pit F5, between sqs 37 and 43.

UBA-8537 E615:99 (*Fraxinus*) cal. AD 259–412 (1691 ± 20 BP) From post-hole in structure (F20).

Returning to the stratigraphic evidence, however, it is clear that trench D2 is sealed by a layer through which trench E is cut (Fig. 4.5, section L^1–L^2). The remaining evidence also tends to negate the idea of retaining palisades associated with bank 1 of phase 3, in particular the absence, apart from the possible short section (trench F, F137) on the east side, of any evidence for such features throughout the rest of the site. Furthermore, the projected lines of trenches D/D1/D2 and E indicate that these extend beyond the line of ditch 1 (F31) and should cut across it on the south-east side (Fig. 2.10).

The three other dates from the residential enclosure, UBA-8535, UBA-8536 and UBA-8537, appear to belong to the final occupation phase in the fourth century AD. UBA-8535 and UBA-8536 should probably be treated as one, given the dates and the context, but together these three dates indicate contemporary, if not synchronous, activity for two stratigraphically related features in phase 3. These are certainly entirely compatible with the archaeological evidence. It is possible that the modifications to the residential enclosure with the insertion of the secondary ditch (F228) and the subsidiary ditch (F227) occurred at this stage.

Conclusions

The radiocarbon evidence has certainly asked some pertinent questions of the archaeological interpretation of the Rath of the Synods. While the dates do not provide precision for the main identified phases, they do suggest continuous activity throughout the late prehistoric period, and perhaps indicate a more complex phasing in the middle Iron Age, *c.* 350–50 BC. The chronology of the residential enclosure suggested by the archaeological evidence is confirmed by the dates of *c.* AD 100–400, although the radiocarbon dates hint at two distinct phases of activity.

It is also clear that while cremation burial, including the barrow, may have been associated with phase 1, or possibly an intermediate stage between phases 1 and 3, the inhumations reflect a period of activity post-dating the abandonment of the residential enclosure. This phase appears to have started with the crouched and flexed burials, such as B, E and I, forming the core of a small cemetery, while the extended inhumation H may indicate a more formally Christian cemetery, possibly centred in the vicinity of the modern churchyard. At least occasional burial in this context continued into the medieval period.

As we have seen, however, there are a number of difficulties with individual dates and serious question marks over the precise context of others. Without further excavation that targets more exact dating material it is essential to use this current series with considerable caution. Nevertheless, these dates provide some interesting insights into the complex archaeology of the Rath of the Synods and provide a stimulus for further debate.

APPENDIX K

FINDS REGISTER

Kim Rice

Find	Material	Description	Context	Cutting	Sq.	Date	Phase	Appendix	Figure
E615:001	Ceramic	Base sherd, Central Gaulish	Uncontexted		6	Roman	3	G & H	Plate 4
E615:002	Glass	Glass setting	F142 (trench D)	16		Post-medieval	2	H	2.11 & Plate 1
E615:003a	Clay pipe	Two clay pipe stems (E615:3 & E615:3a)	Top of stone layer under humus						
E615:003b	Glass	Glass sherd	Uncontexted		1	Post-medieval	4	H	
E615:003c	Clay pipe	Stem	Uncontexted		1	Post-medieval	4	H	
E615:004	Iron	Fragment of iron with hollow stem	Sod		6		4	G & H	
E615:005	Ceramic	Roman pottery, body sherd. Fragment of mortarium	Sod		6	Roman		G & H	
E615:006	Iron	Oval penannular strip—possible scabbard mount	F143 (trench D1)		8		2	A	
E615:007a	Clay pipe	Bowl fragment	Depth of 0.36m		4	Post-medieval		H	
E615:007b	Flint	Flake	Uncontexted					D	
E615:008	Glass	Two body sherds	Uncontexted					H	
E615:009	Glass	Three body sherds	Uncontexted					H	
E615:010	Ceramic	Body sherd, Severn Valley ware	Ditch 1: layer 3, immediately under band of shale, sticky grey layer	1		Roman	4	G	Plate 2
E615:011	Iron	Blade fragment	Dark grey sticky fill near the base of ditch 1, rampart 1	2			4		
E615:012	Flint	Flake	Stony surface at outer edge of ditch 1, rampart 1	1				D	
E615:013	Flint	CANCELLED							
E615:014	Flint	Flake	Uncontexted					D	
E615:015	Stone	Fragment of polished stone axe, fine-grained volcanic stone	Uncontexted		3	Prehistoric	4	D	
E615:016	Iron	Square-sectioned stem	Uncontexted		9		2		
E615:017a	Ceramic	Base sherd, Central Gaulish	Uncontexted		8	Roman	3	G & H	Plate 4
E615:017b	Ceramic	Base sherd, Central Gaulish	Uncontexted		8	Roman	3	G & H	Plate 4
E615:018	Flint	Flake	Uncontexted		36		4		4.15
E615:018a	Flint	Utilised flake	Ditch 1	1			4		4.15
E615:018b	Chert	Nodule	Ditch 1	1			4	D	
E615:018c	Quartz	Two water-rolled quartz pebbles	Ditch 1	1			4		
E615:018d	Iron	Stem fragments	Ditch 1, close to charcoal spread, rampart 1	1			4		
E615:018i	Chert	Core	Uncontexted		36		4	D	
E615:018ii	Flint	Utilised flake	Uncontexted					D	
E615:018iii	Flint	Flake	Uncontexted					D	
E615:018iv	Chert	Utilised flake	Uncontexted					D	4.15
E615:019		CANCELLED							
E615:020		CANCELLED							
E615:021a	Copper alloy	Round-sectioned penannular ring with overlapping terminals, one tapered	Ditch 1 fill. Rampart 1. Found over F7	2				A	4.15

Find	Material	Description	Context	Cutting	Sq.	Date	Phase	Appendix	Figure
E615:021b	Copper alloy	Incomplete round-sectioned ring	Ditch 1 fill. Rampart 1. Found over F7	2				A	4.15
E615:021c	Copper alloy	Incomplete round-sectioned ring	Ditch 1 fill. Rampart 1. Found over F7	2					4.15
E615:022	Bone	Thin, pointed, chipped bone	Ditch 1, rampart 1	2			4	D	
E615:023		CANCELLED							
E615:024a	Flint	Unutilised flake fragment	Uncontexted						
E615:024b	Iron	Fragments with stone	Ditch 1, rampart 1	1					
E615:024c	Flint	Retouched flake	Ditch 1, rampart 1	1					
E615:025	Flint	Core rejuvenation flake	Uncontexted	15 (ext.)			4	D & H	
E615:025a	Flint	Utilised flake	Uncontexted		4			D	
E615:025b	Flint	Core	Uncontexted		8			H	
E615:026	Stone	Rim fragment of dressed sandstone bowl	F143 (trench D1)		7		2	A	2.11
E615:027	Stone	Section of shale undecorated oval-sectioned ring	Uncontexted				4	A & H	4.16 & Plate 1
E615:028	Flint	Flake	Secondary mound of barrow	5			3	D	
E615:029	Bone	Bone point	Ditch 1, rampart 1. In charcoal and white clay	2			4		
E615:030		CANCELLED							
E615:031	Chert	Flake fragment	Uncontexted	5				D	
E615:031a	Clay pipe	Four clay pipe stems	Uncontexted	5	10			H	
E615:031b	Iron	Fragments	Uncontexted	2	10			H	
E615:032a	Glass	Layered glass inset	Uncontexted	2		Roman		A	4.16 & Plate 1
E615:032b	Iron	Nail	Uncontexted					H	
E615:033a	Glass	Clear body sherd	Uncontexted					H	
E615:033b	Stone	Roof slate	Uncontexted					H	4.16
E615:034		CANCELLED							
E615:035	Ceramic	Body sherd, Severn Valley ware	Uncontexted: bank 3	4	5	1st–2nd C. AD		G & H	Plate 2
E615:036		CANCELLED							
E615:037	Flint	Flake	Dark fill of W post-hole. Enclosure S area	5			4	D	4.13
E615:038a	Iron	Fifteen fragments of stems and staples	Uncontexted			Post-medieval	3	H	
E615:038b	Ceramic	Stoneware, body sherd	Uncontexted				3	H	
E615:038c	Stone	Pair of pebbles					4		
E615:039a	Chert	Chip	Uncontexted	1				D	4.16
E615:039b	Stone	Roof slate	Uncontexted					H	
E615:040		CANCELLED							
E615:041	Iron	Corroded iron disc	In stony spill inside bank 3, rampart 3	4					
E615:042	Iron	Iron rods & whiskey pot sherds	Uncontexted	5					
E615:043		CANCELLED							
E615:044	Chert	Flake fragment	Under inner edge of bank 3, rampart 3	5				H	

Find	Material	Description	Context	Cutting	Sq.	Date	Phase	Appendix	Figure
E615:045	Iron	Corroded stem	Uncontexted		6		4	H	
E615:046	Stone	Hoard of 65 water-rolled pebbles	Uncontexted		9				
E615:047		CANCELLED							
E615:048		CANCELLED							
E615:049	Iron	Nail with rectangular section	Uncontexted	7	9		3	H	
E615:050		CANCELLED							
E615:051	Flint	Core rejuvenation flake	Uncontexted					D & H	
E615:052	Glass	Oval green glass with bevelled edge	Uncontexted					H	Plate 1
E615:053	Iron	Rectangular-sectioned stem fragment	Uncontexted: bank 2	2	6			H	
E615:054	Clay	Elliptical ball of burnt clay	F142 (trench D)		1	Iron Age	2		
E615:055	Stone	Smoothed siltstone cone	Uncontexted		1		4	H	
E615:056	Iron	Chisel, gouge	Uncontexted				4		
E615:057	Clay	Vitrified clay	F16		9		4		
E615:058	Ceramic	Modern pottery?	Uncontexted				3	H	
E615:059	Flint	Flake	Uncontexted	5			3	H	
E615:059i	Flint	Concave scraper						D	
E615:059ii	Flint	Core rejuvenation flake	Bottom of ditch 2, rampart 2	7				D	
E615:060	Stone	Polished red disc-shaped pebble	F145 (trench E)	1	10		2		
E615:061	Iron	Staple	F145 (trench E)				2		
E615:062	Iron	Corroded fragments of iron and small piece of amber	F142 or F144 (trench D/D2)		6		2		
E615:063	Chert	Core	Fill of ditch 1, rampart 1	8	11			D & H	
E615:064	Iron	Fragment of five-sided stem	Uncontexted						
E615:065	Stone	One half of two-piece oval mould of micaceous sandstone	Uncontexted	8				A & H	4.16
E615:066	Copper alloy	Incomplete shank of tapering pin or needle shank in two pieces	Bank 1. Deep black pit containing bone and charcoal, inside inner bank, rampart 1	2			4	A	4.15
E615:067	Ceramic	Roman—waster	Uncontexted: ditch 1	10	10	4th century AD	4	G & H	
E615:068	Ceramic	Body sherd, possibly Wilderspool ware	Fill of ditch 1, rampart 1					G	Plate 2
E615:069	Flint	Retouched flake	F4	13	10		1	D	2.11
E615:070a	Ceramic	Small ball of yellow ironstone/haematite	Uncontexted	13		Roman	3	G	
E615:070b	Glass	Body sherd of green glass	Uncontexted				3		
E615:071	Glass	Dark blue globular bead (Guido group 7iv)	Outside outer edge of ditch 1, rampart 1	8			4	A	4.15
E615:072a	Iron	Hooked rod with square section and hooked end	Uncontexted	10				H	
E615:072b	Glass	Two body sherds of blue/green glass	Uncontexted	10				H	
E615:073	Copper alloy	William and Mary halfpenny	Uncontexted		16	1698			
E615:074	Flint	Flake	Uncontexted	6			3	H	

Find	Material	Description	Context	Cutting	Sq.	Date	Phase	Appendix	Figure
E615:075	Stone	Thirty water-rolled pebbles worn from rubbing. Gaming pieces?	F142 (trench D)	2			2	H	
E615:076	Iron	Spatulate object	Uncontexted	5 & 8			4	H	
E615:077	Iron	Pointed stem	F142 (trench D)	2			2	H	
E615:078	Iron	Nail	Ditch 1, outer edge, rampart 1	8					
E615:079	Copper alloy	Semicircular object, possibly button	Uncontexted			Roman	3	H	
E615:080	Copper alloy	Victorian penny	Uncontexted	7			3	H	
E615:081	Iron	Incomplete square-sectioned nail with square head	Uncontexted	10			4	H	
E615:082	Iron	Pin or nail stem	F142 (trench D)				2	H	
E615:083	Iron	Blade	Secondary mound of barrow	12			3		
E615:084	Stone	Disc which has broken from circular-sectioned rod of sandstone (whetstone?)	Barrow	13			3	A	
E615:085	Ceramic	Stoneware, body sherds	Uncontexted	5		Post-medieval	3	H	
E615:086	Glass	Three body sherds of bubbled green glass	Uncontexted	12			3	H	
E615:087	Quartz	Flake	Uncontexted	9				H	
E615:088a	Silver	Modern silver plate terminal	Uncontexted	6			3	H	
E615:088b	Ceramic	Modern body sherd	Uncontexted	6			3	H	
E615:088c	Glass	Rim of vessel	Uncontexted	6			3	H	
E615:089a	Iron	Rectangular-sectioned stem fragment with expanded head	Uncontexted	12			3	H	
E615:089b	Clay pipe	Stem	Uncontexted	12	8		3	H	
E615:090	Iron	Round-sectioned nail	F142 (trench D)	2			2	H	
E615:091	Clay pipe	Four stems	Uncontexted	5				H	
E615:092	Copper alloy	Mushroom-headed stud/nail	Uncontexted	1	22	Roman	4	H	
E615:093	Copper alloy	18th-century coin	Uncontexted		15	18th century		D & H	
E615:094a	Stone	Two pebbles worn from rubbing	Uncontexted		15			H	
E615:094b	Iron	Stem with rectangular section tapering to round terminal	Uncontexted						
E615:095	Ceramic	Three stoneware body sherds	Uncontexted	12				H	
E615:096	Iron	Stem	Upper fill of ditch 1	2	2			H	
E615:097	Iron	Nail	Uncontexted	4	4		4	H	
E615:098		CANCELLED							
E615:099	Glass	Body sherd of blue glass vessel	Uncontexted	6			3	H	
E615:100a	Iron	Three stems	Uncontexted	1			4	H	
E615:100b	Flint	Unutilised flake	Uncontexted	1			4	D & H	
E615:101	Glass	Body sherd	Uncontexted: bank 2	2	16			H	
E615:102	Iron	Nail	Uncontexted					H	
E615:103	Clay pipe	Stem	Uncontexted				3		
E615:104	Copper alloy	Fragments	Ditch 1, rampart 1	10				H	
E615:105	Glass	Six body sherds and one rim	Uncontexted	1				H	
E615:106	Glass	Body sherd	Uncontexted	10					
E615:107	Glass	Setting with white inset and round base	Uncontexted		18			H	Plate 1
E615:108		CANCELLED							

Find	Material	Description	Context	Cutting	Sq.	Date	Phase	Appendix	Figure
E615:109	Iron	CANCELLED							
E615:110	Iron	Bar	F142 (trench D)				2		
E615:111	Iron	Stem	F100 (trench B)				2		
E615:112	Antler	Stem	Uncontexted	10	14		2	A	
E615:113	Iron	Tapered circular-sectioned nail/pin	F142 (trench D)	2			3		4.16
E615:114	Antler	Cut antler	From barrow, primary silt of ditch	9					
E615:115	Silver	Ringed pin with round head	Uncontexted		3 & 4	Roman	4	H	
E615:116	Glass	Half of cobalt blue glass cylinder bead with both ends obliquely cut	F4 (trench C)				2	A	2.11
E615:117		CANCELLED							
E615:118	Flint	End scraper	On side of ditch 1, rampart 1	1			4	D	
E615:119	Iron	Nail	Uncontexted		7			H	
E615:120	Flint	Tanged flake	Uncontexted	7			3	D & H	
E615:121	Flint	Burnt flake	F4 (trench C)				2	D	2.11
E615:122	Iron	Object with two arms and rectangular section	Uncontexted	10				H	
E615:123	Ceramic	Base sherd, Central Gaulish	Uncontexted			Roman		G	Plate 4
E615:124	Lead	Lead-alloy seal, oval impression with raised figure of a bird	Upper level of habitation, northern area		42		4	A	4.10 & Plate 1
E615:125	Copper alloy	One half of penannular brooch with zoomorphic terminal (Fowler type E or Ei)	Upper level of habitation, northern area		55	Late 3rd–late 4th century AD	4	A	4.10
E615:126a	Copper alloy	Portion of circular-sectioned cast pin	F174		42		4	A	4.10
E615:126b	Iron	Part of circular-sectioned stem	F174		42		4	A	
E615:127	Ceramic	Spindle-whorl of Severn Valley ware	Dark habitation layer, top of hard stony surface		52	Roman	4	G	4.13 & Plate 2
E615:128	Iron	Large nail with square-sectioned shank	Dark layer, upper habitation level		42		4		4.12
E615:129	Iron	Portion of a circular-sectioned ring	Dark charcoal-rich layer		42		4	A	4.13
E615:130a	Glass	Spherical translucent dark blue bead with cylindrical perforation	Habitation level		52		4	A	4.13
E615:130b	Glass	Translucent annular cobalt blue bead (Group 6 ivb)	Habitation level		52	3rd–4th century AD	4	A	4.13
E615:131	Glass	Mid-blue opaque cylinder bead of tapering rectangular section	From top of stony habitation level		55		4	A	4.13
E615:132	Glass	Small annular bead of opaque turquoise glass (Group 6 vii)	Habitation level		42		4	A	
E615:133	Iron	Tapered circular-sectioned rod with rounded head	Dark layer, upper habitation level		42		4	A	4.11
E615:134	Copper alloy	Penannular ring of rounded section with one blunt and one rounded terminal	Habitation level		42		4	A	4.10
E615:135a	Iron	Portion of oval-sectioned ring	Upper habitation level, northern area		52		4	A	4.11

Find	Material	Description	Context	Cutting	Sq.	Date	Phase	Appendix	Figure
E615:135b	Iron	Circular-sectioned tapering rod	Upper habitation level, northern area	52	52		4	A	4.11
E615:135c	Flint	Flake	Upper habitation level, northern area				4		4.13
E615:136	Glass	Portion of ultramarine glass bracelet	Uncontexted				4	C & H	4.16 & Plate 1
E615:137	Ceramic	Body sherd, possibly Wilderspool ware	SE sector from stony hard brown clay		47	Roman	4	G	4.13 & Plate 2
E615:138	Copper alloy	U-sectioned binding strip	Habitation level		37		4	A	4.10
E615:139a	Iron	Nail with damaged bar head and rectangular-sectioned shank	Upper stony habitation level		55		4	A	4.12
E615:139b	Iron	Fragment of circular-sectioned rod	Upper stony habitation level		55		4	A	4.12
E615:140	Glass	Rim sherd of small mould-blown or mould-pressed bowl of clear colourless transparent metal	Upper habitation level, northern area		38	2nd–4th centuries AD	4	C	4.14
E615:141		CANCELLED							
E615:142	Amber?	Amber or glass fragment	Edge of black area	15	44			H	
E615:143	Iron	Nail	Uncontexted				2	A	
E615:144	Iron	Fragment of oval-sectioned ring	F100 (trench B)		53		4	A	
E615:145	Glass	Two fragments of green glass and one fragment of clear glass	Top of stony habitation layer		53	Roman	4	C	4.14
E615:146	Ceramic	Twelve body sherds of Central Gaulish Samian ware	Top of habitation layer in F16		53	Roman	4	G	4.13 & Plate 3
E615:147a	Iron	Fragment of oval-sectioned rod	Upper stony habitation level, in pit		54		4	A	4.12
E615:147b	Iron	Stem of round-sectioned nail	Upper stony habitation level, in pit		54		4	A	4.12
E615:148	Iron	Top portion of Type 1 Roman nail with flattish pyramid head and square-sectioned stem	F5		37	Roman	4	A	4.12
E615:149	Copper alloy	Penannular ear-ring of oval section	F4 (trench C)		54	Late 1st–2nd century AD	2	A	2.11
E615:150	Ceramic	Body sherd, Samian	Uncontexted			2nd–4th centuries AD	4	G & H	4.16 & Plate 2
E615:151	Glass	Clear colourless body sherd of bowl	Uncontexted		42		4	C	4.14
E615:152	Iron	Fragment of circular socket with copper core and straight-sided blade	Stony habitation layer		52		4	A	
E615:153	Iron	Rectangular-sectioned stem of nail	F5		37		4	A	4.12
E615:154	Glass	Nine adjoining body and rim sherds of a cone beaker of soda glass	Upper habitation layer		52	4th century AD	4	C	4.14
E615:155	Iron	Seven stems, four round-sectioned, one oval-sectioned, one square-sectioned and one disintegrated stem	Stony habitation layer		53		4	A	
E615:156	Iron	Blade fragment	Enclosure, N area		44		4	A	
E615:157	Iron	Rectangular-sectioned strip staple	Uncontexted		38		4	H	

Find	Material	Description	Context	Cutting	Sq.	Date	Phase	Appendix	Figure
E615:158	Iron	Oval-sectioned rod with pointed end	Upper habitation level, W of F20		47		4	A	
E615:159a	Iron	Nail with square-sectioned stem and bulbous head	Habitation level		36		4	A	4.12
E615:159b	Iron	Circular-sectioned rod with tapered end	Habitation level		36		4	A	4.12
E615:160	Iron	Plate with parallel sides	F8		37		4	A	4.11
E615:161	Copper alloy	U-sectioned dagger chape binding	F137 (trench F)		38/39		2	A	2.11
E615:162	Iron	Blade fragment	Uncontexted		52		4	H	
E615:163	Iron	Loop with double spike, strip curve and lozenge-sectioned arms	Uncontexted		53		4	A & H	
E615:164	Iron	Stud with circular-sectioned shank and incomplete trefoil head	Stony habitation layer		45		4	A	4.11
E615:165a	Iron	Square-sectioned stem	Stony habitation layer		52		4		4.11
E615:165b	Iron	Flat plate with rounded tip, blade?	Stony habitation layer		52		4	A	
E615:165c	Iron	Stem	Stony habitation layer		52		4		
E615:165d	Ceramic	Body sherd, Samian	Stony habitation layer		52		4	G	Plate 2
E615:166a	Iron	Circular-sectioned stem with globular head and expanded rounded end	Dark habitation layer. Enclosure, N area		37		4	A	4.12
E615:166b	Iron	Portion of nail with square-sectioned shank and incomplete disc head	Dark habitation layer. Enclosure, N area		37		4	A	4.12
E615:166c	Iron	Square-sectioned shank of nail, bent at right angle	Dark habitation layer. Enclosure, N area		37		4	A	4.12
E615:166d	Iron	Fragment of triangular-sectioned blade	Dark habitation layer. Enclosure, N area		37		4	A	4.12
E615:167	Iron	Roman barrel padlock—Type 1a (Donaghy 1991)	Upper level of F16. Enclosure, N area (habitation layer)		37	Roman	4	B	4.11
E615:168	Glass	Portion of ultramarine glass bracelet	Dark area. Enclosure, N area		43		4		4.10 & Plate 1
E615:169	Stone	Grinding stone of sandstone or quartz, elliptical, both faces flat	Uncontexted		52		4	H	
E615:170a	Iron	Circular-sectioned stem with bulbous ends, possible pivot bar for buckle	Stony habitation layer. Enclosure, N area		44		4	A	4.11
E615:170b	Iron	Rectangular-sectioned stem	Stony habitation layer. Enclosure, N area		44		4		
E615:170c	Stone	Disc-shaped water-rolled yellow pebble	Stony habitation layer. Enclosure, N area		44		4		4.13
E615:171	Stone	Spherical stone of calcareous sandstone	Uncontexted		43		4	H	
E615:172	Copper alloy	Two fragments of a strip ring with overlapping terminals and tapered ends, outer face decorated with two longitudinal grooves	Uncontexted		35		4	A & H	4.16
E615:173	Iron	Nail with bulging rectangular-sectioned shank and large solid ball head—Roman Type 1	Habitation level, top of dark charcoal layer (F16). Enclosure, N area		37	Roman	4	A	4.12
E615:174	Ceramic	Body sherd, Wilderspool	NE corner of extension on charcoal layer. Ditch 1, rampart 1		15		4	A	4.15 & Plate 2

Find	Material	Description	Context	Cutting	Sq.	Date	Phase	Appendix	Figure
E615:175	Bone	Perforated bone pin	From the neck of burial E (F97)				3		2.11
E615:176	Iron	Fragment of ring of tapering circular section	Above abdominal region, burial E (F97)				3	A	2.11
E615:177	Copper alloy	Flat elliptical perforated knife guard, undecorated	Burial E (F97)		43/44		3	A	2.11
E615:178	Copper alloy	Small circular disc. Possibly a coin	Burial E (F97)		36		3	A	
E615:179	Iron	Nail or tack	Uncontexted				4	H	
E615:180	Iron	Fragment of strip collar with out-turned edges	Habitation layer. Enclosure, N area				4	A	
E615:181a	Iron	Nail with rectangular-sectioned stem and disc head	In dark charcoal fill of pit (F5). Enclosure, N area		37/43		4	A	
E615:181b	Iron	Tack or small nail with square-sectioned stem and round head	Baulk, in dark charcoal fill of pit (F5).		37/43		4		
E615:182	Glass	Globular blue bead, roughly spherical with cylindrical perforation (Group 7iii)	Enclosure, N area		36/37		4	A	4.13
E615:183a	Ceramic	Roman pottery	S face of extension. Ditch 1, rampart 1		59		4	G	4.15 & Plate 2
E615:183b	Ceramic	Roman pottery	Overlying ditch 1, rampart 1		59		4	G	4.15 & Plate 2
E615:184a	Flint	Flake	Stony habitation layer. Enclosure, N area		53		4	D	4.13
E615:184b	Flint	Incomplete retouched flake	Stony habitation layer. Enclosure, N area		53		4	D	
E615:185	Iron	Tanged chisel	Bank 2 (F240)		63		4		
E615:186	Chert	Utilised flake	Secondary ditch (F228)				D		
E615:187	Copper alloy	Roman fibula spring for brooch, oval-sectioned wire in eight sections	Dark charcoal layer in fill of ditch 1, secondary ditch (F228)	21		Roman	4	A	4.15
E615:188a	Iron	Round-sectioned nail/pin with globular head	Dark habitation layer. Enclosure, N area		52		4		
E615:188b	Ceramic	Rim fragment of crucible with red vitreous glaze	Dark habitation layer. Enclosure, N area		52				
E615:189a	Iron	Tapering square-sectioned shank with wide fanned head and circular-sectioned rivet	Dark charcoal and bone spread. Bank 2, rampart 2		21			A	4.15
E615:189b	Iron	Triangular mount on stem							
E615:190	Iron	Tapering rectangular-sectioned rod with rounded end	Dark habitation level.		52		4	A	

Find	Material	Description	Context	Cutting	Sq.	Date	Phase	Appendix	Figure
E615:191	Silver	Fragments with inscription or design in relief	Enclosure, N area. Top of habitation level.		44/65		4		
E615:192	Iron	Stem	Enclosure, N area		59		4	A	
E615:193	Copper alloy	Penannular striated ring decorated with transverse ribbing	Ditch 1, rampart 1		36/37		4	A	4.10 & Plate 1
E615:194	Iron	Rectangular-sectioned strip with one blunt and one narrowed end	Habitation layer. Enclosure, N area		45		4	A & H	
E615:195	Copper alloy	Decorated bracelet with circular section with band of transverse grooving on outer face of curve	Ditch 1, dark area in inner ditch. Rampart 1		59	Roman	4	A	4.15
E615:196	Iron	Blade or strip	Uncontexted		54		4	H	4.16
E615:197	Iron	Disc	Uncontexted		44/52		4	H	4.14
E615:198	Glass	Clear colourless body sherd of bowl	In the dark fill of the secondary ditch (F228)	21		2nd–4th centuries AD		C	4.14
E615:199	Iron	Nail	Uncontexted		53		4		
E615:200	Glass	Clear colourless body sherd of bowl or squat jar	Habitation layer		55	Late 3rd–early 4th century AD		C	4.14
E615:201									
E615:202	Ceramic	Four body sherds, grey with yellow glaze	Uncontexted	21				H	
E615:203	Copper alloy	Halfpenny *Grati*	Uncontexted	23				H	4.13
E615:204	Glass	Globular green bead with cylindrical perforation, possibly recycled Roman glass (Group 7iii)	Habitation layer (F20). Enclosure, N area		46/54			A	
E615:205	Iron	Stem	Top of palisade. Bank 2, rampart 2		63				
E615:206	Glass	Body sherd	Uncontexted		59			H	
E615:207	Iron	Nail with short oval-sectioned shank and disc head	Uncontexted					A & H	
E615:208	Iron	Stem	Secondary ditch (F228)		21		4	H	
E615:209	Glass	Seven pane fragments	Uncontexted		44/52		4	H	
E615:210	Iron	Stem fragments	Uncontexted		43/44			H	
E615:211	Copper alloy	Fragment of curved sheet with parallel edges	F240, inner edge of bank 2, on stony fill of palisade. Rampart 2					A	4.15
E615:212	Copper alloy	Fragment of sheet with two parallel straight edges	Habitation level. Enclosure, N area		38/42		4	A	
E615:213a	Copper alloy	D-sectioned strip	Habitation level, stony layer. Enclosure, S area		20		4	A	4.13
E615:213b	Iron	Stem	Habitation level, stony layer. Enclosure, S area		20		4		
E615:214	Glass	Fragment of cobalt blue glass waste, possibly from bead-making	Habitation layer (F20). Enclosure, N area		52		4	A	
E615:215	Iron	Stem	Stony material in the middle of bank 2		62				
E615:216	Glass	Spherical blue bead with opaque white	From 'top of packing		37/43		4	A	4.13

Find	Material	Description	Context	Cutting	Sq.	Date	Phase	Appendix	Figure
		marvered vertical stripes	stones of dark charcoal and bone pit'.						
E615:217	Copper alloy	U-sectioned sheet moulding or binding	Habitation layer. Enclosure, N area		35		4	A	4.10
E615:218	Copper alloy	Fragment of pin	From fill of F163. Habitation layer. Enclosure, N area				3		
E615:219	Copper alloy	CANCELLED							
E615:220	Copper alloy	Oval-sectioned shank of pin from penannular brooch	Grave-good from burial E. From charcoal fill of pit over skull in pit (F97)		43		4	A	4.10
E615:221	Clay pipe	Parnell pipe bowl with stem fragment. Stamped with 'The Parnell MP Pipe'	Stony habitation layer. Enclosure, N area		63	Post-medieval		H	4.15
E615:222	Copper alloy	CANCELLED							
E615:223a		Fragment	Uncontexted						
E615:223b	Iron	Circular-sectioned nail stem	Habitation layer. Enclosure, N area		59		4	A	
E615:224	Iron	Unidentifiable fragments	Enclosure, N area		59		4	A	
E615:225	Copper alloy	Two strips with parallel sides, flat backs and shallow convex faces	Grave-good from burial E. From pit (F97) Rath na Ríogh				3	A	
E615:226	Iron	Small wide-headed nail with square-sectioned shank and disc head	Rath na Ríogh				3	A	
E615:227	Copper alloy	Button with loop for fastening	Uncontexted					H	
E615:228		CANCELLED							
E615:229		CANCELLED							
E615:230	Iron	Incomplete circular-sectioned rod	House (F16). Enclosure, N area		45		4	A	
E615:231	Iron	Bar of rectangular section with oval-sectioned rounded end (joiner's dog)	Rath na Ríogh					A	
E615:232	Iron	Rectangular-sectioned rod with oval-sectioned rounded end	Rath na Ríogh					A	
E615:233	Iron	Nail and clay pipe stem	Uncontexted	16					
E615:234	Clay	Crucible in two parts. Triangular-shaped and of grey clay	Extension N, immediately under burnt area and on top of red layer. Ditch 1, rampart 1	15			4	H	4.16
E615:235	Iron	Nail with rectangular shank and incomplete disc head	Near base of charcoal-rich pit (F5). Enclosure, N area		37/43		4	A	4.12
E615:236		CANCELLED							
E615:237		CANCELLED							
E615:240a	Iron	Plate fragments with slag accretions	Habitation layer.		44/45		4	A	

Find	Material	Description	Context	Cutting	Sq.	Date	Phase	Appendix	Figure
E615:240b	Iron	Corroded sheet	Enclosure, N area		44/45		4	A	
E615:241	Iron	Two small wide-headed tacks or nails	Habitation layer. Enclosure, N area		44		4	H	
E615:242	Iron	Stem with bifurcated terminal	Stony material, bank 2, rampart 2		62				
E615:243		CANCELLED							
E615:244		CANCELLED							
E615:245	Clay pipe	Stem	Uncontexted					H	
E615:246	Iron	Bar of rectangular section with down-turned ends	Rath na Ríogh		19			A	
E615:247		CANCELLED							
E615:248		CANCELLED							
E615:249		CANCELLED							
E615:250a	Flint	Utilised flake	Uncontexted		21			D & H	
E615:250b	Lead	Shot	Uncontexted		21			H	
E615:250c	Clay pipe	Seven bowl fragments	Uncontexted		21			H	
E615:251	Copper alloy	Pair of dividers; arms have flat backs and faceted face hinged by circular rivet at pointed head	Top of stony layer under thick humus, secondary ditch (F228)		16			A	4.15
E615:252		CANCELLED							
E615:253	Iron	Blade strip with parallel edges ending in tang	Rath na Ríogh					A	
E615:254	Stone	Roof slate with aperture	Uncontexted					H	
E615:255	Stone	Palette, roughly circular flat sandstone pebble with one well-polished face	F101 (trench A)	11			2	A	
E615:256	Stone	Grinding or rubbing stone of sandstone. Circular in shape and elliptical in section	Uncontexted					H	
E615:257	Stone	Spherical pebble	Uncontexted		41		4	H	
E615:258	Stone	Coarse micaceous sandstone pebble, rubbing stone/gaming piece	F101 (trench A)		42		2	A	
E615:259	Stone	Water-rolled sandstone pebble, rubbing stone/gaming piece	F142 (trench D)				2	A	
E615:260	Bone	Object	Grave-good, burial H. Found near the vertebrae in pit (F96)				3		
E615:261	Glass	Opaque green glass vessel sherd	Uncontexted		63			H	
E615:262	Copper alloy	Fragments	Uncontexted		52/53		4	H	
E615:263	Iron	Flat stem with rivet	Uncontexted		23			H	
E615:264	Iron	Nail	Uncontexted		23			H	
E615:265	Iron	Stem	Uncontexted					H	
E615:266	Iron	Stem	Rath na Ríogh					A & H	
E615:267	Iron	Rectangular-sectioned shank that terminates in a wedged head	Uncontexted						
E615:268	Quartz	Flake	Uncontexted		59			H	
E615:269	Chert	Flake	In primary fill of ditch 1	1					

Find	Material	Description	Context	Cutting	Sq.	Date	Phase	Appendix	Figure
E615:270	Glass	Inset for ring or brooch	Uncontexted					A & H	
E615:271	Chert	Flake	Burnt layer. Enclosure, N area		54		4		
E615:272	Quartz	Two pebbles worn from rubbing	Stony layer, top of habitation. Enclosure, N area		52		4		
E615:273	Chert	Flake	Habitation layer. Enclosure, N area		44		4		
E615:274	Chert	Flake	F16		54		4		
E615:275	Stone	Two rubbing stones/gaming pieces	F144 (trench D2)		4		2		
E615:276	Antler	Two pieces of antler with root stem and worn tine	Post-hole of inner palisade of bank 3, rampart 3	23			4		
E615:277	Antler	Antler with signs of wear but not worked	Post-hole of inner palisade of bank 3, rampart 3	23			4		
E615:278	Antler	Section of partially worked antler tine, cut at both ends and faceted	F227		63		4		
E615:279	Antler	Antler tine partially worked with tool marks at one end and five chop marks	F227		63		4		
E615:280	Antler	Antler with three incomplete tines	F250	23			4		
	Coin	Roman coin hoard	18 inches beneath the sod, over or close to a 'trench', either the primary ditched enclosure or the inner ditch of the ringfort				4	E	

APPENDIX L

BURIALS REGISTER

Kim Rice

Site	Burial	Type	Bone coffin	Location	Description	ID	Depth	Phase	Square	Cutting	Weight
Rath of the Synods	A	Cremation deposit		Lost	Unprotected cremation on top of the boulder clay at the outer edge of ditch 1 of the residential enclosure	Adult female	0.35m	3?	40		1,385g
Rath of the Synods	B	Complete, also cremated bone	399	National Museum of Ireland: Collins Barracks	No further information						
Rath of the Synods	D	Complete, also some animal bone	399	National Museum of Ireland: Collins Barracks	Extended inhumation aligned ESE–WSW	Male?	0.50m	3		17	
Rath of the Synods	E	Complete	400	National Museum of Ireland: Collins Barracks	No further information						
Rath of the Synods	F	Cremation deposit		National Museum of Ireland: Collins Barracks	Uncontexted: possibly under the bank of rampart 2 to the S of modern field wall, under 'humus layer'			3		23	429.07g +39.72g +413.26g (in 3 bags)
Rath of the Synods	G	Cremation deposit		Lost	No further information			3		23	147.38g
Rath of the Synods	H	Complete—extended inhumation	401	National Museum of Ireland: Collins Barracks	In oval pit (F96), aligned E–W —secondary burial	Adult male		3	43 & 44		
Rath of the Synods	I	Crouched inhumation		Lost	Lay on a 'stony layer' which was on the boulder clay and covered with a layer of redeposited clay—secondary burial	Adult		3			
Rath na Ríogh	J	Skull & animal	401	National Museum of Ireland: Collins Barracks	No further information						
Rath of the Synods	K	Skull only	401	National Museum of Ireland: Collins Barracks	No further information						
Rath of the Synods	L	Cremation deposit		Lost	Primary cremation deposit sealed by the barrow—primary burial	Young adult	0.40m	3			
Rath of the Synods	M	Cremation deposit		Lost	Primary cremation deposited on or in the undisturbed sod layer beneath the primary barrow— primary burial		1.79m	3			
Rath of the Synods	N	Cremation deposit		Lost	Rested on area of burnt clay on the northern side of the barrow —secondary burial		0.45m	3			
Rath of the Synods	O	Cremation deposit		Lost	Unprotected deposit within the secondary natural sod layer over the line of the ditch—secondary burial		?	3			
Rath of the Synods	P	Cremation deposit		Lost	Cremation scatter in the upper levels of the stone core 2m SE of the centre of the barrow— secondary burial		0.10m	3			

Site	Burial	Type	Bone coffin	Location	Description	ID	Depth	Phase	Square	Cutting Weight
Rath of the Synods	Q	Cremation deposit		Lost	From the ditch on the SE side of the barrow—secondary burial		1m	3		
Rath of the Synods	R	Cremation deposit		Lost	Deposited among the large stones of the upper level of the barrow core. Part of the burial underlay the inhumation burial U—primary burial		0.40m	3		
Rath of the Synods	S	Cremation deposit		Lost	Unprotected deposit 2m from the W edge of the barrow and immediately beneath the natural sod layer of the barrow—primary burial		0.15m	3		
Rath of the Synods	T	Cremation deposit		Lost	Unprotected deposit beneath the natural sod layer over the barrow—primary burial	Adult	0.10m	3		
Rath of the Synods	U	Crouched inhumation		Lost	Inserted over the centre of the barrow—secondary burial			3		
Rath of the Synods	V	Cremation deposit		Lost	Quantity of cremated bone found on and in the immediate vicinity of a large earthfast boulder		0.40–0.55m	3	37 or 2	
Rath of the Synods	W	Cremation deposit		Lost	Cremation deposit in oval pit (F6)—secondary burial		0.65m	3	37	
Rath of the Synods	1	Complete	398	National Museum of Ireland: Collins Barracks	No further information					
Rath of the Synods	10	Complete, also some cremated bone & animal bone	399	National Museum of Ireland: Collins Barracks	No further information					

APPENDIX M

SAMPLE REGISTER

Kim Rice

Sample	Description	Context	Cutting	Square	Depth	Phase	Weight	Radiocarbon date
1	Iron slag	Post-hole A in trench D (F142)				2		
2	Iron slag	Uncontexted		8	0.35m			
3	Iron slag	Uncontexted: bank 1, W side of square		9	0.50m	4	16g	
4	Lump of bloom	Uncontexted: 'found beside silver coin' (E4m/N6.20m)		10	0.96m	4		
5	Iron slag	Uncontexted: from burnt stony layer		44, 52		4		
6	Slag & burnt clay	Bottom of ditch 1	2	55	1.4m	4	58g	
7	Slag & burnt clay	Uncontexted: ditch 1	2		1.65m	4	95g	
8	Iron slag	Bottom of ditch 1	2		1.85m	4	1,610g	
9	Iron slag & small piece bronze slag	Ditch 2 (0.8m SW)	2		1.8m	4		
10	Iron slag	Uncontexted	1					
11	Iron slag	Bank 3 (W 0.5m, c. 25m)	4		0.42m			
12	Iron bloom	Uncontexted: from upper levels of Rath na Ríogh ditch	23					
13	Iron slag	Uncontexted: from lower levels of Rath na Ríogh ditch	23		1.45m			
14	Iron bloom	From 'black stony layer' under Rath na Ríogh bank (25cm S of south peg)	23		0.35m			
15	Crucible fragments and bits of charcoal	From 'black stony layer' under Rath na Ríogh bank (S 1.30 N to S 4.30 N)	23					
16	Iron slag	CANCELLED						
17	Iron slag	CANCELLED						
18	Iron slag & charcoal	From 'black layer' under Rath na Ríogh bank	23					
19	Iron slag & iron fragments	From charcoal-rich fill of F142 (trench D)	23	6	0.50m	2	200g	
20	Burnt clay	CANCELLED						
21		CANCELLED						
22		CANCELLED						
23		CANCELLED						
24	Iron pyrites	Uncontexted: from SW sector of cutting	21		0.46m			
25	Bone, cremated bone & charcoal	Uncontexted: under topsoil	21					
26	Three fragments of ribs	Uncontexted: rampart 1, residential enclosure	2			4		
27	Burnt bone & charcoal	Uncontexted: habitation layer		36 & 37		4		
28	Teeth	Uncontexted: rampart 1, residential enclosure	2		1.1m	4		
29	Bone & charcoal	Bank 3	24			4		
30	Daub	Uncontexted		9				
31	Burnt clay	Uncontexted		15				
32	Fifteen fragments of wood	Uncontexted: c. 21m W 1.00m, from E bridge face	1		0.10m			
33	Clay and seven pieces of vitrified organic material	Barrow: 0–50cm, 5–7m on top of mound; above and amongst stones	5		0.30m	3		
34	Cremated bone & charcoal	Uncontexted: trench in central area, E of post-hole						
35	Black coal-like substance	Inner edge of bank 3						
36	Cremated bone & charcoal (Quercus)	From palisade trench D2 (F144)	5	20				
37	Pig teeth & burnt bone	From dark clay & post-holes. Small blackened pig teeth from W post-hole, large pig teeth from W and N post-hole		5	0.20m	4		The late middle Iron Age AD 86–249
38	Cremated bone	Uncontexted: from trench C1 (F134)		2		2		
39	Animal bone fragments	Uncontexted: from levels above habitation level		38		4		

Sample	Description	Context	Cutting	Square	Depth	Phase	Weight	Radiocarbon date
40	Human teeth & bone	From stiff yellow clay of accumulation of small stones; 09.65m W, 562cm from N edge of cutting						
41	Small pieces of bone	On stones at base of outer ditch, c. 41m W 75cm	1		1m	4		
42	Six shells	Uncontexted: from fill of Rath na Riogh ditch	23					
43	Traces of white clay	Secondary fill of ditch 1, rampart 1	1		0.82m	4		
44	Charcoal & bone	Uncontexted		8				
45	White clay	On outer edge of primary ditch (F260)	2		0.90m	1		
46	Bone	Palisade in S end of cutting 23, S of ditch of Rath na Ríogh. From 10.8 to 11.8 S of S peg, W side of cutting	23		0.34m			
47	Charcoal, soil & bone	From trench D (F142)				2		
48	Wood and bone fragments	Uncontexted: below sod	11	10	0.70m	3		
49	Charcoal	Uncontexted						
50	Cremated bone	From grave fill of burial C				3		
51	Charcoal, bone & slag	Uncontexted						
52	Charcoal & cremated bone	Uncontexted		55, 56		4		
53	Iron, clay & charcoal (Quercus)	From red fill of pit F157, immediately N of burial I		43				The late middle Iron Age 169 BC–AD 1
54	Charcoal	From ash pit F5 near burial E		37, 38, 42, 43		4		
55	Charcoal	From ash pit to S and E of burial C				4		
56	Charcoal (Fraxinus)	From ash pit F5		37, 38, 42, 43				Final Iron Age AD 259–412
57	Charcoal	Uncontexted: from baulk				4		
58	Charcoal	Uncontexted: from baulk		37, 38, 42, 43				
59	Charcoal (Fraxinus)	From ash pit F5				4		Final Iron Age AD 257–400
60	Charcoal	From palisade trench inside inner bank	5	29		2		The late middle Iron Age AD 21–210
61	Charcoal (Fraxinus)	Palisade E (F145), from large bed of charcoal, all one post						
62	Charcoal	Secondary ditch, black fill of inner fosse near accumulation of jawbones	8		0.70–0.80m	4		
63	Charcoal	Black fill of inner fosse near accumulation of jawbones	8		0.70–0.80m	4		
64	Charcoal	Uncontexted: from fosse	8		0.66–0.92m	4		
65	Charcoal	Black fill of inner fosse near accumulation of jawbones	8		0.70–0.80m	4		
66	Charcoal	Uncontexted: from fosse	8		0.66–0.92m	4		
67	Charcoal	From inner ditch—rampart 1	2		0.70m			
68	Charcoal, cremated bone & burnt clay	Uncontexted		15				
69	Charcoal & cremated bone	Uncontexted		15		4		

Sample	Description	Context	Cutting	Square	Depth	Phase	Weight	Radiocarbon date
70	Charcoal & cremated bone	From hearth F187 in S area		7		4		
71	Charcoal	Uncontexted: just under cinders in grass sod						
72	Ferrous material	Uncontexted						
73	Burnt clay	From palisade trench C1 (F134), running from sq. 2 into deep black wall trench		2		2		
74	Burnt clay	Hut foundation (F20), W end of central area		4		4		
75	Burnt clay	Hut foundation (F20), W end of central area		4		4		
76	Burnt clay	Hut foundation (F20), W end of central area				4		
77	Burnt clay	Hut foundation (F20), W end of central area				4		
78	Burnt clay	Hut foundation (F20), W end of central area				4		
79	Charcoal	From dark area in W side of square 10 at inner edge of bank	1	10	0.53m	4		
80	Charcoal	From 'black spread' in palisade trench D (F142), inside inner bank	2	6, 8, 10, 14		2		
81	Charcoal	Uncontexted: post-hole at E of N–S baulk in central area c. 6.20 N				4		
82	Charcoal	From N–S trench N, c. 10m W 2m		4	0.60m	4		
83	Charcoal	In palisade trench D2 (F144), c. 9.1m W		4	0.80m	2		
84	Charcoal	Uncontexted: from S part of the cut of hut, 1.30m		2		4		
85	Charcoal	Uncontexted: trench in second ditch	1	1	0.45m			
86	Charcoal	Uncontexted: 46m W, 7m S		5				
87	Charcoal	From 2m cutting in rampart 1, c. 3.3m W–c. 35.70m W	1		0.45m	4		
88	Burnt clay and charcoal (Corylus)	In undisturbed area in centre of barrow, under large stones	5		1.1m			Late Neolithic 3366–3104 BC
89	Charcoal	Uncontexted		14				
90	Charcoal (Fraxinus) & cremated bone	Primary ditch (F260), extension E, 0–2.5m (this sample was probably taken from feature that was cut into F260)	10		0.76m			The late middle Iron Age AD 24–255
91	Burnt clay, charcoal, cremated bone	Uncontexted: in clay at E edge of barrow & at same depth as barrow material at this edge	12			3		
92	Bone, slag & charcoal	Uncontexted		45		4		
93	Charcoal	Uncontexted: W baulk, from habitation layer		55		4		
94	Bone & charcoal	From palisade trench D2 (F144), c. 16m W, 2m		4	0.60m	2		
95	Bone & charcoal	From burnt pit F5		36		4		
96	Bone & charcoal	Uncontexted		38				
97	Bone & charcoal	Uncontexted: from stony undisturbed layer—Small volume of burnt and half-burnt animal bones most of which came from swine, but a few fragments probably cattle'		52		4		
98	Charcoal	Uncontexted: from dark habitation layer c. -70cm		37		4		
99	Charcoal (Fraxinus)	From post-hole (F62) in central area of structure (F20), c. 40m E, 7.0m N				4		AD 259–412
100	Bone & charcoal	Uncontexted: from NE pit in habitation area, E of structure (F66)		37		4		
101	Charcoal	Uncontexted		12		4		
102	Charcoal	From hard stony layer within structure (F20)		53		4		
103	Charcoal (Quercus)	From NW corner pit F163		36		4		Middle Iron Age

Sample	Description	Context	Cutting	Square	Depth	Phase	Weight	Radiocarbon date
104	Bone & charcoal	Uncontexted		46				359–176 BC
105	Bone & charcoal	From post-hole and pit fillings in structure (F20)		45, 46, 53, 54		4		
106	Bone & charcoal (Quercus)	From post-hole F103 under E baulk		36				Middle Iron Age 372–197 BC
107	Charcoal	Uncontexted: on dark stony habitation layer under N baulk leading into ext. N of sq. 52		52		4		
108	Bone & charcoal	Uncontexted: from under N baulk at habitation level		45		4		
109	Charcoal	From SW corner of palisade trench G (F135)		23		2		
110	Charcoal	Inner bank of palisade trench C1 (F134)				2		
111	Charcoal (Fraxinus) & cremated bone	Ditch 1 (F31) from among large stones at bottom of ditch, rampart 1	1					The late middle Iron Age AD 77–216
112	Charcoal	From post-hole in spread of burnt material in palisade trench D (F142)		4		2		
113	Charcoal	Palisade trench D2 (F144)			0.73m	2		
114	Bone & charcoal	0.5m S, in dark soil in second ditch—rampart 2	8		0.55m			
115	Bone & charcoal (Alnus)	Palisade trench D1 (F143)		14		4		Early Iron Age 765–416 BC
116	Bone & charcoal	Uncontexted: from 'dark layer' in ext. 59						
117	Bone, charcoal & slag	Uncontexted						
118	Bone & charcoal (Quercus)	From central area of slot-trench in structure (F20)		59		4		Middle Iron Age 359–179 BC
119	Bone & charcoal	Pit with bone (F5)		37		4		
120	Bone & charcoal	From habitation layer (F16), E of structure (F66) under N baulk		44		4		
121	Bone & charcoal	Uncontexted: from burnt layer in structure (F20)		54		4		
122	Bone & charcoal	Uncontexted		36		4		
123	Charcoal (Corylus)	From base of pit in palisade trench B (F100), baulk of squares 55 & 56		55 & 56	0.65m				The late middle Iron Age 36 BC–AD 128
124	Charcoal, cremated bone & burnt clay	Uncontexted: from post-hole, c. 5.5 E, c. 6.5 N		42 & 43				
125	Charcoal (Quercus)	From pit (F158) under baulk, around burial I. The sample also originally included 'one good sized dog (or wolf), fragment of shed antler of red deer, several pigs, one horse tooth, several ox of various ages. Some bone burnt'—from Ó Ríordáin's field notes						Early medieval AD 414–540
126	Charcoal	Uncontexted						
127	Bone & charcoal	Uncontexted: S sector of square						
128	Charcoal	c. 30m W–c. 32.7 W, inside bank 3	1	43	0.75m	4		

Sample	Description	Context	Cutting	Square	Depth	Phase	Weight	Radiocarbon date
129	Slag	Uncontexted		6	0.25–0.33m			
130	Shell	Uncontexted						
131	Horn	From base of palisade trench B (F100), c. 2.8m W, 4.8m N		54	0.65m	2		
132	Charcoal & cremated bone	Uncontexted						
133	Fragments of copper-alloy waste	On south edge of square in area of much charcoal. Slag also found in vicinity. Phase 3 habitation		10	0.38m	4		
134	Fragments of bronze & iron	From dark layer -93cm, ext. 59, phase 3 habitation				4		
135		CANCELLED						
136	Bone	Bone with object touching skull of burial E		13				
137		CANCELLED						
138	Cremated bone	Uncontexted		4		4		
139	Cremated bone	Uncontexted		10				
140	Six fragments of bone		9					
141	Cremated bone	Uncontexted: bank 3	4					
142	Cremated bone	Uncontexted: stony habitation level		44		4		
143	Bone, epiphysis	Uncontexted: bank 3	4					
144	Bone	Uncontexted: residential enclosure, extension of rampart 1	15	4		4	120g	
145	Cremated bone	Uncontexted: British-Israelite rubble, c. 10.50m W	10	4		3		
151	Bone and teeth	Uncontexted: inner edge of ditch	9			3		
156	Fragment of human skull							
166	Twenty fragments of animal bone, including one tooth	Uncontexted: outside 'outer' ditch	5		0.60m	3		
167	Two fragments of animal bone	Uncontexted: E part of cut under sod	10	2		3		
168	Cremated bone	Uncontexted				3		
177	60 fragments of animal bone, teeth and tusk	Uncontexted: fill of ditch 1	11					
178	Animal bone	Uncontexted: 'trench' in central area	7					
182	Animal bone	Uncontexted		30				
185	Cremated & human bone	Uncontexted: from 'pit'		2		3		
198	Slag	Uncontexted			1m			
199	Cremated bone & charcoal	Found at the edge of the 'black area' in association with E615:142, c. 3.90m N, c. 4.40m E		44	0.70m	3		
204	Wood	Uncontexted	9					
205	Animal bone	Uncontexted			0.49m			
207	Animal bone	Uncontexted	15					